Issues in Realist Cri

Sage Contemporary Criminology

Series editors

John Lea ● Roger Matthews ● Jock Young

Sage Contemporary Criminology draws on the best of current work in criminology and socio-legal studies, both in Britain and internationally, to provide lecturers, students and policy-makers with the latest research on the functioning of the criminal justice and legal systems. Individual titles will cover a wide span of issues such as new developments in informal justice; changing forms of policing and crime prevention; the impact of crime in the inner city; and the role of the legal system in relation to social divisions by gender and race. Throughout, the series will relate theoretical problems in the social analysis of deviancy and social control to the practical and policy-related issues in criminology and law.

Already published

Jeanne Gregory, *Sex, Race and the Law: Legislating for Equality*
John Pitts, *The Politics of Juvenile Crime*
Roger Matthews (ed.), *Informal Justice?*
Nigel South, *Policing for Profit: The Private Security Sector*
Roger Matthews (ed.), *Privatizing Criminal Justice*
Tony Vass, *Alternatives to Prison*

Issues in Realist Criminology is a companion volume to
Rethinking Criminology: The Realist Debate edited by
Jock Young and Roger Matthews

Issues in Realist Criminology

edited by
Roger Matthews and Jock Young

SAGE Publications
London ● Newbury Park ● New Delhi

First published 1992

 SAGE Publications Ltd
6 Bonhill Street
London EC2A 4PU

SAGE Publications Inc
2455 Teller Road
Newbury Park, California 91320

SAGE Publications India Pvt Ltd
32, M-Block Market
Greater Kailash – I
New Delhi 110 048

British Library Cataloguing in Publication data
Issues in Realist Criminology.—
(Sage Contemporary Criminology Series)
I. Matthews, Roger II. Young, Jock III. Series 364

ISBN 0-8039-8624-6
ISBN 0-8039-8625-4 (Pbk)

Two-volume set: *Rethinking Criminology*
ISBN 0-8039-8484-7
ISBN 0-8039-8485-5 (Pbk)

Library of Congress catalog card number 92-050108

Typeset by GCS, Leighton Buzzard, Bedfordshire
Printed in Great Britain by Hartnolls Ltd, Bodmin, Cornwall

Contents

Contributors

David Brown, Law School, University of New South Wales.

Pat Carlen, Department of Sociology, Keele University.

Russell Hogg, Law School, MacQuarie University.

Roger Matthews, Centre for the Study of Public Order, University of Leicester.

Frank Pearce, Queen's University, Ontario.

Richard Sparks, Keele University.

Steve Tombs, The Business School, Liverpool Polytechnic.

Sandra Walklate, University of Salford.

1 Questioning left realism

Jock Young and Roger Matthews

Left realist criminology, although having roots in the debates of the mid-1970s, has only really emerged in the period post-1985. For many, 'left' or 'radical' realism has been seen as an essentially British phenomenon, but as the range of subjects covered in these chapters (and *Rethinking Criminology: The Realist Debate*) signify, the debate around criminological realism has an international significance. These debates touch upon a number of theoretical, political and strategic developments which are present in many advanced western countries (see Matthews and Young, 1992).

As the debate becomes more widespread and the range of responses increases from commentators in different countries, it is likely that differences of emphasis and meaning will arise. As some of the commentaries occurring to date signify, there are different under-standings and adaptations of realism in different countries (Brown and Hogg, Chapter 7). In some cases, left realism remains undifferentiated from other radical strands in criminology; while in other cases, critics simply miss the target (Mugford and O'Malley, 1991; Mathieson, 1990).

As radical realism develops and the range and depth of debate increases, these problems will, no doubt, intensify. The principal aim of this chapter is to clarify some of the more prevalent (mis)con-ceptions of left realism which have arisen in the literature to date. One question which is repeatedly and understandably asked of left realism is: is it new?

Has left realist criminology anything new to say?

It is often suggested that realism is simply a revamped version of traditional criminology: victimization statistics replacing crimes known to the police, the traditional goal of the search for causes of crime merely re-elaborated, with the role of the criminal justice system being criticized at a superficial rather than a fundamental level. It is true that realism does not reject out of hand the traditions of socio-logical criminology. It does not represent a paradigm which seeks to create a critical criminology which has an abrupt hiatus with the past. It could not do so because its starting point is that the various competing 'old' criminologies, to varying degrees, possess a kernel of truth. Their problem is that they attempt to explain the reality of crime by focusing on only one part of the phenomenon. The square of crime should make this clear: all crime involves two dyads: that of social action and reaction and of victim and offender. Yet the competing criminologies attempt the impossible in explaining crime rates by focusing on one of these four points (see Lea, 1992).

Let us concentrate on the action/social reaction dyad. This dyad has been the basis of the debate between individual positivism and neoclassicism and between sociological positivism and labelling theory. The positivist side of the equation has focused on why people commit crimes, their opponents on the reaction to crime. But a full-blown criminology must problematize both why people commit crimes and why certain actions are criminalized. And, of course, it must do more than this: it must examine the interaction between actors and those reacting against them, the interplay between crime and 'non-criminalized behaviour', and social censure and approval. In the case of the pivotal debate between social positivism and labelling theory (subsequently social constructionism), it must look both at the *structural* causes of crime and the reasons and consequences of the *administration* of certain acts as criminal or otherwise. It must problematize on *both* levels and it is quite incorrect of critics such as Colin Sumner (1990) to recognize the need for both levels of analysis, yet choose to focus solely on moral censure, or for Brian MacLean (1991) to suggest that the crisis of current criminology is just that of a definitional level while discarding the problem of the aetiology of criminal behaviour. At the very least both the sociology of law making and law breaking are irrevocably linked. As David Matza pointed out a long time ago (1969), the positivist school attempted the impossible – to separate the study of crime from the study of the state. It would be a pity if in the process of creating a critical criminology we simply produced a mirror image of positivism.

Partiality: the focus on part of the phenomenon of crime in order to explain its totality is, of course not merely restricted to the formal constituents of criminology (the state, informal social control, the offender and the victim), but to notions of human nature (the focus on the individual as freely willed or determined), and society (the focus on the micro – or macro – levels of society). It is in its recognition of the need to surmount these false alternatives that realism has close affinities with subcultural theory. For it is the subcultural tradition which has recognized the need to understand the nature of human praxis in changing determinate circumstances, of the necessity of coupling micro- with macro-analyses of society, of the relationship between consensus and diversity and of the constant interplay between social action and the reaction of the wider society to the developing sub-culture (Lea and Young, 1984). It was subcultural theory, both in its structural functionalist and Marxist variants, which responded most creatively to the debate with labelling theory during the 1970s. The move towards a criminological synthesis was on the cards, yet much of this project was abandoned in the new wave of left idealist and establishment criminology of the 1980s (Young, 1986). This was the theoretical agenda set down in *The New Criminology*; it is a project which has yet to be completed. Considerable work is necessary; to this extent, realism, by examining crime and indicating the questions which a fully social theory must answer, serves to set up a series of pointers for this task. For example, if we are to have a subcultural under-standing of the offender, we need also to situate the subculture of the victim, the formal agencies of control (such as the police) and the various public agencies involved in informal control (see Young, 1992). The development of such an analysis is a firm basis on which to create a criminology capable of comprehending the diverse nature of human behaviour and censure.

Does realism constantly regress to either neoclassicism or social positivism?

This type of criticism, seemingly paradoxically, accuses realism either of merely reasserting the primacy of the police and the criminal justice system in tackling crime (see Garland, 1987; Mathieson, 1990), or of reverting to social positivism (e.g. Walklate, Chapter 5; MacLean, 1991). First of all, it should be noted that the paradox is resolved in that realism insists that intervention in the control of crime should occur at all points of the square of crime (state agencies, public involvement, the structural causes of offending and victim support). Coercive legal interventions on the level of the state are necessary (hence the accusa-tion of neoclassicism), interventions directed at the social causes of crime are vital (hence the accusation of a rekindled social positivism). In addition, to complete the square of crime, the role of informal control is stressed (Matthews, 1988), as is support, protection and the mobilization of the victim.

Thus realism straddles the divide between the control of crime by means of interventions from the criminal justice system (neoclassicism) and those divided at the social structure (social positivism). However, the endemic problems of society at large, namely, gross economic inequality and patriarchy – that is, *structural* problems – are of greater importance in the creation and control of crime than unfairness and injustice in the *administration* of justice. Intervention to control crime must, therefore, prioritize social intervention over criminal justice intervention. All of this must be tempered by the realist notion of *specificity*. That is at certain points of time, with regard to certain crimes, and over specified parts of the intervention process, criminal justice interventions can be both judicious and effective. The legacy of social positivism must be maintained, structural intervention prioritized over the, at best, band-aid and, at worst, exacerbating effects of legal intervention. To tackle the causes of crime is of greater weight than to punish or prevent its consequences. The central weakness of social positivism was, as we shall see, its extraordinarily simplistic view of causation and its naïveté with regard to the problems of service delivery. It constructed both the causes of crime and the intervention against it in a most mechanistic fashion. Furthermore, it belittled the role, albeit minor, of the criminal justice system in the control of crime, in that it underestimated where and at what points judicial intervention could be effective and, with regard to the causes of crime, in that it was unaware of the way in which unjust, judicial reactors could be the precipitating causes in the generation of criminality.

To emphasize the social prevention of crime involves a twofold agenda. First of all dealing with, *as far as is politically possible*, structural inequality: that is, the provision of jobs with long-term security (Currie, 1990), of housing which people can be proud and secure in, of a built environment conducive to human civility and development. Secondly, and closely related, to build up the informal control system of the neighbourhood, the peer group and the family – the social immune system – which is the major basis of social control. If the first task was naïvely tackled by social positivism, the second is simply touched upon by control theory.

Let us look at the differences with neoclassicism. This is not the place to detail the major tenets of neoclassicism, nor to engage in a thorough criticism (for a fuller discussion, see Young, 1980).

First, the most vital difference with neoclassicism is that realism does not view legal constraints as the major bulwark against crime. Crime is produced by inequalities within the social structure and by the breakdown of informal, non-legal controls. This being said, legal intervention can, across a wide range of specified situations, be an effective back-up to the wider systems of social control. Yet it can also, in certain situations, be counterproductive. Indeed, inappropriate legal intervention by the police and the courts can be the precipitating causes which transform social discontent into a more committed criminality (the process of criminalization).

Secondly, realists would agree with neoclassicists that due process, the protection of the rights of the offender, the pursuit of equal treatment in the courts, irrespective of age, class, gender or race, is an important objective. Yet the pursuit of formal equality before the law in a world of substantive inequalities – which both generate unequal propensities to crime and make the impact of equal punishment, irrespective of social situation, inequitable – is a transitional aim (Young, 1979). To take a current example, there undoubtedly exists a disproportionate number of blacks and ethnic minorities in the prison systems of most western countries. To an extent such disproportionality would be alleviated by a justice which was colour blind, but it would scarcely tackle the fact that poor people (and hence blacks) are under greater pressure to commit the crimes which are at present the focus of the criminal justice system and prisonization (Currie, 1985; Reiman, 1979).

Thirdly, on the face of it realism and neoclassicism are in agreement: for both espouse a minimalist position in terms of the interventions of the criminal justice system. But the minimalism is different by virtue of the fact that neoclassicism and realism differ in their interpretation of what is the minimum legal coercion necessary to maintain a civilized social order. Libertarian neoclassicists, in particular, would whittle down legal intervention to a basic minimum. They would, for example, remove legal sanction from the so-called 'crimes without victims' because of their 'free' contractual nature and, across a wide spectrum of offences, prefer informal public and non-policing institutional interventions to that involving state coercion. Although realism would seek to minimize coercive interventions it would make the following distinctive caveats. 'Crimes without victims' are a mixed bag of offences, some of which – such as marijuana regulation – need no more than regulations akin to those pertaining to the sale of other relatively innocuous substances (that is, legal safeguards concerning purity and places of sale). Others, such as heroin use, necessitate medical regulation backed by coercive sanctions applied to strategically ascertained sections of the black market. Just because consensual crimes involve free contractual relationships does not, by definition, obviate intervention. Freedom in an unequal society does not involve contracts between equals. In the case of prostitution, to legalize simply means the delivery of a large number of economically and socially vulnerable women to the tender mercies of the marketplace (Matthews, 1986).

Fourthly, realism is acutely aware of the limitations and counterproductive nature of much coercive intervention. Draconian action against, for example, juvenile delinquents, prostitutes or heroin users, is more likely to exacerbate than resolve their problems. Harm minimization is an important goal, stressing as it does the necessity of intervention, yet the limits of what is possible at any particular point in time and the fact that any intervention has its costs in terms of both offenders and victims (Dorn and South, 1987). Yet an across-the-board minimization of legal intervention as espoused by neoclassicists is not necessarily effective or more tolerant. There are instances of relatively minor crimes where adroit police intervention would be effective, and there are instances of major crimes where regulative rather than criminal justice means would be more appropriate (see Pearce and Tombs, Chapter 4). Furthermore, there are a whole series of crimes (such as racist attitudes, domestic violence, child abuse) for which the present cover provided by the criminal justice system is inadequate. To this extent net-widening in some areas as well as the reduction of the net of social control in others would be advocated. Lastly, it should be stressed that very often informal controls and the interventions of public authorities can be more coercive and illiberal than those of the criminal justice system.

Next, just as social positivism has been unsuccessful in tackling the problem of crime, so has neoclassicism. In the latter instances, deterrence theory based on individuals, each with the same rational calculus and with an equal stake in the social order, is inevitably flawed. Deterrence, however formally just, has a vital, yet only partial, effect on crime rates. Our problem is to find where criminal justice system interventions do work, with the following factors in mind:

1 the costs in terms of resources and the comparative efficacy of other parts of the multi-agencies which have a purchase on crime control (social services, housing, education, etc);
2 the impact on the offender as well as the social protection of the likely victim;
3 the impact on specific crimes rather than crime in general, and the particular delimited sector of the criminal process in which coercive legal sanctions should be applied (Young, 1992).

All of this is a far cry from the neoclassicist notion of the criminal justice system universally and impartially tackling the whole range of sufficiently serious wrongdoing in our society. In terms of domestic violence, for example, it would ask what agencies should be involved against what type of domestic violence and at what point of its development?

The accusation of realism as relapsing into social positivism is ironic. Realism is avowedly anti-positivist in that it views crime as a product of behaviour *and* social definition. Crime is not an objective datum outside the definitions of social actors (see the critique of Eysenck and Gudjonsson, 1989, in Young, 1989). Furthermore, it pinpoints the ferment in criminology since the 1960s as a product of the aetiological crisis (Young, 1986, 1988a). That is, social positivism – the notion that 'bad' conditions lead invariably to 'bad' behaviour – was undermined by the fact that as social conditions markedly improved the crime rate rose rapidly. The roots of realism lie, therefore, in a critique of positivism and in the failure of social positivism, in particular. At the same time, realism is critical of the various manifestations of idealism (left idealism, labelling theory, social constructionism, moral panic theory, abolitionism, etc), which, by focusing on the social reaction to crime, lose sight of the need to explain criminal behavior altogether. Hence, the need to focus on criminal action and reaction, on the victim and the offender, on one hand, and the informal and formal reactions to crime, on the other. Of course, such a stress on the need to explain crime rates and criminalization by the interplay of victim, offender, the state and the public could result in merely a more complex positivism with a fourfold aetiology rather than one solely encompassing the offender. A social positivism of the offender could be combined with a positivist victimology, an instrumentalist theory of the state and a reductionist view of public opinion. But realism does not do this, because it insists that the reality of crime involves not only its formal components (the square) but also, substantively, the fact that human action involves choice within determinant circumstances. For example, the increased public intolerance of violence, which has arisen in the last 20 years, cannot merely be reduced to a reflection of the widespread material changes that have occurred, but to the fact that human actors have continually redefined what is permissible. Likewise, the fears and anger of victims about crime are not merely a positivistic reflection of their different rates of victimization, but of the various levels of tolerance which groups have evolved concerning an acceptable social order.

Lastly, let us turn to the traditional stalking horse of social positivism: the offender. Social positivism seeks universal laws such as 'unemployment leads to crime'. Of course, this is not even good positivism: much crime necessitates employment and there is no invariant relationship between unemployment and crime (Lea and Young, 1984). Indeed, as realists in the philosophy of science have stressed, even if the social world were identical with the material, it would be most unusual for laws to be easily established by observing event B as invariably following event A in a situation outside a laboratory or in the relevantly controlled situation of interplanetary space (Bhaskar, 1980). For the real world is an open system with a host of different causalities impinging on each other.

Social positivism is imbued with a sense of the objective, the mechanical and the instantaneous. Realism, by stressing the role of human consciousness within determinant circumstances, as in the tradition of subcultural theory, denies all of this. It does not do this by denying the social determinants of crime, but by granting space for the actor's assessment of these circumstances. Relative deprivation – one of the major causes of crime – involves the subjective assessment by the actor of injustice. And this sense of injustice can have many sub-cultural outcomes (political and religious, for example, as well as criminal), depending on the fashion in which individuals forge their response within the national and cultural possibilities which present themselves. There is, therefore, nothing mechanical about the relation-ship between social circumstances and crime. Absolute deprivation, an objective cause, is patently insufficient even to explain the conven-tional crimes of the working class. Social injustice, however severe, can be opaque to the individuals involved. It is only in certain circumstances mediated through the eyes of particular subcultures that crime is a chosen option. Not all poor people commit crime, as conservative critics constantly and obviously point out, but crime does not, as they would have it, involve a moral choice in a vacuum (cf. Carlen's depiction of realism, Chapter 3).

The notion of an instantaneous response to a change in social circumstances is a corollary of such a mechanistic viewpoint. For example, unemployment seemingly gives rise to crime immediately: you push the table and the table moves. Subcultures, however, take a time to build up, they involve the conscious evolution of collective responses and individual moral careers. Because of this, the effect on a locality of structural employment may take years to develop as people 'grow' into the situation. The reverse of this, the belief that the sudden provision of employment, will, in the short term, reduce crime rates, is thus equally problematic.

Positivism, furthermore, suffers from the problem of undifferen-tiated categories. It attempts to relate, in our example, unemployment to crime, as if both sides of the equation consisted of homogeneous entities. Unemployment can be the prerogative of the idle rich, the temporary movement between jobs, the sudden redundancy of those who have worked all their lives, the structural unemployment of those who have known nothing else, etc. And its experience is mediated by age, class, gender and race within particular subcultures, located spatially in areas with totally different experiences of unemployment. So-called hard facts must be constantly unpacked into the varied specifics of lived realities. And crime itself is far from a unitary phenomenon. It can involve insider dealing, various crimes of the workplace, white-collar infractions, interpersonal violence, ranging from domestic to armed robbery, property crimes of every sort, shape and variety. Even when we focus on a seemingly homogeneous phenom-enon such as burglary, we are melding together behaviour with totally different actors, motivations and targets – witness the contrast between the 'opportunistic' burglary of young kids on the street and the calculated break-in of the professional burglar.

At the very least, therefore, various types of unemployment may have different, and often contrary, effects on the rates of differing crimes. This is not to suggest that official statistics are unusable: they are often the only statistics we have, particularly at the national level. Rather, they must be unpacked carefully, and socially situated, with considerable attention given to weighting for hidden and occluded figures (see Hindess, 1973). In order to achieve such interpretations triangulation with quantitative and qualitative research, using such situated categories, is vital.

What is of importance to stress is that realism, while insisting at a formal level that *all* crime involves the interaction of each part of the square of crime and human actors acting voluntaristically in determinant circumstances, has no truck with the notion that crime and its causes are unitary on a substantive level (cf. Brown and Hogg, Chapter 7). If we are to look for the causes of crime we must, therefore, mobilize concepts such as differential association and relative deprivation which are of a formal nature. This, in the latter instance, what actually people are relatively deprived about, will vary substantively with their particular subculture. Eileen Leonard (1984), for instance, in her powerful feminist critique of mainstream criminology, indicates how Mertonian anomie theory would have to be completely reformulated in order to deal with the actual goals pursued by women, and the means available and tolerable to them. And even on the level of such formal categories, realism, despite its great interest in relative deprivation as a cause of crime, would rule out any notion of mono-causality. All that it would insist on is that the concept has great explanatory power, and that it need not be restricted to crimes committed by the poor. There is, after all, no inbuilt notion of poverty in the term *relative* deprivation (Lea, 1992). In fact, even restricting oneself to the means-end formulation of Merton, there is a considerable variation in the possibilities which would lead to crime, of which relative deprivation is only one (see Young, 1992; Simon and Gagnon, 1986).

Furthermore, the traditional dichotomy in criminology between the social causes of crime (the 'background' factors of unemployment, poverty, etc, in the case of conventional crime) and the 'foreground' causes of criminalization (the responses of the criminal justice system) which manifests itself in such debates as that between social positivism and labelling theory, is patently inadequate. The commonplace distinction between social structure and the administration of criminal justice is important, yet confusing in that it grants too great and almost a symmetrical importance to the justice system, and suggests a temporal sequence: first the propellant, social structure and then the consequence, judicial reaction.

The administrations of the state (including that of the criminal justice system) are, of course, part of the social structural position of the citizen. They contribute to both the limitations and possibilities of people and their contribution varies with people's position in society, dependent on their circumstances from cradle to grave. For some individuals living in areas with high crime rates, the criminal justice system is scarcely something which is encountered *after* a deviant infraction is discovered by the law; it is omnipresent from childhood, as the autobiographies of many a subsequently professional criminal will testify. The watertight separation of the two was a fault inherent in labelling theory (Taylor et al., 1973: ch. 5), and is reproduced in all subsequent criminological debates. Of course, in terms of the criminal career, the intensity of the intervention of the criminal justice system tends to increase throughout the offender's life. Indeed, in the case of the labelled criminal, typically passing from the prison to regular suspicion on the street back to the prison again, the criminal justice system becomes *the* paramount feature of social structure. It is because of this realism, while agreeing with social positivism that the major thrust of what creates (and controls) crime is extraneous to the criminal justice system, would not negate the influence in controlling (and creating) crime suggested by neoclassicists, labelling theorists and contemporary social constructionists. Any study of the causality of crime must, therefore, take note of both sources emanating from civil society and the state; any worthwhile intervention in the control of crime must speak of interventions in both spheres.

Does realism merely reflect conventional definitions of crime?

Realism attempts to understand the 'construction' of crime as a process. Crime, it argues, occurs at the intersection of a number of lines of force involving four central elements – the offender, the victim, the state and the public. It recognizes that 'crime' occurs within a certain time–space continuum and that there is nothing intrinsic in the 'act' itself, which defines it as a crime. Changes in crime, therefore, are a function of the changing dynamics of this *relational* process. For this reason realists do not and cannot take or accept official definitions of crime unquestioningly.

The aim of radical criminology is, in part, to unpack this complex relation and to attempt to understand its dynamics. It is misleading, therefore, to suggest that radical realists either accept public or commonsense definitions of crime uncritically or adopt essentialist conceptions (Sumner, 1990; Carlen, Chapter 3). In contrast, realists have sought to explore in some detail the problems of disorder and crime as well as the 'fear of crime'. As Matthews (Chapter 2) suggests, the question of disorder, or incivilities as he prefers to call it, are central to realist concerns. It is not at all accidental that the problem of disorder, or incivilities, was one of the first points of confrontation between left and right realists (see Matthews, Chapter 2; Kinsey et al., 1986; Wilson and Kelling, 1982; Skogan, 1988). In this debate the meaning of disorder, its social and political mobilization are key issues, and the relation between disorder, crime and community safety becomes a central focus.

Similarly, the issue of the 'fear of crime' has been addressed by realists. Realists have taken issue with those who have seen fear of crime as irrational – particularly in the case of women and the elderly (Painter et al., 1990). Fear of crime, however, remains something of an ideological category. All too often fear of crime is treated as if it were a unitary phenomenon. As Crawford et al. point out: 'The subject is often treated as though fear, like crime, were undifferentiated. There lies a danger in treating responses to vague and ambiguous questions relating to fear of crime as raw data without first eliciting exactly what we are discussing' (Crawford et al., 1990: 39). Richard Sparks (Chapter 6) argues that, although realists have made important strides in unpacking the notion of fear of crime, it remains a complex and amorphous concept and that the fear of crime has to be analysed within a broader socioeconomic matrix of anxieties, fears and aspirations.

Even when realists extend the parameters of enquiry to include issues of disorder and fear of crime, there remains the charge that the focus is almost exclusively on 'street crime' and that there is a noticeable, and significant, neglect of white-collar and corporate crime. Frank Pearce and Steve Tombs (Chapter 4) examine this question. The issue which Pearce and Tombs address is whether radical realism has neglected white-collar and corporate crime because it is ideologically blinkered or whether it is because the theories and approaches which have been developed by realists are inadequate or inappropriate when analysing white-collar and corporate crime. In relation to conceptions of aetiology, the role of the police and other regulatory agencies, methods of investigation and the like, it is suggested that different sets of problems arise. Analysing corporate crime, they argue, involves a distinctly different framework of analysis and mode of investigation than radical realists have normally adopted. However, Pearce and Tombs argue that although criminological realism has, to date, failed to engage in such analysis – it is not because it cannot do so. They argue for a 'modification of realism, conceptual categories, and a broadening of its field of interest'.

Is realism 'merely' pragmatism?

Left realist criminologists are often accused of pragmatism. By this it is usually meant that interventions are pursued for opportunistic or contingent reasons, with little or no reference to any long-term strategies or principles. This type of approach which might more accurately be referred to as 'instrumentalism' which, although becoming prevalent in certain criminological circles, is not endorsed by radical realists. Realism may, however, be seen as a form of pragmatism to the extent that it refers to that which can conceivably be achieved within the existing structures and constraints. A definition of this kind does not preclude the possibility of longer-term aims and objectives, but recognizes that decisions and choices are not voluntaristic but made within certain parameters and under definite material conditions.

The relation between short-term interventions and longer-term strategies is the perennial problem of all approaches which pursue the path of 'progressive' reforms. In pursuing the logic of this position, realism attempts to avert the negativity of the 'nothing works' and non-interventionist positions on one hand, as well as the 'anything works' position of naive, liberal reformers on the other.

Over the past decade or so we have learnt a great deal about how not to intervene. Liberal pessimists and conservatives have argued that our aim ought not to be 'to do good' but rather 'to do no harm'. The logic of this position is a gradual withdrawal from the policy-making arena and a return to the domination of market principles. It is these principles, however, which, if left uncontrolled, can create the necessary conditions for a criminogenic society (Currie, 1990). The effect of abdicating responsibility for policy formation, therefore, is to leave decision making in the hands of those who have traditionally kept their hands on the levers of power and simultaneously to encourage an unmediated free-for-all in which the powerless are left without defences.

The liberal pessimists are, no doubt, correct to point to the dangers and uncertainties of reform, but it is wrong to assume that reforms can never be successful or that non-intervention constitutes a realistic and constructive option. The real choice, as Travis and Cullen (1984) have argued, is between pursuing 'progressive' interventions and abandoning criminal justice to the right.

The growing volume of postmodernist critiques have lent weight to the scepticism about the possibility of 'progress' (Alexander, 1990). Progress, it is clear, is not automatically a linear or evolutionary process. Although these critiques, like the liberal versions of 'non-interventionism', provide some valuable reminders about the problems and pitfalls of reforms, they too easily lead into cyncism, impossibilism and pessimism (Smart, 1990).

Taking social reform seriously is a central element of radical realism. Within the realist literature, some general objectives of reform in the criminal justice system have been touched upon – democratization, greater personal security, increased public accountability, improved cost effectiveness, and the like (Kinsey et al., 1986; Lea and Young, 1984; Matthews, 1989). These objectives within the criminal justice system are linked to wider social and political objectives of greater equality, opportunity and freedom of choice. Thus, as opposed to the limiting and sceptical critiques of progress which the postmodernists identify as a failure of reason and of modernism, a radical realist approach involves a restatement and rethinking of modernism and reform. As Claus Offe has argued, the increase in options and choices was, at one time, seen as a function of 'modernization'. Now the pressing problems facing modern societies are not so much a further expansion of these options, but of coordinating them and synthesizing them in a more compatible and constructive way. As he puts it:

> A provisional result of these considerations is that the characteristic and decisive criteria of modernity consists not only in the increase in options available in action but equally and contrariwise, in the existence of regulative mechanisms that steer the actually occurring selection of options in such a way that these options are brought into a relationship of harmony and mutual accommodation, and at least do not wreak havoc upon one another and thus destroy one another *as* options. (Offe, 1987: 7)

In an attempt to rethink the problem of reform and to avoid the excesses of pessimism and optimism, Offe indicates some of the complexities and possibilities in thinking about 'progressive' reforms. This involves moving beyond individualistic notions of 'freedom of choice' and towards more systemic considerations. There are issues of strategy and agency which urgently need to be addressed. Strangely enough, however, many of those 'radicals' who have called realism to account because of its 'pragmatism' appear to have surprisingly little to say about how worthwhile social change can be achieved.

Does not realism merely represent a new empiricism based on victimization studies?

In this critique, realism is seen as merely replacing the uncritical acceptance of police figures with an equally uncritical use of victimization data. On the immediate level, victimization studies present us with a much clearer picture of the prevalence of crime than has been available in the past. In particular, the local victimization study, with its high geographical and social focus, utilizing sympathetic interviewers, has uncovered much that is invisible about the dark figure of crime. Both feminist and realist surveys have done much to uncover the criminal victimization of vulnerable groups within the population (Hanmer and Saunders, 1984; Hall, 1985; Jones et al., 1986). Furthermore, they are not, as is frequently suggested, restricted to merely replicating, in an improved fashion, the conventional focus of criminal statistics: street crime such as robbery, burglary and interpersonal violence between strangers. Studies of crimes against women, such as marital rape and domestic violence, are greatly illuminated by victimization studies (Russell, 1982; Painter, 1988; Mooney, 1991). Crimes of powerful groups such as the police are regularly documented (Jones et al., 1986; Painter et al., 1990), while Frank Pearce's work with the *Second Islington Crime Survey* has extended the focus from conventional to commercial crimes (1990). And even certain areas where the public are unaware of their victimization could be covered. For example, it would be quite easy to add to a criminal victimization survey, a medical epidemiological questionnaire in order to measure the prevalence of illness caused by chemical pollution. Both their subjective awareness and the objective impact of pollutants could be established. Moreover, unlike police statistics, victimization studies can provide data as to the impact of crime on different subgroups of individuals, the prevalence of victimization in terms of their economic and social vulnerability and, in many instances, the relationship between the offender and the victim. They do not, therefore, merely provide a series of figures which regard each incident as a crime against an 'equal' isolated victim, but provide the basis for at least a preliminary social contextualization of who is victimized.

It must be stressed at this juncture that a victimization study is a misnomer for the type of empirical research which has been the basis of realist work. The 'second generation' survey includes, as we have seen, a wider range of victim questions, but it goes far beyond this area. It includes self-report data on offences committed, public evaluation of police and other agency service delivery and level of legitimacy, police–public encounters, public attitudes to the punishment appropriate to various crimes, avoidance behaviour with regard to spatial characteristics of the area, etc. Indeed, it covers every aspect of the square of crime: victimization questions often being in the minority (see Crawford et al., 1990). In the majority of instances it does not merely produce more adequate crime statistics than those available from the police, it produces data which are not available from any other source. Even if analysis were to remain on a purely empiricist level – which is clearly untrue – it would, at the bottom line, provide the empirical evidence necessary for any criminological understanding of an area.

Quantitative studies alone, of course, are not sufficient. They give an overview and, by using large samples, can separate out the very different patterning of experiences and attitudes by subgroups divided by a combination of the major axes of age, class, gender and race, and can allow focused representative generalization. But although questionnaire schedules appear objective they display the subjective values of the social scientist and are differentially interpreted according to the subjective values of each subgroup. To take the values of the social scientist first: the menu of possible answers allowed the interviewee is determined by the questionnaire. In the most obvious instances, they tend to view the modal victimization as akin to the burglary. That is a clear, distinct event – the sort of crime that would occur against a middle-aged, middle-class, male researcher. Incessant crime, such as many examples of domestic violence, is scarcely grasped by this method (Genn, 1988; Mooney, 1991). Similarly, the schedules are obsessed with fear of crime when, perhaps, a truer reflection of many subgroups might be anger.

As for the interviewees themselves, they answer the questions from their own values and perspectives. This results in anomalies, particularly in the area of violence where we frequently find that educated women report more violence against them than those less educated (Sparks, 1981) and, even more paradoxically, white men in the United States report more violence than do blacks. Part of this is due to differential disclosure, part due to different values and therefore differential tolerance of permissible violence (Hough, 1986; Young, 1988b). To an extent these problems can be solved technically (Mooney, 1991), but a considerable substratum cannot be solved by quantitative research. Quantitative research is constantly needed in order both to interpret survey data and indeed to move from the discovery of correlations to the imputation of social causality (Young, 1991; Sayer, 1984; Harre, 1979).

Is realism a form of political populism?

We have been accused of political populism, of merely moving from a public, 'commonsense' attitude to one of policy (Mugford and O'Malley, 1991). Such criminological populism is definitely not the aim of realism. We have repeatedly stated that policy cannot be simply read off the computer printout of public opinion (Crawford et al., 1990). Data has to be contextualized and situated. On the most empiricist level, the individual member of the public does not know the collective problems of an area; on a practical level, he or she does not instinctively know whether various control strategies are effective or not (neighbourhood watch being a prime example); on the theoretical level, people are often unaware of the unintended consequences of their actions and the background causes of their behaviour with regard to crime (see Walklate, Chapter 5). But sociological explanation demands that we start from the subjective definitions of the situation, the cultural meanings, with which actors endow the world. Only rank positivists would deny this. And democratic politics bids us take heed of the problems and priorities of the citizen. We take explicit issue with top-down politics, where experts bestow on the population *their* definition of what are problems (Corrigan et al., 1988). Indeed, as, for example, surveys on women's attitudes to crime have shown, the general population very often has a better understanding of the problems facing them than so-called experts. We do not, however proceed from top-down expertise or bottom-up public opinion, but try to incorporate the two. On a theoretical level this involves situating subcultural attitudes within the context of the wider society. On a political level, this involves a debate between the criminological expert and the public. Sandra Walklate (1991) depicts this process as a sleight of hand: first we grant Joe and Jayne Public their opinions, then we, as experts, take it from them. This simply denies the nature of social explanation and the debate which is a necessary part of democracy. It is unreal about social reality and unrealistic about real politics.

References

Alexander, J. (1990) 'Between progress and apocalypse', in J. Alexander and P. Sztaka (eds), *Rethinking Progress*. London: Unwin Hyman.

Bhaskar, R. (1980) *A Realist Theory of Science*. Brighton: Harvester.

Corrigan, P., Jones, T., Lloyd, J. and Young, J. (1988) *Socialism, Merit and Efficiency*. London: Fabian Society.

Crawford, A., Jones, T., Woodhouse, T. and Young, J. (1990) *The Second Islington Crime Survey*. London: Middlesex Polytechnic Centre for Criminology.

Currie, E. (1985) *Confronting Crime: an American Challenge*. Pantheon: New York.

Currie, E. (1990) '"Crime and market society": lessons from the United States'. Paper presented to the Conference on Crime and Policing, Islington.

Dorn, N. and South, N. (eds) (1987) *A Land Fit for Heroin*? London: Macmillan.

Eysenck, H. and Gudjonsson, G. (1989) *The Causes and Cures of Criminality*. New York: Plenum Press.

Garland, D. (1987) 'Review of *Losing the Fight against Crime*', *Contemporary Crises*, 11(2): 198–201.

Genn, H. (1988) 'Multiple victimisation', in M. Maguire and J. Pointing (eds), *Victims of Crime: A New Deal*. Milton Keynes: Open University Press.

Hall, R. (1985) *Ask Any Woman*. Bristol: Falling Wall Press.

Hanmer, J. and Saunders, S. (1984) *Well-founded Fears*. London: Macmillan.

Harre, R. (1979) *Social Being*. Oxford: Blackwell.

Hindess, B. (1973) *The Use of Official Statistics in Sociology*. London: Macmillan.

Hough, M. (1986) 'Victims of violence and crime: findings from the *British Crime Survey*', in E. Fattah (ed.), *From Crime Policy to Victim Policy*. London: Macmillan.

Jones, T., Maclean, B. and Young, J. (1986) *The Islington Crime Survey*. Aldershot: Gower.

Kinsey, R., Lea, J. and Young, J. (1986) *Losing the Fight against Crime*. Oxford: Blackwell.

Lea, J. (1992) 'The analysis of crime', in J. Young and R. Matthews (eds), *Realist Criminology: The Realist Debate*. London: Sage.

Lea, J. and Young, J. (1984) *What is to be Done about Law and Order?* Harmondsworth: Penguin.

Leonard, E. (1984) *Women, Crime and Society*. New York: Longman.

MacLean, B. (1991) 'In partial defence of socialist realism', *Crime, Law and Social Change*, 15: 213–54.

Mathieson, T. (1990) *Prison on Trial*. London: Sage.

Matthews, R. (1986) 'Beyond Wolfenden, prostitution, politics and the law', in R. Matthews and J. Young (eds), *Confronting Crime*. London: Sage.

Matthews, R. (1988) 'Reassessing informal justice', in R. Matthews (ed.), *Informal Justice?* London: Sage.

Matthews, R. (1989) 'Alternatives to and in prison: a realist approach', in D. Cook and P. Carlen (eds), *Paying for Crime*. Milton Keynes: Open University Press.

Matthews, R. and Young, J. (1992) 'Reflections on realism', in J. Young and R. Matthews (eds), *Rethinking Criminology: The Realist Debate*. London: Sage.

Matza, D. (1969) *Becoming Deviant*. New Jersey: Prentice-Hall.

Mooney, J. (1991) *Domestic Violence: Research Problems and Strategies*. London: Middlesex Polytechnic Centre for Criminology.

Mugford, S. and O'Malley, P. (1991) 'Heroin policy and deficit models: the limits of left realism', *Crime, Law and Social Change*, 15: 19–36.

Offe, C. (1987) 'The utopia of the zero-sum option', *Praxis International*, 7(1): 1–24.

Painter, K. (1988) *Lighting and Crime: The Edmonton Project*. London: Middlesex Polytechnic Centre for Criminology.

Painter, K., Lea, J., Woodhouse, T. and Young, J. (1990) *Hammersmith and Fulham Crime and Policing Survey*. London: Middlesex Polytechnic Centre for Criminology.

Pearce, F. (1990) *Commercial and Conventional Crime in Islington*. London: Middlesex Polytechnic Centre for Criminology.

Reiman, J. (1979) *The Rich get Rich and the Poor get Prison*. New York: Wiley.

Russell, D. (1982) *Rape in Marriage*. New York: Macmillan.

Sayer, A. (1984) *Method in Social Science*. London: Hutchinson.

Simon, W. and Gagnon, J. (1986) 'The anomie of affluence', *American Sociological Review*, 82: 356–78.

Skogan, W. (1988) 'Disorder, crime and community decline', in T. Hope and M. Shaw (eds), *Communities and Crime Reduction*. London: HMSO.

Smart, C. (1990) 'Feminist approaches to criminology, or postmodern woman meets atavistic man', in L. Gelsthorpe and A. Morris (eds), *Feminist Perspectives in Criminology*. Milton Keynes: Open University Press.

Sparks, R. (1981) 'Surveys of victimization – an optimistic assessment', in M. Tonry and N. Morris (eds), *Crime and Justice Review*, Vol. 3. Chicago: University of Chicago Press. pp. 1–58.

Sumner, C. (1990) 'Contemporary socialist criminology', in C. Sumner (ed.), *Censure, Politics and Criminal Justice*. Milton Keynes: Open University Press.

Taylor, I., Walton, P. and Young, J. (1973) *The New Criminology for a Social Theory of Deviance*. London: Routledge & Kegan Paul.

Travis, L. and Cullen, F. (1984) 'Radical non-intervention: the myth of doing no harm', *Federal Probation*, 29–32.

Walklate, S. (1991) 'Researching victims of crime: critical victimology', *Social Justice*, 17(3): 25–42.

Wilson, J.Q. and Kelling, G. (1982) 'Broken windows', *The Atlantic Monthly*, March.

Young, J. (1979) 'Left idealism, reformism and beyond', in B. Fine et al. (eds), *Capitalism and the Rule of Law*. London: Hutchinson.

Young, J. (1980) 'Thinking seriously about crime', in M. Fitzgerald et al. (eds), *Crime and Society*. London: Routledge & Kegan Paul.

Young, J. (1986) 'The failure of criminology: the need for radical realism', in R. Matthews and J. Young (eds), *Confronting Crime*. London: Sage.

Young, J. (1988a) 'Radical criminology in Britain: the emergence of a competing paradigm', *British Journal of Criminology*, 28: 159–83. Reprinted in P. Rock (ed.), *The History of British Criminology*. Oxford: Clarendon Press.

Young, J. (1988b) 'Risk of crime and fear of crime: the politics of victimization studies', in M. Maguire and J. Pointing (eds), *Victims of Crime: A New Deal*. Milton Keynes: Open University Press.

Young, J. (1989) 'Making good', review article on *The Causes and Cures of Criminality*, *Nature* 342, 9 November: 138.

Young, J. (1992) 'Ten points of realism', in J. Young and R. Matthews (eds), *Rethinking Criminology: The Realist Debate*. London: Sage.

2 Replacing 'broken windows': crime, incivilities and urban change

Roger Matthews

It is no accident that the debate about crime, incivilities and public order should mark one of the earliest confrontations between the 'new realists' and the 'radical realists'. This debate focuses upon an underlying interest in street crime and community cohesion which is a central focus of both these groups of criminologists. Although they approach the issue from different political and theoretical vantage points, both sides are clear that these issues are seminal to any viable 'law and order' policy.

The debate, however, remains unresolved. The 'new realists' represented by James Q. Wilson and George Kelling continue to express support for the prioritization of order maintenance issues in relation to policing; while the 'left realists' have argued that the police's proper role is controlling crime and it is on their ability to reduce crime rates that they should be judged (Kinsey et al., 1986; Wilson, 1986; Kelling, 1987).

The focal point of this encounter has been the classic article on 'Broken windows' by Wilson and Kelling (1982), in which they laid out their now-familiar thesis on the role of incivilities in promoting neighbourhood decline. They summarize this thesis in the following terms:

> A piece of property is abandoned, weeds grow up, a window is smashed. Adults stop scolding rowdy children; the children, emboldened, become more rowdy. Families move out, unmarried adults move in. Teenagers gather in front of the corner store. The merchant asks them to move, they refuse. Fights occur. Litter accumulates. People start drinking in front of the grocery, in time, an inebriate slumps to the sidewalk and is allowed to sleep it off. Pedestrians are approached by panhandlers. (Wilson and Kelling, 1982: 32).

For Wilson and Kelling the visible evidence of drunks, panhandlers and youths hanging around the area indicates that 'no one cares' and that the area is a vulnerable target for criminal activities. As the more mobile and more respectable families move out, the existing system of informal controls breaks down and the mechanisms for regulating social interaction become less effective. In consequence, both crime and incivilities proliferate.

The primary indicator of decline is the growth of incivilities, and where these problems become intensified, aggressive policing is seen as necessary to prevent their continuation. The better-off areas experience relatively low levels of street crime and incivilities, while in the majority of the poorer areas these problems are so entrenched that it makes sense, Wilson and Kelling argue, to target those neighbourhoods which are identified as being in danger of 'tipping' into decline.

This thesis is undoubtedly attractive and eminently plausible. It draws upon a range of criminological and sociological material and touches upon some real experiences of urban life. By arguing for a strategic intervention, aimed at preventing decline, it offers a more hopeful response than simply throwing more and more money at the problem. It is this strong realist edge, combined with an imaginative attempt to link crime, incivilities and urban change, which has encouraged so many criminologists and policy makers to adopt this thesis in various forms. Over the past few years 'Broken windows' has become one of the most widely referenced articles in criminology and is currently in danger of becoming one of the subject's 'folk wisdoms'. In a discipline characterized by deep disagreements the widespread adoption of this thesis is both surprising and significant. It is surprising in that it has been adopted with only a minimal degree of empirical support. It is significant in that the relationship between crime and incivilities – despite the prioritization often given to the latter by the public – remains largely unexplored.

One of the few responses which has been critical of the Wilson–Kelling approach is that offered by Kinsey and his colleagues (1986) in their *Losing the Fight against Crime*. In this book they take issue with the Wilson–Kelling thesis and argue that the prioritization of order maintenance problems amounts to letting the police 'off the hook' in terms of accountability and the formal criterion of performance – the clear-up rate. Moreover, they argue that much of what Wilson and Kelling depict as order maintenance issues – gang fights, domestic disputes and the like – are, in fact, crimes. The police may 'no crime' or treat these infractions 'informally' in order to dispose of them rapidly, but this does not mean that we have to accept these definitions or practices.

Kinsey et al. (1986) conclude that 'order maintenance' is something of an ideological category and that 'those incidents which might be regarded as disturbances but which do not involve illegalities, are surely not the areas in which the police should intervene'. Thus, for them, it is crime control which ought to remain the focus of police work and this rationalization of effort is seen to be an important element in improving the service and accountability of the police. There is no dispute that the police ought to deal effectively with minor crimes. The issue is whether or not they should be encouraged to deal with that range of activities – which we will refer to as incivilities – that would not normally be considered as crimes, but which are a cause of social concern.

In general Kinsey et al. are correct in pointing to these ambiguities and limitations of the Wilson–Kelling thesis. However, as Wilson and Kelling point out, 'order maintenance' problems are of major concern to many members of the community – particularly the poor – and need to be addressed. And, although there may be some overlap between what Wilson and Kelling identify as incivilities and crime, there are a number of activities related to noise, low-level harassment and intimi-dation which would not normally be considered as criminal acts but which can have a profound effect on the quality of life in particular neighbourhoods. If we are interested in developing a criminology which responds to public interests and concerns, then it is necessary to take both crime and incivilities seriously.

Within this brief exchange between these 'realists' a number of questions remain unanswered. First, we are left with the problem of determining the exact relationship between crime and incivilities. Is this relationship arbitrary and contingent, or is there a causal con-nection? The second issue which is left unresolved is the extent to which the hypothesis of neighbourhood decline and its proposed association with crime and incivilities is credible. Thirdly, we are left with some uncertainty about the most appropriate and effective system of regu-lating incivilities.

In addressing these questions we are encouraged to rethink the relationship between crime and community safety, the 'seriousness' of crime, the problem of displacement, different forms of policing, as well as the spatial dimension of crime and disorder.[1] Although there is clearly an overlap of interests between 'left' and 'right' realists on these issues, there are also some substantial differences. In order to begin to identify some of these points of divergence it is necessary to re-examine some of the key elements of the Wilson–Kelling hypothesis.

Re-examining the Wilson–Kelling hypothesis

When neighbourhoods go into decline they often exhibit the type of characteristics which Wilson and Kelling identify. There is often evidence of high crime rates as well as a growth of a range of other social problems. There is also likely to be an increased sense of vulnerability and sensitivity to the 'signs of decline', as well as changes in the composition of the local population. The initial question, however, is whether declining areas normally exhibit these character-istics and whether or not these processes are actually set in motion by the presence of physical or social incivilities. That is, we need to determine the relation – both logically and historically – between incivilities, crime and neighbourhood decline. For it is Wilson and Kelling's contention that:

> ...at the community level disorder and crime are usually inextricably linked in a kind of developmental sequence. Social psychologists and police officers tend to agree that if a window in a building is broken and *is left unrepaired,* all the rest of the windows will soon be broken. This is as true in nice neighbourhoods as in run-down ones. (Wilson and Kelling, 1982: 78)

There are three central issues which arise from this often-quoted statement. The first involves the degree to which crime and incivilities are inextricably linked. The second is whether 'broken windows' – either metaphorically or literally – have the same effect in different areas; and the third involves the accuracy of the developmental sequence which is suggested. These questions are important, since they have a direct bearing on the formulation of policy concerned with preventing neighbourhood decline.

The 'inextricable' link between crime and incivilities

Crime and incivilities can and do occur together – but not always. There are, it should be noted, areas with high crime rates and low levels of incivilities, just as there are areas with a high incidence of incivilities and relatively low levels of crime (Lewis and Salem, 1986). But, as Wilson and Kelling suggest, there is evidence which indicates that crime and incivilities do tend to occur together. This has been one of the main findings of Home Office researchers who have attempted to assess the applicability of the 'broken windows' thesis to the British situation. The *British Crime Survey* (1984), for example, incorporated measures of crime and incivilities in different parts of the country. To the question: 'What would you say are the worst things about living in your area?', responses were given as shown in Table 2.1.

What these figures indicate is that areas with low concern about crime tend to have lower concern about incivilities. If we put the figures for rural areas aside and concentrate on the urban areas, we find that in designated 'high-risk' areas the concern about crime is high but the identification of incivilities is slightly lower than that presented for 'medium-risk' areas. In 'medium-risk' areas only 5–8 percent of the

TABLE 2.1 *The worst thing about the local area, by Acorn neighbourhood group (Percentages)*

	Crime and vandalism	In- civilities	Shopping facilities/ amenities	Poor transport	Too much traffic
Low-risk areas					
A Agricultural areas (*n* = 460)	1	1	16	24	7
C Older housing of intermediate status (*n* = 1936)	3	8	15	7	12
K Better-off retirement areas (*n* = 443)	4	6	12	10	13
J Affluent suburban housing (n = 1589)	3	5	13	11	11
B Modern family housing higher incomes (*n* = 1475)	4	8	17	8	10
Medium-risk areas					
E Better-off council estates (*n* = 975)	5	10	14	8	10
D Poor quality older terraced housing (*n* = 735)	6	10	10	3	16
F Less well-off council estates (*n* = 1129)	8	14	10	2	7
High-risk areas					
I High status non-family areas (*n* = 573)	7	7	7	4	19
H Multi-racial areas (*n* = 379)	12	9	7	2	11
G Poorest council estates (*n* = 523)	17	10	8	2	5
National average	5	8	13	7	11

Source: Hough and Mayhew, 1985

interviewees considered crime and vandalism as the worst problem, but the incivilities score ranged from 10 to 14 percent. However, in 'high-risk' neighbourhoods – multi-racial areas and high rise council estates – some 17 percent said that crime and vandalism were the worst problems. In these areas the level of incivilities registered was less than in the 'medium-risk' areas (7–10 percent). These figures do not indicate what the objective relationship between crime and incivilities might be, but do suggest that highest levels of perceived incivilities were not recorded in the 'highest-risk' areas, but in the 'medium-risk' areas.

An attempt to explore this relationship further – again using the data from the 1984 *British Crime Survey* – has been presented by Michael Maxfield (1987). His reworked data shows much closer correlation between areas with high levels of incivilities and victimization. These findings have also been broadly supported by the figures produced from the same data source by Tim Hope and Mike Hough (1988). Their results show, not surprisingly, a similar distribution with the level of incivilities roughly the same in medium- and high-risk areas except on the 'better off' and 'poorer' council estates (see Table 2.2).

TABLE 2.2   *Perception of incivilities, by Acorn neighbourhood group*

	Perceived incivilities		
	Drunks, tramps on streets % saying 'common'	Litter lying around % saying 'v. common'	Teenagers hanging around % saying 'v. common'
Low-risk areas			
A Agricultural areas (*n* = 476)	1	4	3
C Older housing of intermediate status (*n* = 2001)	9	14	12
K Better-off retirement areas (*n* = 463)	11	13	8
J Affluent suburban housing (*n* = 1659)	4	8	7
B Modern family housing high incomes (*n* = 1537)	5	11	11
Medium-risk areas			
E Better-off council estates (*n* = 1018)	9	17	18
D Poor quality older terraced housing (*n* = 759)	16	32	20
F Less well-off council estates (*n* = 1175)	14	25	23
High-risk areas			
I High status non-family areas (*n* = 609)	25	21	12
H Multi-racial areas (*n* = 400)	19	34	17
G Poorest council estates (*n* = 543)	19	40	31
National average	10	17	14

Weighted
Source: British Crime Survey, 1984

Hope and Hough's (1988) account which was designed explicitly to examine the Wilson–Kelling thesis found that the 'rates of perceived incivilities are more strongly related to levels of fear of crime ($p < .05$) and neighbourhood satisfaction ($p < .01$) than the level of victimization itself'. Thus Hope and Hough find only a 'loose' relationship between incivilities and crime but do suggest that incivilities may strongly influence feelings of personal and neighbourhood security.

Maxfield's (1987) evidence, on the other hand, indicates that in the areas in which the level of incivilities increased, there was a corresponding increase in the estimated levels of burglary and mugging. Interestingly, his reworked data showed that it was on the poor inner-city council estates that the level of incivilities is highest. These figures, however, do not show, it should be emphasized, that there is any causal relationship between crime and incivilities or that they are 'inextricably' linked.

Unfortunately, these types of studies which have set out to correlate various crimes and incivilities provide only a snapshot. However, the picture which is presented is far from clear. This is partly because the research on which it is based suffers from two major limitations. First, the methodology which underpins national victimization studies is often imprecise and tends to lump together significantly different types of responses. Respondents are often asked whether they 'worry' about certain things, for example. Questions of this kind are too vague to draw any sound conclusions, and no amount of statistical manipulation can compensate for these conceptual difficulties. The second problem is that there is little attempt to separate the effects of specific types of incivilities on specific crimes. To some extent Wilson and Kelling's approach encourages this lack of specificity since, in their analysis, they maintain that it is the spread of incivilities *in general* which is seen to encourage a range of criminal activities. This is also possibly why, in their analysis, there is a tendency to conflate 'environmental' or 'physical' incivilities – 'broken windows', graffiti and litter – with 'social' incivilities such as rowdyism, harassment and intimidation. But physical and social incivilities can give out significantly different messages and it is not always the case that an increase in one leads to an increase in the other. The two are not synonymous and they do not necessarily occur together.

The case for incivilities inviting crime remains weak, whether or not crime is measured by official statistics or victimization rates. The lack of a strong correlation between crime and incivilities has led researchers to turn to the potentially more fertile area of the impact of incivilities on the fear of crime. Michael Maxfield (1987) has attempted to examine some aspects of the Wilson–Kelling thesis in relation to the fear of crime, and claims that the prevalence of incivilities in an area appears to affect neighbourhood and personal risk assessment. He suggests that, although incivilities may not be directly related to actual crime levels, they may, nonetheless, affect what people think about crime. In particular, he reports that burglary and mugging were thought to be common by those who saw incivilities as rife.

In examining the relation between incivilities, victimization rates and fear of crime, Maxfield is aware that different groups express different levels of concern about future victimization. In contrast to Wilson and Kelling's generalized thesis, he finds that, even in areas with high recorded levels of incivilities, only certain crimes are a major cause of concern. Unfortunately, he does not provide data on the actual victimization levels of different groups, and therefore it is impossible to assess the relationship between objective and subjective dimensions of risk and fear of crime, but what he does provide, which is useful, is a reworking of the Wilson–Kelling thesis, which tends towards a rethinking of the relationship between crime and incivilities.

What Maxfield tries to show is that there is a relation between the experience of certain incivilities and estimates of neighbourhood and personal risks of victimization. As opposed to Wilson and Kelling's propositions, he suggests that there are variations, both in the sense that certain incivilities appear to have little or no impact on the fear of crime, while others only have an influence on certain groups under certain conditions. In introducing greater specificity into the relation, Maxfield examined the differential impact of particular incivilities; namely noisy neighbours, groups of teenagers, graffiti, tramps and litter. He found that:

> Of these five items, the belief that 'drunks and tramps on the street' were common was more consistently related to worry and anxiety about personal safety than were the other incivilities. To a lesser extent 'noisy neighbours and loud parties' also increased worry about burglary and mugging. With one important exception, the degree to which incivilities were widespread was *inversely related* to their effects on worry and anxiety for personal safety. Litter and groups of rowdy teenagers were the most common incivilities, but had the least impact on the attitudes of most respondents. (Maxfield, 1987: 33, emphasis added)

Assessments of risk appear to vary considerably by age and gender, and different types of incivilities seem to figure differently among the different populations. Interestingly, litter, which although the most common of all incivilities and presumably one of the most visible signs that 'no one cares', has, according to Maxfield, 'no independent impact on fear'.

The direction in which Maxfield is driven by the logic of his investigations appears to be away from the kind of global relation which Wilson and Kelling propose and towards a more specific enquiry into the connections between crime, fear of crime and in-civilities. His findings would ultimately seem to negate some of the basic assertions of the Wilson–Kelling hypothesis. In its place Maxfield points towards an alternative hypothesis which links estimates of personal risk for particular populations, with the perceived prevalence of certain incivilities.

Drawing upon Maxfield's discussion, it is possible to develop an approach which posits a link – both subjective and objective – between incivilities, crime and fear of crime. It suggests the formulation of an alternative hypothesis. This hypothesis involves three assumptions. The first is that people make rational assessments about their risks of victimization and in adopting avoidance behaviour. The second is that different kinds of incivilities will have an impact on different populations in various ways, and the third assumption is that there is not necessarily a relationship between the spread of incivilities in an area and the increase of crime in general, but that *certain* incivilities may be directly or indirectly linked with certain kinds of crime.

An increasing recognition of the rational nature of much of what is referred to as the 'fear of crime' has been an important element of radical realist work (Crawford et al., 1991). Through the use of local victimization surveys, it has been shown that many of those assessments which were once seen as 'irrational' were, in fact, much more accurate assessments of risk than the unfocused national crime surveys indi-cated. Also, there is a growing awareness of the elaborate and complex calculations which people make in developing avoidance strategies. Using different streets, travelling only at certain times of the day, staying in the house or even moving into another area, are only a few of the multiplicity of strategies which people routinely employ to avoid victimization (Painter, 1989).

At the same time, it would seem reasonable to suppose that different incivilities have a different significance for different groups. It is widely reported that, although young males are frequently the victims of interpersonal violence, they often express a low level of fear, whereas other groups, whose exposure to interpersonal violence is relatively low, may experience a high level of fear. Fear of crime, therefore, appears to be a function of vulnerability, perceived risk and levels of tolerance (Maxfield, 1984).

Certain crimes and incivilities seem to occur together, and the fear which is associated with them may, in part, be based on assessments of an overlap of those involved in perpetrating *both* crime and incivilities. Thus, in contrast to Wilson and Kelling's thesis which claims that incivilities attract outsiders into the neighbourhood, it may be that in a range of crime and incivilities, the perpetrators are in fact the same people.

We might, therefore, hypothesize that members of the public make a range of calculations about the possible relationship between the risk of victimization and the prevalence of certain incivilities. Just as there is no necessary link between the incidence of different types of crimes, so there is no necessary relationship between crime in general and incivilities. Rather, there may be perceived links between different crimes and between certain crimes and particular incivilities. Where these links are seen to occur, we have what might be referred to as 'crime maps' or 'crime sets' (Smith, 1986). By these terms is meant that among certain groups, a number of key variables are perceived to be connected in a number of ways. Increased exposure to certain incivilities may be seen quite reasonably as increasing the likelihood of future victimization, which may, in turn, heighten the fears associated with particular crimes. What would appear to be critical in these calculations is when crime and incivilities are:

1 perceived to involve the same set of victims and offenders;
2 identified as involving the transgression of certain areas of social or defensible space;
3 to be seen as related in a temporal or developmental sequence.

Research carried out by Warr on fear of crime among women and the elderly lends some weight to this hypothesis. He found that among different groups, different offences were grouped together, and that: 'For example, begging is closely associated with a variety of serious personal and property offenses (e.g. assaults, robbery, murder, threats with a weapon among elderly females, but not among young males. Similarly, robbery is much more closely associated with assault, murder and threats with a weapon among elderly females' (Warr, 1984: 696). Each group, Warr suggests, makes its own calculations and links between the perpetration of certain offences and the likelihood of other related offences happening in the future. Each of these offences will have a different impact among each of these groups, which may be ultimately underpinned, as in the case of women, by a perennial fear of sexual attack.

The 'excessive' fear which women, in particular, are seen to express in relation to crime is explicable, not only in terms of the greater spread of criminal victimization to which women are subject, but also, in terms of their vulnerability to a wide range of incivilities which occur in those public spaces in which they may feel most vulnerable. Taking exposure to incivilities and experience of crime together may well indicate that women's assessment of their risk of victimization may be far more accurate than they are given credit for by many criminological researchers.

Just how well-founded these fears and assessments are needs to be determined by a mixture of subjective and objective measures which are sensitive to the varying levels of tolerance exhibited by certain groups. At present, despite the efforts which have been made to investigate the applicability of the 'Broken windows' thesis to the British situation, the research remains largely inconclusive. The type of 'snapshot' which has been provided through the *British Crime Survey* data points to certain possibilities but can tell us little about the *relation* between incivilities, crime and urban decline. The variations on the conclusions reached through the weighted and unweighted figures, however, do provide a reminder of the dangers of taking the findings of national victimization surveys at face value, irrespective of how apparently sophisticated the statistical techniques employed are.

The enduring problem with the type of statistical correlations presented by the Home Office researchers is that crime correlates positively with almost every other negative social indicator (such as unemployment, poverty, mental illness, poor housing, low educational achievement, poor transport and the like). There is always a tendency to try to impute a direct causal relationship between crime in general and any of those variables. Such attempts rarely hold up (Box, 1987). What is clear, however, is that there is a predictable concentration of all these negative social indicators in certain inner-city areas and among particular populations, which produces a compounding effect and which, ultimately, heightens the impact of crime. Certain groups of people living in these areas suffer from a double jeopardy. On one side they are victims of an uncertain and segmented labour market; while on the other side, they are often subject to low levels of security and service provision.

Unravelling the relationship between crime, incivilities and urban change, requires that we consider the relations between specific incivilities and crimes within different contexts and try to better understand the types of assessments which people make about their future victimization. To do this requires that we understand something about the process of neighbourhood decline.

The process of neighbourhood decline

Understanding the processes by which particular inner-city neighbourhoods sink into decline is difficult because change is rarely linear. Identifying the role of any one factor in this process is even more difficult, but there have been some longitudinal studies which have directly and indirectly attempted to address this issue.

One ambitious attempt to examine the effect of crime on neighbourhood decline in Los Angeles between 1950 and 1970 has been presented by Schuerman and Kobrin (1986). Their analysis indicates that it is socioeconomic change and related subcultural transformations which, in turn, affect family types and relational networks. Changes in the form of investment and sites of industrialization invariably alter the composition of the local population; social networks often fragment, and areas become characterized by instability and normative ambiguity. The end result is often an increase in crime rates. The developmental sequence which they identify suggests – in common with many other urban sociologists – that these changes tend to be 'over-determined' by economic and political developments. The question which we are left with is what role do incivilities play in this process? The answer appears to be that they are relatively marginal to the processes of decline and that both crime and incivilities are a function of underlying transformations. Rather than incivilities encouraging crime, it may well be that the growth of crime spawns various incivilities. A great deal seems to depend on the particular age and social composition of the populations remaining in these declining areas, the rate of decline, and the nature of surrounding areas.

Although Schuerman and Kobrin do not directly address the role of incivilities in neighbourhood decline, they do seem to suggest that physical incivilities tend to occur separately from and to precede social incivilities, and that run-down housing, litter and damaged facilities tend to follow shortly after the initial socioeconomic changes take place. The sequence which they identify involves a significantly different dynamic to that suggested by Wilson and Kelling, who are noticeably reticent about the role of economic change, the changing structure of the labour market, and the processes of social and economic marginalization. Incivilities and disorder may be serious problems and greatly affect the quality of life in inner-city neighbourhoods, but their role within the process of urban change, it would seem from this study at least, is far from central. At best certain incivilities may act as catalysts in this process. This possibility, although relatively far removed from the original formulation, is, in developmental terms, a more tenable proposition and one which requires further investigation.

In part the apparent atractiveness of the incivilities–crime–neighbourhood decline model is that incivilities are often the most directly visible element in this process. However, it would appear that removing incivilities, even if it were possible, would offer little possibility of halting or reversing these structural processes. They may be more of a symptom than a cause. A further difficulty in identifying the causal and historical relationship between crime and incivilities is that, in the process of rapid social change and the accompanying normative uncertainty, 'incivilities' can become transformed into 'crimes'. That is, the breakdown or reconstruction of informal controls can mean that incidents which once were dealt with through informal mechanisms are increasingly referred to formal agencies. This is not, as Wilson and Kelling suggest, simply a function of the increased seriousness or prevalence of certain 'problematic situations', but may reflect the unwillingness or inability of local residents to deal effectively with these problems. It may even involve, in some cases, a 'civilizing process', in which conflicts which were once dealt with by interpersonal violence or some form of vengeance, become dealt with by more formal and impersonal agencies. Informal control is not always benign and is rarely equitable (Abel, 1982; Matthews, 1988).

One interesting way of considering the relationship between incivilities, crime and neighbourhood decline is to invert it. That is, to examine the process of gentrification which has become an equally pronounced development within many urban areas in the post-war period. It seems to involve a reversal of the flight to the suburbs and the neglect of central inner-city areas. The corollary of the Wilson–Kelling thesis would, presumably, be that the prevalence of incivilities and disorder in inner-city areas would be a barrier to gentrification and that gentrification would tend to occur in those areas where incivilities and crime were relatively low.

Significantly, what seems to have occurred among the predominantly young, professional sections of the middle classes, who prefer the 'mean streets' to the leafy suburbs, is that they have bought up large run-down properties, often in areas characterized by high crime rates and incivilities. Paradoxically, certain inner-city areas with very high rates of incivilities have become very fashionable and sought-after areas. Places like the Lower East Side and Greenwich Village in New York, Georgetown in Washington, downtown Seattle, as well as various areas in London, seem almost to have become gentrified because of the high level of incivilities, if not crime, since this is 'where the action is'. Interestingly in one area of central London, Camden Town, the range and prevalence of social incivilities and disorder grew as the area became gentrified. Street traders and street musicians, noisy bars and rudimentary 'ethnic' restaurants were all seen to give the area 'character' and make it a desirable place to live. Gentrification, it should be noted, is a destabilizing process and often involves the replacement of families by single people and unmarried, childless couples. The high levels of crime and disorder in the neighbourhood do not seem to prevent this process.

There is no doubt that in other inner-city areas, the perceived risk of victimization and the visibility of incivilities will affect the value of property (Taub et al., 1984). But, as Wesley Skogan put it, 'concern about crime does not, *in itself*, determine levels of investment, the confidence of residents in the future or property values. Rather, it is one strand in a bundle of features which make up a community's character. Where people are optimistic about the bundle as a whole, crime counts for less' (Skogan, 1988: 56). Interestingly, in many areas in America which were gentrified during the 1970s and 1980s, the crime rates remain relatively high. Thus, just as crime does not necessarily increase with urban decline, neither does it decrease as a result of gentrification (McDonald, 1986). It does seem, however, that there is a relationship between the stability of neighbourhoods and crime rates.

In terms of the relation between incivilities, neighbourhood decline and fear of crime, Lewis and Salem (1986) found that 'the communities' political and social resources appeared to constitute a major mediating force between the perception of crime and other neighbourhood problems and the subsequent expression of fear'. The political infrastructure of neighbourhoods is a crucial feature of urban life, but it is something about which Wilson and Kelling have relatively little to say. Presumably one of the reasons why high levels of crime and incivilities are less of a problem for the young urban professionals living in gentrified areas is that they are aware that they possess political clout as well as the resources to cushion or deflect the impact of these phenomena. This raises the important issue of the differential impact of crime and incivilities.

The differential impact of crime and incivilities

Although Wilson and Kelling obviously see the process of urban decline as fairly universal, they do not see it as inevitable. It can be stopped, slowed down or reversed if the appropriate action is taken. However, they do make the bold claim that the process works in exactly the same way in 'nice' neighbourhoods as in run-down ones. This is a strange contention. It is at odds with most of what we know about the distribution and differential effects of social processes in different areas. Moreover, it portrays little understanding of the ability of different neighbourhoods to absorb and resist pressures towards decline, and at the same time, of how incivilities might be differently interpreted among different populations.

On the first issue it seems palpably obvious that some derelict houses, or some abandoned cars, in relatively affluent areas are likely to make little impact on the sense of vulnerability in the area. Residents in better-off areas know that they have the resources and political influence to absorb and deflect the effects of these 'signs of decline' (Byrne and Sampson, 1986).

Just like crimes, the meaning and significance of incivilities is defined by time and space. Space is becoming increasingly recognized as a critical factor in the equation and as a prime determinant in the 'construction of problematic events'. Time and space are critical variables in defining the relationship between offenders and victims. As such, they will substantially condition the reaction of both the public and the state. Thus it is not surprising to find that similar activities can have substantially different – even oppositional – meanings in different areas. Youths hanging around in one area may be widely perceived as a nuisance or a threat, whereas in others they may be seen as protecting community 'turf'.

In a similar vein, it may well be that in poorer areas where there is a high level of serious crime, 'problems' such as litter, graffiti and disorder may be seen as trivial and non-threatening. On the other hand, it could well be that, in middle-income areas where the housing market is changeable, residents may be more sensitive to minor infractions (Skogan, 1988). Sensitivity and concern with incivilities, it would seem, may be as much a function of social location as the objective incidence of such events.

There are two other considerations which are identified elsewhere by Wilson and Kelling which can significantly affect the impact of crime and incivilities in different areas and which we should readily acknowledge. The first is that the impact of crime and incivilities is not simply a function of the number of incidents involved. The difference between two youths and 30 youths hanging around in an area, is often not just a numerical one. At a critical point a qualitative difference occurs in the nature of the problem. When such a shift occurs it invariably necessitates a significant change in the mode of intervention. This observation is important in reminding us that the meaning and impact of problems cannot be simply read off from statistical tables, and that the scale, shape and density can condition how they are conceived. In short, it is a useful antidote to both idealism and empiricism while sensitizing us to the complexities of the theory–practice relation.

A second and related point which on one level seems blatantly obvious, but which is often forgotten, is the difference between individual and social and visible and invisible effects. That is, certain problems (such as drugs, pollution, traffic, etc) may not be identified by most individuals as a serious problem. They may not directly or consciously experience particular activities as causing harm. However, these activities may cause considerable long-term damage to neighbourhoods or may only become apparent to individuals a long time after the event. This process of 'hidden' or invisible victimization raises a number of important questions in relation to the differential impact of crime and incivilities. It raises questions, not only about the validity and reliability of individualized victimization surveys, but also about the value of 'public opinion' when it is measured as the accumulation of individual responses. By the same token, it puts into relief the role of 'public opinion', as expressed through mass surveys, in the prioritization and formulation of policies.

The implications which follow from these two points, although important, do not fit very well with the contention that incivilities have the same impact in different areas. Rather, they suggest that the meaning of different kinds of incivilities will vary considerably from place to place. They also seem to suggest that if we are to take into account the social impact of crime and incivilities, then it is on the poorest and least resourced neighbourhoods that we should focus our attention, rather than those which are described as 'tipping into decline'. This is where these problems are compounded and where the ability of residents to withstand them will be limited.

Addressing these problems would realistically involve locating the concern with incivilities within a wider context of community resources. Wilson and Kelling, as has been suggested above, are particularly neglectful of the role of the political organizations through which policies would have to be channelled. Also, what most urban sociologists would consider to be prime movers in the process of urban decline – corporations, industrial and finance capital and political groupings – play a virtually non-existent role in their presentation. Instead the focus is on the development of more aggressive policing of the 'low lifers' and obstreperous youths who are deemed to be the instigators of urban decline.

The problems of policing disorder

Controlling incivilities and maintaining order raises a number of problems. George Kelling has himself identified some of the central issues:

> Police order maintenance activities are important but controversial. They are controversial because there is no clear and consistent definition of what constitutes disorder and because the justification of police intervention in disorderly situations is uncertain. Some behaviour that creates disorder is illegal and the basis for intervention is clear: the law. Other behaviour that creates disorder is not illegal; instead, it violates community or neighbourhood expectations of what constitutes appropriate civil behaviour. Under such circumstances a primary basis for police intervention is the political will of the community. (Kelling, 1987: 90)

Finding an effective method of policing these problems is difficult, Kelling argues, because of the growing levels of individualism and egoism which have made inner-city streets less ordered and more precarious. High levels of incivilities in these areas tend to heighten fears and decrease the 'quality of life'.

Despite these problems, Kelling insists that focusing on order maintenance has a number of advantages. On one side, he argues, the reduction of disorder has immediate benefits for the community, while providing a unique opportunity for crime control on the other (Kelling, 1985). Policing disorder can, he claims, affect crime control by preventing disorderly behaviour from escalating into criminal acts, by encouraging the moral self-defence activities of citizens and by decreasing the demand for the police's service functions as a result of greater contact on the street. Order maintenance, Kelling argues, has historically been the primary role of the police and it is only in the relatively recent past that crime control has been emphasized.

Before we examine these specific assertions it is necessary to address some of the general problems in effectively policing disorder. Kelling claims that a major distinction arises from the fact that there is 'no clear and consistent definition of disorder and unlike crimes which are defined in relation to *acts*, disorder is a *condition*'. This is an important point, but the distinction is not quite as clear-cut as Kelling suggests due to the non-specific nature of much disorder and the absence, in most cases, of any direct victim. There is a second, and arguably more important, distinction, however, which arises from the lack of public consensus over the 'problem' and the nature of these 'conditions'.

For these reasons there are serious limitations in leaving these 'problems' to be dealt with by the police, whose authority is largely tied to the mobilization (real or threatened) of the criminal law, since many of these activities do not involve specific acts and, as a result, the police, who are charged with controlling them, are often forced to adopt extra-legal means. Since Wilson and Kelling believe that order maintenance ought to be the police's primary function, they unequivocally endorse the use of extra-legal methods and the need to 'kick ass' to keep people in order. Significantly, the asses of the people they want kicked are winos, street prostitutes, panhandlers and juveniles. Wilson and Kelling want the police to respond to the responsible and respectable interests of the community and to disperse these 'undesirables'. However, many of the neighbourhoods where incivilities are common are marked by a general lack of consensus. In this context the police may have no clear mandate and may be seen as acting on behalf of one section of the community (Skogan, 1990). Amidst conflicting sets of values and relying on the often inappropriate instrument of the criminal law, the police are at risk of alienating sections of the community and thereby interfering with the flow of information on which their crime control function depends. Thus, in contrast to Kelling's claim that vigorously policing disorder is the way to reduce crime, it would seem that it is equally likely to impair the police's crime control function. We have seen only too clearly in recent years when the police try to control 'disorder' in the form of strikes, demonstrations and the like in an aggressive manner, they can alienate, not only a significant number of individuals and groups, but, as in the case of the miners' strike in Britain, they can alienate a whole community (Green, 1990).

In fact, Kelling's contention that policing disorder will reduce crime is confounded by his own research carried out in Newark, which found that, while the introduction of foot patrols increased people's sense of security, it had no measurable effect on crime at all (Police Foundation, 1981; Klockars, 1985). One evaluation of the foot patrol experience in Newark concluded that, while it had some effect on residents' perceptions of disorder, it appears to have had no significant effect on victimization, recorded crime or the likelihood of reporting crime (Pate, 1986). It should also be added that the suggestion that order maintenance was historically prior to crime control overlooks the fact that the movement away from order maintenance was part of a development aimed at controlling police abuses, limiting discretion, and increasing professionalism (Walker, 1984).

In relation to Newark, which has no doubt been the beneficiary of some innovative policies in recent years, the key problem during the 1970s in the police department was the excessive use of force, corruption and the lack of accountability. All of these basic problems had to be addressed before any reform was possible. According to Skolnick and Bayley (1986), the main problems facing Newark's police department during this period was poor relations with the public, the increase in the rates of serious crime, and the tendency to operate according to hidden norms which were unacceptable to the local population. In these situations it is not surprising to find the police department was swamped with complaints and law suits filed against them for 'harassment' and other 'excesses'. Dealing with endless complaints substantially increases the costs of policing.

During the 1980s projects were carried out in both Newark and Houston which were greatly influenced by the writings of Wilson and Kelling and which were specifically designed to reduce the fear of crime (Pate, 1986). These were fairly comprehensive programmes involving several community policing strategies. The programmes produced mixed results. Although there was some indication of reductions in perceived disorder, perceived crime levels and improved citizen evaluations of the police, Rosenbaum comments that:

> One noticeable failure in the Houston–Newark Fear Reduction Project was the 'signs of crime' program, which attempted (a) to reduce fear and related problems by reducing social disorder (through foot patrols and aggressive order maintenance) and (b) to reduce physical deterioration (through more intense city services and a youth clean-up program). The lack of positive police–citizen contact and the random implementation of the program may

help to explain the *complete lack of effects*, but in view of the amount of resources devoted to this strategy, some might question the 'incivility' theory and the 'crime attack' model that served as the rationale for the approach. (Rosenbaum, 1988: 373, emphasis added)

The influence of Wilson and Kelling has also been felt elsewhere. In Denver, for example, order maintenance was emphasized through what was called the ESCORT (Eliminate Street Crime on Residential Thoroughfares) Strategy, which attempted to improve order and safety on the streets in the Capitol Hill area by controlling the marginal populations by way of a strategy of 'skilled harassment'. Using an array of legal sanctions, the strategy involved combing the streets for minor violations, rowdyism and drugs. In this run-down area, aggressive policing was justified in terms of protecting the poor and powerless in the neighbourhood and to provide the necessary conditions for the minimum level of security for local citizens. In their examination of ESCORT Skolnick and Bayley concluded that:

> It is hard to tell if ESCORT has been successful. It has certainly been popular, and the department has been asked continually to expand it to other neighborhoods. As one would expect, ESCORT officers generate impressive totals of practice enforcement. They are surely a felt presence. The department believes ESCORT has been effective in reducing crime, although the evaluation has been rough and ready. For example during ESCORT's first twenty months (1975–77), reports of rapes and both simple and aggravated assaults declined significantly. Burglaries declined too, but only slightly. Despite a continuing high incidence of crime, many politicians and business people credited ESCORT with stabilizing transitional areas that otherwise would have become blighted and uninhabitable. (Skolnick and Bayley, 1986: 141).

The experience of Denver appears to give some qualified support for promoting order maintenance activities. But it should be noted that in this case policing was closely monitored and tied to *legal* controls, and that the area concerned was atypical and subject to extreme problems. It was not an area 'tipping' into decline, but paradoxically one which would probably have been depicted by Wilson and Kelling as being 'beyond reclamation'.

Many of the problems which Wilson and Kelling identify – rowdy youths, noisy neighbours, drunks and vagrants – remain incivilities precisely because the public, by and large, do not think that they ought to be dealt with by the criminal justice system. When the public report these problems to the police, it is often not because they want a heavy-handed, truncheon-wielding army of police officers descending on their neighbourhood, but because there is not an available alternative. In recent years there has been a move by local councils in Britain to deal with a range of disorder problems – particularly those related to noise, harassment of neighbours and litter. Wilson and Kelling's contention that the police are the key to controlling disorder is, it would seem, becoming less tenable in this country at least. In fact, in many of the more imaginative and successful interventions which have occurred in recent years to control both crime and incivilities, the police have played an increasingly subordinate role. In some noteworthy initiatives they have been conspicuously absent. In Kelling's own research on reducing the level of graffiti on the New York subway, it was not tougher policing, or even better target hardening which proved successful, but, rather, reducing the motivation of graffiti artists by removing graffiti immediately from the trains and preventing offenders from 'getting up' (Sloan-Howitt and Kelling, 1990).

The notion of 'community policing' has a great deal of prominence these days and it is widely recognized that fostering the relationship between the police and the public is crucial in improving the service which the police provide. However, the critical issue concerns the proper nature of this relationship. The kind of model which Wilson and Kelling offer is inadequate, it has been suggested, in a number of ways. First, its implementation seems to be largely dependent on the 'goodwill' of police chiefs and particular officers. The police in this model are presented as the 'good guys', who only have the interests of the community at heart (Wilson and Kelling, 1989). The reality, however, is that this goodwill is a limited commodity within urban police forces and that the police have other interests. One of the most difficult jobs for senior police managers is to keep these various interests in check. In a situation in Britain, where one half of the police force is currently under investigation by the other half, the view that the police constitute a band of committed 'do-gooders' is a little myopic. Secondly, patrol work and dealing with low level disorder is low priority and low status work for the police. Thirdly, it must be said that it is also a little naive to believe that the police have a total commitment to remove crime and incivilities altogether. There are bureaucratic and organizational pressures to maintain a 'manageable' level of crime. For these reasons we need to be careful about always allowing these 'community policing' strategies to be police-led. Also, a great deal is made by Wilson and Kelling of the effects of uniformed foot patrols, and certainly their research indicates that this increases people's sense of security. But it may well be that a range of uniformed patrols could fulfil this function and that, in some areas, there may be other agencies who could perform this function more cost-effectively.

Dennis Rosenbaum (1987) has rightly pointed to the limits of what he calls the 'implant' approach to crime control. In many cases there is little to be gained from implanting new organs into decaying bodies. Although there are no doubt some significant short-term and localized gains to be made from developing more imaginative and responsive styles of policing, there is a growing recognition that if problems are not to be simply displaced or postponed, then more comprehensive and socialized forms of policing need to be developed. For the vast majority of minor infractions, interpersonal conflicts, and a range of 'incivilities', neither the full authority of the police and the criminal law, nor the threats and intimidation of self-styled moral guardians in the form of citizen patrols, seem particularly appropriate. Between these two extremes there are a number of alternatives which may be more relevant.

The growing experimentation with multi-agency approaches to crime control has, on one hand, focused attention on the effectiveness of certain agencies in dealing with particular problems which were once seen as the province of the police; while on the other hand, they have encouraged a serious rethink about the appropriate *point* of intervention, both in relation to the 'evolution' of the problem and to the development of the person(s) involved (Forrester et al., 1988; Matthews, 1986). It has, by implication, involved a re-examination of the complex relationship between formal and informal modes of regulation.

Moreover, in recent years there has been a growing awareness of the value and effectiveness of various 'intermediary' agencies in regulating social (mis)behaviour. Paradoxically, this interest has occurred at a time when many of these agencies are in decline. In a sense it is the very absence of such agencies which allows the problem of regulation to be posed in terms of an opposition between formal policing and citizen patrols. Many of the once-familiar regulatory bodies – park-keepers, station guards, etc, as well as many of the social and political organizations – working mens' clubs, trade union associations, church organizations, etc – which once acted both as channels of political and social participation and as vehicles of expression and control within the public sphere, have either gone into decline or disappeared (Habermas, 1989). In consequence, the nature of the public sphere has been significantly transformed, and this has a profound effect upon the nature of urban living and, in particular, on the organization of social space.

One immediate example of this change is a massive reduction in the number of people operating transport systems. As a result, buses and trains have become a kind of 'no man's land' in many cities. Many transport systems are characterized by high levels of vandalism, unmediated aggression and, in some cases, high levels of fare evasion. Attempts have been made to try to resolve these problems in recent years. In Holland, for example, one useful initiative involved engaging about 1200 unemployed people as transport officers who were introduced to try to improve the security and to reduce the number of fare evaders. The results were impressive. Security was increased, the levels of vandalism and graffiti decreased, and there was a reduction in petty crime and fare evasion (Andel, 1989).

A similar type of strategy has been developed in a number of countries to provide a relatively low level, but effective, regulation on council estates. This involves the use of concierges or receptionists whose role is to monitor activities around the estate. This strategy is normally linked to entry control systems and the aim is that the receptionist is not only concerned with helping to reduce crimes like burglary and vandalism, but also to act as a focal point for the people living in the block and to help to improve the management of the blocks. The evaluations which have been carried out suggest that these schemes are very effective, both in terms of reducing crime and disorder on estates and also in improving the quality of housing and repair services (Poyner and Webb, 1987). Both of these examples were reasonably cost-effective and point to the possibilities of developing middle-range interventions which can reduce both crime and the fear of crime in particular areas. These strategies are not so much 'implants' as mechanisms for developing a more integrated regulatory infrastructure.

A different kind of initiative which has proved beneficial in England is the 'Priority Estates Project'. This involves developing a comprehensive policy for 'difficult to let' or 'sink' estates which are identified as suffering from high levels of crime as well as a range of other social problems, including poor maintenance, vandalism, and high tenant turnover. These estates are often unpoliced, badly designed and poorly protected. It is these estates where residents' fear of crime is notoriously high and where there is a prevalence of graffitti, vandalism, litter, drunks and rowdy youths. There is a disproportionate number of young people on these estates, many one-parent families, and a great deal of unemployment. Through a range of policies, including the setting up of tenants' associations, youth clubs, the clearing up of litter, police patrols, and prompter housing repairs, substantial improvements have been made. Importantly, these initiatives have centred on residents' ability to influence events. The experience of the Priority Estates Project is that, if crime and incivilities are to be reduced in these areas, 'some combination of resident organisation, youth leadership, estate-based housing management, residential employment initiatives, communal guarding, beat policing and anti-crime measures (doors, locks and lighting, securing access-ways, vandal-proof fittings, etc) is needed' (Power, 1989).

The Priority Estates Project is particularly impressive because it has managed a rare achievement in the field of crime control; it has produced extremely beneficial results in high-crime areas which might otherwise be written off. This multi-faceted initiative also underlines the deep-seated motivation even in depressed areas to improve security and to reduce crime. As our understanding and involvement in these neighbourhoods grows we see that the areas are neither characterized solely by egoism and individualism on one side, or a pre-given 'community' on the other. Instead, we find divisions and conflicts – but also overlapping levels of interest, associations and communality. Shifting the balance from individualism to collectivism, from conflict to consensus, and from depression to confidence, appears to be largely dependent on building social networks and developing a range of intermediary agencies – both locally and generally – which can effectively channel and regulate social actions (Braithwaite, 1989). Policing plays a relatively minor back-up role in this empowering process. Aggressive and discriminatory policing employing extra-legal methods can produce, as we have seen, more disorder and, in some cases, has led to full-blown riots (Gifford, 1986). Building 'communities' is not a matter of creating a monolithic set of values or, for that matter, reducing dissensus, but rather creating the mechanisms through which different values and aspirations can be mobilized, discussed and realized. Developing such mechanisms is an important part of creating a pluralistic, social democratic state.

The experience of the Priority Estates Project shows that various incivilities can be removed through the organization of facilities, the provision of basic resources and changes in housing policies. Similarly, many of the problems associated with youths hanging around have been resolved through the provision of youth clubs, training facilities and the like. Vagrancy and public drunkenness can similarly be reduced through the provision of housing, hostels and clinics.

Wilson and Kelling express little interest in developing mechanisms and agencies which may empower the poor and the powerless, and they seem even less interested in directing resources towards the disadvantaged and marginalized. Instead, their main concern is to remove these undesirables' from respectable areas, and since they do not want to do very much about their condition, they will, presumably, be deflected towards those poorer areas which already have more than their fair share of social problems. In their diatribe against decriminalization and decarceration, they seem to be suggesting that 'if only we got really tough' on these people and put them in prison for longer, then urban decline in respectable areas could be prevented. The reality is, of course, that decarcerated populations invariably gravitate towards the run-down inner-city ghettos (Scull, 1977). Since Wilson is against rehabilitation and seems to be largely impervious to the debilitating and alienating effect of incarceration, preferring instead a policy of incapacitation, there is no indication of how the continual flow of increasingly marginalized offenders back into the poorer urban areas is to be overcome (Wilson, 1983; Cullen and Gilbert, 1982). In fact, the policy of selective incapacitation which Wilson and some of his more punitive conservative associates support, is precisely the policy which currently operates both in Britain and America. Its undesirable effects are all too apparent (Currie, 1986). Decriminalization is a more complex problem and the debate over legal and non-legal modes of regulation for different types of activities cannot be fully discussed here, but it should be noted that, while there has been a monumental expansion in the number of new laws passed over the last decade, it is also the case that some forms of decriminalization have occurred in recent years, not because of a new wave of 'permissiveness', but because a number of statutes have proved unenforceable.

Summary and discussion

In reviewing the literature related to the crime incivilities and neighbourhood change, very little support has been found for the 'Broken windows' hypothesis or to the central contentions of the Wilson–Kelling thesis relating to the relationship between crime and incivilities. The dynamics of urban decline and the differential effects of disorder appear extremely weak. Most significantly, the model of decline which Wilson and Kelling present which involves the following sequence:

$$\text{Incivilities} \rightarrow \begin{array}{c} \text{Decrease in} \\ \text{informal control} \end{array} \rightarrow \begin{array}{c} \text{Increased} \\ \text{crime} \end{array} \rightarrow \begin{array}{c} \text{Increased} \\ \text{fear} \end{array}$$

was found to have little empirical support. Instead, incivilities appear to be the dependent variable and seem relatively marginal to the process of urban decline (and gentrification), and only tenuously linked to crime. There does appear to be some relationship between the levels of incivilities, victimization and the subsequent 'fear of crime', but it has been suggested that this needs to be examined in relation to the temporal and spatial relations involved. Taking the objective incidence of crime and incivilities together may indicate that the 'fear of crime' among specific groups in particular areas is more rational and realistic than it is often portrayed.

The evidence drawn from the *British Crime Survey* indicates a loose correlation between crime and incivilities, but allowing for different levels of tolerance and sensitivity to incivilities, it seems that these problems are predominantly located in those poorer neighbourhoods which score highly on other negative social indicators and receive generally inadequate services.

The disturbing feature of Wilson and Kelling's proposals is that they would invariably compound these problems by displacing crime and incivilities from the more 'respectable' to the less 'respectable' areas. Since they are not interested in providing the resources to deal with these problems and thereby reducing them, their objective is to move them from those areas which are probably better equipped to deal with them to the less well-equipped areas. What appears at first sight is a relatively altruistic strategy to prevent neighbourhood decline, turns out, on closer inspection, to be the cleaning up of one area at the expense of other less well-endowed ones. It is not difficult to see how such proposals might be attractive to radical conservative adminis-trations during periods of increased social inequality. It provides a clear rationale for writing off poorer areas as 'unreclaimable', while identifying vagrants, drunks and disenchanted youth as the instigators rather than the victims of neighbourhood decline and economic change. It is a short step from this familiar ideological inversion to the critique of deinstitutionalization and decriminalization, and to blaming inner-city ills on the mood of 'permissiveness'. Instead they advocate more 'get tough' policies, greater use of imprisonment, and the extension of selective incapacitation. At the same time, they want, not only more legal sanctions, but also endorse the use of extra-legal tactics by the police and seem to suggest that the appropriate response to intimidation and harassment on the street is more intimidation and harrassment by the police.

The 'Broken windows' hypothesis comes complete with all this conceptual baggage. It is, no doubt, attractive to those who want to write off deprived inner-city areas and who think that marginal populations do not deserve the same safeguards as the rest of the population, who feel comfortable about endlessly recycling (often minor) offenders through a debilitating penal system, and who are basically uninterested in developing more democratically accountable forms of policing.

Although Wilson distances himself from the 'try 'em and fry 'em' brigade on one hand, and radical non-interventionalists on the other, his particular brand of 'realist' criminology incorporates most of the major elements of conservatism (Wilson, 1986). His approach includes a mixture of instrumentalism ('What works?') phenomenalism (a disdain for 'root' causes), biologism (that people are inherently 'wicked'), essentialism (criminality is a function of 'human nature'); combined with an underlying punitiveness which is reserved largely for the poor, the 'feckless' and the marginalized (Wilson, 1983; Wilson and Herrnstein, 1985). These essential ingredients of conservative criminology are given a new slant by Wilson, who presents his ideas in a commonsensical way.[2]

Like much commonsense theorizing, however, the work is littered
with untheorized and unmediated dichotomies – the wicked and the
innocent, respectable and non-respectable, individual and community,
the salvageable and the unsalvageable. The continual use of these oppositions injects the writing with a series of often untenable and unrealistic
choices and alternatives. This particular brand of 'new realism' is,
therefore, underpinned by a constraining dualism. Within the confines
of this approach there are a number of noticeable omissions. The wider
economic and political configurations and the processes by which
certain groups become marginalized are hardly referred to. The focus
is almost exclusively on predatory street crime and a wide range of
interpersonal and white-collar crime – all of which play an important
part in the complex dynamics of urban living – are rarely touched
upon. These omissions and the narrow focus of the work leads
invariably to skewed and partisan policy proposals. As Elliott Currie
has argued:

> In the absence of that ('socio-economic') the conservative emphasis upon
> culture, values and tradition degenerates into wistful nostalgia, or worse,
> into a self-righteous, punitive demand for more corporal punishment.
> Harsher discipline in the family and schools and the indiscriminate use of
> the prisons as holding pens for the urban underclass we have decided to give
> up on.
>
> The conservative model turns out to be shot through with contradictions.
> In a world of dramatic national variations in criminal violence, it blames
> crime on an invariant human nature. In a society that ranks amongst the
> most punitive in the developed world, it blames crime and leniency on the
> justice system. In a country noted for its harsh response to social deviation,
> it blames crime on attitudes of tolerance run wild. (Currie, 1986: 436)

There is a further tension involved in this approach. On one side there
is a sense of desperation which arises from the view that these problems
are so widespread that only a thoroughgoing response will go any way
towards dealing with them; while on the other hand there is the worry
that change might be too 'radical' and far-reaching.

As we have seen, many of these policies and proposals are based on
very flimsy evidence, and even the work carried out and reported by
the authors themselves provides little support for their central contentions. Thus, what at first appears to be a hard-headed, no-nonsense
approach concerned only with 'what works', turns out to be less of an
explanation and more of a rationalization. The real issue seems to be
'what works for whom?'

It is not that the writings of Wilson and his colleagues do not contain
a sense of realism, but that they are often not realist enough. Their
work relies heavily on the immediate and outward appearances being
guided ultimately by irrepressible ideological beliefs. There is a thin

veneer of scientificity in all this, just as there is a formal concern for the plight of urban communities. Ultimately, however, it does not offer much of a solution, since it is based on a political philosophy which accepts growing social inequalities, which argues for reduction of state intervention, which sees the growth of crime as a necessary by-product of a 'free market' society and argues for the extension of those aggressive policing practices which rely on 'informal' means to resolve problems of crime and disorder.

In contrast, a 'left realist' approach would offer a different set of strategies and modified objectives. From this oppositional vantage point it is suggested that besides the need to address the underlying socio-economic determinants of crime and disorder, there are a number of alternative proposals which should be considered:

i) *The equalization of victimization* The unequal nature of victimization across different groups residing in different areas has been repeatedly identified. Multiple victimization is often compounded by the social and geographical concentration of various other social problems. It was one of the original propositions of radical realism that a great deal of crime was intra-class rather than inter-class. Although there is considerable variation in the distribution of victimization between different categories of crime, it remains the case that the poor and the vulnerable are disproportionately victimized (Sparks, 1981). This is not a 'natural' occurrence. Significant changes in the impact and distribution of victimization can be effected, as some of the above examples indicate. A democratic crime control policy would attempt to equalize the risk and the effects of victimization.

ii) *The prevention of displacement* A prevalent characteristic of a great deal of crime prevention initiatives which have been implemented to date is their extremely specific and parochial nature. Although a number of crime prevention measures have been successful in terms of specific individuals, many have resulted in the displacement of the problem into other areas or on to other individuals. The net result of much crime prevention undoubtedly has been to heighten inequalities in the distribution of victimization by shifting the crime from the better to the less well-protected. It is difficult to know the precise displacement effects of specific initiatives, since measures of displacement have only rarely been incorporated into research designs. We know, however, that crime prevention tends to work better where it is needed least and, therefore, in situations in which there continues to be an increase in virtually all categories of crime, it would seem that the consequence of many strategies (such as neighbourhood watch) is to displace crime into the less well-protected areas (Bennett, 1989; Rosenbaum, 1987).

Such displacement is far from inevitable, but the blinkered and individualistic vision which has underpinned so many recent crime prevention initiatives is reflected in the fact that the prevention of displacement is rarely considered an essential element in evaluating the 'success' of these measures.

iii) *Encouraging 'benign' displacement*   The prevention of displacement must be the major objective. However, controlling displacement effects can be extremely difficult. Displacement can take a number of forms – temporal, occupational and situational. But since an element of displacement is often involved in the selection of victims – 'crime patterns at any point in time are frozen displacement patterns' (Barr and Pease, 1990) – the aim must be to encourage 'benign' forms of displacement. The policies advocated by Wilson and Kelling only serve to intensify these problems by advocating the displacement of crime away from the more 'respectable' neighbourhoods. A social democratic response should aim to avoid displacement or, alternatively, attempt to facilitate those forms of displacement, which would aim to limit the level and impact of victimization by deflecting crime and incivilities away from the most vulnerable populations.

iv) *The minimization of social injury*   As we have seen, both crime and incivilities make an impact on different populations in various ways. The younger and wealthier sections of society have more physical and social resources to deal with crime-related problems. However, the minimization of social injury requires, on one hand, support and compensation services (such as Victim Support, group insurance, etc) to reduce the impact of crime, particularly among the more vulnerable and least resourced populations; on the other, it involves the reduction of those crimes and incivilities which have the most damaging effects. Pursuing these joint strategies may well go some way to reducing the fear of crime and its consequences. As Lewis and Salem (1986) put it: 'a fear reduction policy, like a poverty reduction strategy, attempts to redistribute a value, in this case, security.'

v) *The development of intermediary agencies*   In opposition to encouraging the development of more aggressive policing and punitive penal policies, it has been suggested that various forms of inter-agency cooperation can be effective – particularly when the police are sensitive and responsive to the views and interests of local residents. Such strategies have been important in encouraging us to think more clearly about the role of non-police agencies in regulating a wide range of social behaviour and in inviting us to examine, in more detail, the role of different agencies at different points in the process.

Strategies, however, which seek to 'implant' a solution without influencing the complex matrix of social relations in a particular locality are likely to be of limited effectiveness. Beneficial crime control measures seem to involve residents in taking responsibility and interest in their neighbourhood and the development of organizations which allow them to exert influence on local developments.

vi) *The targeting of resources into areas of high crime rates and incivilities* Problems of disorder can have a devastating effect on the quality of life for certain inner-city dwellers. However, we now have a considerable amount of information about which groups and which areas need to be targeted to reduce crime and other social problems. Unlike the old 'welfare' policies which were too general and often missed their target, a more diligent and imaginative use of resources is needed. We know that a range of incivilities could be substantially reduced by providing hostels, youth clubs, drop-in centres and clinics. All these services, it might be argued, cost money, but as targeted programmes they probably compare very favourably with the cost of police patrols, court procedures and prisons – not to mention the personal and social costs of continually recycling the same marginalized population through the criminal justice system. A great deal could be done to reduce this costly recycling process.

Endnote

Finally, it could be argued with some justification that this evaluation of the 'Broken windows' hypothesis has been mounted from a predominantly British vantage point and that the problems of crime and disorder in US cities are quantitatively and qualitatively different and, therefore, require a different type of response. The complex relationship between federal and state agencies as well as the size and organization of US cities is likely to make direct comparisons impossible. However, in examining the evidence, a range of US literature has been used and this, in general, provides little support for the 'Broken windows' thesis. The questions which have been posed in relation to this thesis are theoretical and logical, as well as empirical.

The current 'Americanization' of British social policy, however, involving the developments of a 'safety net' state and the widening of economic inequalities, together with the encouragement of competitive individualism and acquisitiveness, has fostered a situation in which the gap between the two countries in relation to crime and disorder appears to be narrowing at a disturbing rate.

Notes

1. The terms 'incivilities' and 'disorder' are often used interchangeably in the literature. In general, however, 'incivilities' is used to refer to both physical and social phenomena, whereas 'disorder' is normally limited to the latter. Thus, although the term 'incivilities' is a little awkward, I have used it rather than the term 'disorder'. Also, as opposed to disorder, it is used to identify a range of problems which would not normally come under the heading of crime.
2. For the sake of convenience and clarity, it is assumed that there is a wide degree of agreement in political and theoretical terms between Wilson and Kelling. However, since most of Kelling's work is more practical, the degree of overlap between these two writers is difficult to determine. To some extent the personal variations, however, are of relatively little importance, since the aim of this chapter is to respond to a particular tendency within criminology which has become identified as 'new realism'.

References

Abel, R. (1982) *The Politics of Informal Justice* Vol. 1. New York: Academic Press.

Andel, H. (1989) 'Crime prevention that works: the case of public transport in the Netherlands', British *Journal of Criminology*, 29(1): 47–56.

Barr, R. and Pease, K. (1990) 'Crime displacement and placement', in M. Tonry and N. Morris (eds), *Crime and Justice* Vol. 12. Chicago: University of Chicago Press.

Bennett, J. (1989) 'Factors related to participation in neighbourhood watch', *British Journal of Criminology*, 29(3): 207–19.

Bottoms, A. and Wiles, P. (1981) 'Housing tenure and residential community crime careers in 1986 Britain', in A. Reiss and M. Tonry (eds), *Communities and Crime*. Chicago: Chicago University Press.

Box, S. (1987) *Recession, Crime and Punishment*. London: Macmillan.

Braithwaite, J. (1989) *Crime, Shame and Reintegration*. Cambridge: Cambridge University Press.

Byrne, J. and Sampson, R. (eds) (1986) *The Social Ecology of Crime*. Berlin: Springer-Verlag.

Crawford, A., Jones, T., Woodhouse, T. and Young, J. (1991) *Second Islington Crime Survey*. London: Routledge.

Cullen, F. and Gilbert, K. (1982) *Reaffirming Rehabilitation*. Cincinnati: Anderson Publishing Co.

Currie, F. (1986) 'Crime and the conservatives', *Dissent*, Fall: 427–37.

Forrester, D., Chatterton, M. and Pease, K. (1988) *The Kirkholt Burglary Prevention Demonstration Project*. Crime Prevention Paper 13. London: Home Office.

Gifford, Lord (1986) *Broadwater Farm Inquiry*. London Borough of Haringey: HMSO.

Green, P. (1990) *The Enemy Without: Policing and Class Consciousness in the Miners' Strike*. Milton Keynes: Open University Press.

Habermas, J. (1989) *The Structural Transformation of the Public Sphere*. London: Polity Press.

Hope, T. and Hough, M. (1988) 'Area crime and incivility: a profile from the *British Crime Survey*', in T. Hope and M. Shaw (eds), *Communities and Crime Reduction*. London: HMSO.

Hough, M. and Mayhew, P. (1985) *Taking Account of Crime. Key Findings from the Second British Crime Survey*. London: HMSO.

Kelling, G. (1985) 'Order maintenance: the quality of urban life and police: a line of argument', in W. Geller (ed.), *Police Leadership in America: Crisis and Opportunity*. New York: Praeger.

Kelling, G. (1986) 'Neighbourhood crime control and the police: a view of the American experience', In K. Heal and G. Laycock (eds), *Situational Crime Prevention: From Theory into Practice*. London: HMSO.

Kelling, G. (1987) 'Acquiring a taste for order: the community and the police', *Crime and Delinquency*, 33(1): 90–102.

Kinsey, R. (1990) *The Edinburgh Crime Survey*. Edinburgh: University of Edinburgh.

Kinsey, R., Lea, J. and Young, J. (1986) *Losing the Fight against Crime*. Oxford: Blackwell.

Klockars, C. (1985) 'Order maintenance, the quality of urban life and police: a different line of argument', in W. Geller (ed.), *Police Leadership in America: Crisis and Opportunity*. New York: Praeger.

Lewis, D. and Salem, G. (1986) *Fear of Crime: Incivility and the Production of a Social Problem*. New York: Transaction Books.

McDonald, S. (1986) 'Does gentrification arrest crime rates?', in A. Reiss and M. Tonry (eds), *Communities and Crime*. Chicago: University of Chicago Press.

Matthews, R. (1986) *Policing Prostitution: A Multi-Agency Approach*, Paper No. 1. London: Middlesex Polytechnic Centre for Criminology.

Matthews, R. (1988) *Informal Justice?* London: Sage.

Maxfield, M. (1984) *Fear of Crime in England and Wales*. Home Office Research Study 78. London: HMSO.

Maxfield, M. (1987) *Explaining Fear of Crime: Evidence from the 1984 British Crime Survey*. Home Office Research and Planning Unit. London: HMSO.

Painter, K. (1989) *Crime Prevention and Public Lighting with Special Focus on Women and Elderly People*. London: Middlesex Polytechnic Centre for Criminology.

Pate, A. (1986) 'Experimenting with foot patrol: the Newark experience', in D. Rosenbaum (ed.), *Community Crime Prevention: Does it Work*? Beverly Hills: Sage.

Police Foundation (1981) *The Newark Foot Patrol Experiment*. Washington DC: The Police Foundation.

Power, A. (1989) 'Housing community and crime', in D. Downes (ed.), *Crime and the City*. London: Macmillan.

Poyner, B. and Webb, B. (1987) 'Gloucester House: a reception service', in B. Poyner and B. Webb (eds), *Successful Crime Prevention Measures: Case Studies*. London: The Tavistock Institute of Human Relations.

Rosenbaum, D. (1987) 'The theory and research behind neighbourhood watch: is it a fear and crime reduction strategy?', *Crime and Delinquency*, 33(1): 103–35.

Rosenbaum, D. (1988) 'Community crime prevention: a review and synthesis of the literature', *Justice Quarterly*, 5(3): 323–95.

Schuerman, L. and Kobrin, S. (1986) 'Community careers in crime', in A. Reiss and M. Tonry (eds), *Communities and Crime*. Chicago: Chicago University Press.

Scull, A. (1977) *Decarceration: Community Treatment and the Deviant*. Englewood Cliffs, NJ: Prentice-Hall.

Skogan, W. (1988) 'Disorder, crime and community decline', in T. Hope and M. Shaw (eds), *Communities and Crime Reduction*. London: HMSO.

Skogan, W. (1990) Disorder and Decline. New York: Free Press.

Skolnick, J. and Bayley, D. (1986) *The New Blue Line*. New York: Free Press.

Sloan-Howitt, M. and Kelling, G. (1990) 'Subway graffiti in New York City: "getting up" is meanin' it and cleanin' it', *Security Journal*, 1(3): 131–7.

Smith, S. (1986) *Crime, Space and Society*. Cambridge: Cambridge University Press.

Sparks, R. (1981) 'Multiple victimisation: evidence, theory and future research', *Journal of Criminal Law and Criminology*, 72: 762–75.

Taub, R., Taylor, D. and Dunham, J. (1984) *Paths of Neighborhood Change: Race and Crime in Urban America*. Chicago: University of Chicago Press.

Walker, S. (1984) 'Broken windows and fractured history: the use and misuse of history in recent police patrol analysis', *Justice Quarterly* 1(11): 75–90.

Warr, M. (1984) 'Fear of victimisation: why are women and the elderly more afraid?', *Social Science Quarterly*, 65: 681–94.

Wilson, J.Q. (1983) *Thinking about Crime*. New York: Vintage Books.

Wilson, J.Q. (1986) 'On crime and the liberals', *Dissent*, Spring: 222–9.

Wilson, J.Q. and Herrnstein (1985) *Crime and Human Nature*. New York: Simon and Schuster.

Wilson, J.Q. and Kelling, G. (1982) 'Broken windows: the police and neighborhood safety', *Atlantic Monthly*, March: 29–38.

Wilson, J.Q. and Kelling, G. (1989) 'Making neighborhoods safe', *Atlantic Monthly*, February: 46–52.

3 Criminal women and criminal justice: the limits to, and potential of, feminist and left realist perspectives

Pat Carlen

The primary purpose of this chapter is to assess the differential potential of both feminism and left realist criminology to inform (a) analyses of women's lawbreaking and criminalization and (b) campaigns and policies aimed at redressing the discriminatory wrongs that women presently suffer in the criminal justice system. The first four parts in turn discuss the limits to, and potential of, feminist and realist perspectives on women's crimes and women's penal regulation. The main argument throughout these first four parts is that although feminist perspectives and left realist criminological approaches have much to offer in terms of political agenda-setting, neither can alone provide the open-ended conceptual system required to explain women's law-breaking and the social response to it. In the fifth part I suggest that in view of the theoreticist, libertarian, separatist and gender-centric tendencies immanent in some recent feminist writings on women, crime and criminology, those wishing to make informed contributions to policies and campaigns to ensure that the penal regulation of women does not increase their oppression as unconventional women, black people and poverty-stricken defendants still further, might find that they have more in common with the aims and priorities of left realists than they have with feminist anti- or gender-centric criminologists. Then, in the final part, and on the basis of a deconstructionist theoretical position, I put forward an agenda for the realization of some attainable ideals both in the deconstruction and theorization of 'women and crime' questions and in the development of policies aimed at increasing criminal justice for women.

Criminal women and criminal justice: the contributions of feminism and feminists

During the last 15 years there has been a much more sustained focus on women's lawbreaking than there had been prior to the mid-1970s

(Adler, 1975; Simon, 1975; Smart, 1976; Smart and Smart, 1978; Heidensohn, 1985; Carlen et al., 1985; Messerschmidt, 1986; Naffine, 1987; Adelberg and Currie, 1987; Allen, 1987; Carlen and Worrall, 1987; Carlen, 1988; Allen, 1988; Cain, 1989; Worrall, 1990). Not all of those working on the topic have explicitly claimed that their works have been informed by 'feminist' concepts and theories, nor have all explicitly styled themselves 'feminist'. Yet because they have variously contributed to the demolition of certain sexist myths concerning women's lawbreaking and the regulation of deviant females, I shall here use 'feminist' very loosely to refer to all those writers who have been concerned to remedy the gender-related wrongs done to women criminals by criminologists, police, courts and prisons. Their writings have been both theoretical and policy-oriented.

Feminist perspectives on women and crime have made three major contributions to the theoretical understanding of the meanings of women's lawbreaking and the differential social response to it. Study after study has revealed, first, that women's crimes are committed in different circumstances to men's – that is, that women's crimes are the crimes of the powerless (Messerschmidt, 1986; Carlen, 1988; Worrall, 1990); and secondly, that the reponse to women's lawbreaking is constituted within typifications of femininity and womanhood which further add to women's oppression (Carlen, 1983; Edwards, 1984; Eaton, 1986). A third contribution has been made by writers who, often (but not always) explicitly eschewing empirical and policy-oriented work, have asked (variously) (a) whether the development of a feminist criminology is a possible theoretical project (Cousins, 1980; Carlen et al., 1985); (b) whether the focus on women lawbreakers is a 'proper' concern of feminism (Allen, 1988; Smart 1989b); and (c) whether a 'feminist' jurisprudence is desirable and/or possible (see Boyle et al., 1985, for Canada; Dahl, 1987, for Norway; MacKinnon, 1987, for the United States; and Smart, 1989a, for England). Fourthly, and conversely, some writers have not disdained an explicit policy orientation and have joined with campaigning organizations and/or women ex-prisoners to publicize conditions in the women's gaols and campaigns for a better deal for women in trouble, before the courts or in prison (Carlen et al., 1985; Seear and Player, 1986; Padell and Stevenson, 1988; Casale, 1989).

Criminal women and criminal justice: the limits to feminism

When I was asked to write this chapter it was suggested that I present my remarks under the title 'Left realism and feminist criminology'. Never having called myself a 'feminist criminologist' I was unable to oblige. And the reason why I have never called myself a 'feminist criminologist' (though I would lay claim to the appellation 'feminist') is because: (a) my own perspective as a sociologist has, since the publication of *Official Discourse* (Burton and Carlen, 1979), involved a deconstructionist approach which strives to work on the contradiction of having to recognize (in the process of politics) but needing to deny (in the process of knowledge-production) the conceptual parameters of both sociology and criminology; and (b) I find it difficult to attribute any meaning to the term 'feminist criminology' which would be either desirable or possible. It would not be *desirable* because any universalizing theories of a taken-for-granted criminality inhering in biological female subjects must be as reductionist and essentializing as the much maligned biological ones. It is not possible for three reasons. First, present knowledge about criminal women and criminal justice has not developed via explanatory concepts which could be called distinctly 'feminist' – unless one counts as explanatory the usually descriptive use of the word 'patriarchy' (but see Cousins, 1978); secondly, once the historically and socially specific discourses and practices within which women's lawbreaking and criminalization occur in Britain, the United States, Canada and Australia are investigated, a concern with gender constructions rapidly merges with questions concerning class, racism and imperialism. Thirdly, no single theory (feminist or otherwise) can adequately explain three major features of women's lawbreaking and imprisonment: that women's crimes are, in the main, the crimes of the powerless; that women in prison are disproportionately from ethnic minority groups; and that a majority of women in prison have been in poverty for the greater part of their lives.

Yet although I do not believe that a 'feminist criminology' is either desirable or possible, both here and in the fifth part of this chapter I take issue with writers who (ironically, given the overall thrust of their writing) do not believe that feminists should study 'women and crime' at all. Two major arguments are advanced by such writers: one I call 'anti-criminology', the other 'deconstructionalist libertarian'.

The anti-criminology position on women and crime argues against the discipline of 'criminology' per se. It implies that specification of empirical referents at the outset of an enquiry must inevitably entail investigations forever trapped in essentialist categories obstructing the production of new knowledge (Cousins, 1980; Brown, 1986; Allen, 1988; Cain, 1989, 1990). This is not such a new insight as anti-criminologists and deconstructionists have claimed. It was an awareness that the empirical referents of social scientific discourses are already endowed with more taken-for-granted and ideological meanings that always already have discursive effects than are discourses in

the physical sciences that led earlier sociologists to develop the notorious 'sociological jargon' (or 'sociologese') so particularly sneered at by their traditionalist opponents.

Yet deconstructionists have access to modes of thought which should diminish the radical theorist's perennial fear of the ideological power of the empirical referent. In particular, they can adopt the methodological protocol of Bachelard (1940), that systems of thought must say 'No' to their own conventions and conditions of existence. Additionally, they can take comfort from Saussurian linguistics which demonstrate that individual words themselves have no essential meaning but only acquire meaning with syntagma which through differentiation assign the value of a specific sign. If then, in taking the assumptions of Bachelard and Saussure (1974) as prescriptive and working on the contradiction that the already-known has to be both recognized and denied, deconstructionists use a 'bricolage' of concepts from other disciplines (Derrida, 1976), there is no reason why they should not *both* take seriously (that is, recognize) *and* deny the empirical referent's material and ideological effects (Burton and Carlen, 1979). Thereafter, whether such investigations are pursued under the political sign of 'feminism' or the academic sign of 'criminology' is important only insofar as such signifiers provide the author with a support group or a salary! From a deconstructionist perspective labels such as 'feminist', 'criminological' (or 'left realist') are irrelevant; none can guarantee the 'truth' of the arguments.

The 'deconstructionist libertarian' stance on 'women and crime' is one sometimes implicit (though not always held to, Smart, 1989a: 165) in the work of Carol Smart (1990). It implies a denial that a reduction in women's crime is a proper concern of criminologists and that therefore criminologists should not seek to justify policy proposals on the grounds that they might help criminal women keep out of trouble in future. (Though according to Allen (1988), who on this takes a line similar to Smart's, it's OK to seek to reduce *men's* lawbreaking!) This is a position very close to that which Jock Young (1986) has called 'left idealist', and together with the 'anti-criminology' reluctance to engage with the empirical reality of women's lawbreaking and criminalization, could result in policy on 'women and crime' being abandoned either to what Smart (1990) has referred to as the 'macho left' (realists?) or to the realists of the right. To my mind, neither alternative would be acceptable.

It should by now have become apparent that (a) I do not believe there is a distinctly feminist theoretical conceptual system which might adequately explain (or call into question) the empirical phenomenon known as 'women and crime'; and (b) I am in any case in agreement with those feminists who would argue against global, essentialist theories seeking to guarantee certain 'truths' – including feminist 'truths'. (The absurdity of the notion that there is a distinctly feminist *method* in criminology or sociology is discussed later.) I do, nonetheless, disagree with feminists who argue for a non-interventionist stance on women's lawbreaking and criminalization. For, as a matter of political calculation (and not as a guaranteed theoretical recipe for a desired outcome), knowledge gained from theoretical work can be used in part to inform policy interventions. The *way* it is used and its effects will be dependent on the balance of competing ideological, material and political conditions of the time, and there is, of course, no reason why any social scientist working on 'women and crime' and calling themselves a feminist should feel obliged to make such interventions. There is a need for all types of work – quantitative, qualitative, rational deductive, ethnographic, purely theoretical, etc. Yet, just as one cannot read off an interventionist politics from a theory, neither too can one read off from any theory a politics of *non-intervention*. My personal view is that if *no* academics were prepared to compromise their claims to theoretical rectitude (or consistency) by committing themselves *as academics* and *as feminists* to campaigns to redress the specific wrongs suffered by women lawbreakers in the criminal justice and penal systems, it would be to the further disadvantage of those very women who not only are among the worst casualties of the gender and poverty traps, but who too often are victims of a gendered racism as well.

Criminal women and criminal justice: the potential of left realist criminology

One of the most notable features of the writing of feminists who take up an anti-criminology position is the extent to which their concerns are reminiscent of some identical concerns of left-wing criminologists of the early 1970s. Fears that radical critique will be neutralized by incorporation into state repressive apparatuses together with an apprehensiveness that any engagement in policy debate will contaminate them with a conservative reformism seems today to be atrophying some British academic feminists' capacity to engage in penal politics in much the same way that 20 years ago the new criminologists temporarily distanced themselves from penal debate for similar reasons. By contrast, today's left realists recognize that such a stance was in part responsible for the hijacking of law and order issues by the radical right and, as a consequence, their major injunction is to take crime and its effects seriously. This is not only because of the need to regain some of the ground predominantly occupied by the new realists on questions of crime control, but also because of a recognition that crime is a real problem, and especially to working-class people who suffer disproportionately both as victims of crime and as apprehended lawbreakers (Young, 1986). In tirelessly confronting the challenge of right-wing administrative criminology (Wilson, 1975) Young and his associates (Lea and Young, 1984; Kinsey et al., 1986; Young, 1987; Lea, 1987; Matthews, 1987) have developed the following tenets:

Theoretical

1   'The basic triangle of relations which is the proper subject-matter of criminology [is] – the offender, the state and the victim' (Young, 1986).
2   Theoretical explanations must be symetrical – there must be the same explanation for social action and social reaction.
3   'Man [sic] is a creator of human nature' (Young, 1987), and therefore explanations of crime should not be deterministic and people should be seen as being responsible for their actions.

Political

1   Crime is a real problem and especially to working-class people who suffer disproportionately from personal crime, such as robbery, assault, burglary, rape.
2   The 'left' should attempt to develop a credible (populist?) approach to crime control in order to prevent the 'right' from having a monopoly of the 'crime problem'.
3   The purpose of theorizing should be to make practical interventions into law and order issues.
4   In order to reduce crime there is a need to achieve a higher level of cooperation between police and public, and this will be best achieved by a democratization of local control of the police.

A vast body of critique of left realist criminology has been developed during the last 10 years (Middlesex Polytechnic, 1989). In the remainder of this section, however, I shall only discuss its potential for informing theoretical and political work on women's lawbreaking and criminalization.

Taking crime seriously – left realism as a politics
As I said above, one of the most important aspects of left realism in criminology is that it explicitly identifies the criminal justice arena as a site of political struggle. Because of the deconstructionist theoretical programme which I have advocated I myself see no reason why feminists should be wary of engaging in theoretical debate about the possible meanings of the peculiar mix of ideological, political and

economic conditions in which 'women as a status group' break the law, are criminalized and, in a minority of cases, are imprisoned.

Realism's advocacy of empirical investigation is an
essential prerequisite of theoretical relevance and
political interventions
In talking of theoretical relevance I am not intending to imply that theoretical concepts have essential relationships with empirical referents. Rather, I am assuming that, because the effects of racism, class exploitation and gender discrimination require different explanations, and because also the discourses and practices of women's lawbreaking and criminalization vary across time and between places, it can never be assumed that discourses and practices of gender differentiation *necessarily* play primary parts in the conditioning of that lawbreaking and criminalization. Close observation and investigation of the empirical phenomenon has a part to play in the shaping of the questions to be asked and the concepts to be used – even though the theoretical system constructed to answer them should also lead to their displacement and the requirement of further theoretical and/or empirical work. Such strategies of investigation and theorizing might or might not involve the use of concepts having claims to be labelled 'feminist'. But, almost certainly, they will often draw on political theories and jurisprudential concepts not primarily concerned with the rights and wrongs of *women* and where political intervention on women and crime issues is premised primarily on concerns about racism or class injustice.

The starting point for realism is the strategy of
democratization
It is in left realism's emphasis (Lea, 1987: 368) on a democratization of the criminal justice system that I see a major (formal, if not substantive) convergence with feminist concerns. For realists not only take lawbreaking seriously, they also take seriously people's experiences of it as *victims*. Indeed, the realists' work on women as victims of crime has been one of their major contributions to both feminist struggle and criminology (Jones et al., 1986). What they have not taken so seriously are people's experiences of crime as suspects, lawbreakers, defendants and prisoners (see below for criticisms of those parts of the 'taking crime seriously' programme which have frequently substituted populism for analysis, and moralism for theory). Yet an understanding of crime and criminal justice from the offender's standpoint is a necessary prerequisite to the reduction of crime (Box, 1987: 29) and to a diminution of the increased oppression which women incur as a result of their lawbreaking (Carlen, 1988, 1990). And this is the main

justification for pursuing qualitative investigations which take seriously women's (and men's) own perceptions and experiences of their offences and the state's response to them. It is not because of any distinctly 'feminist method' which 'allows women to speak for themselves' (Jupp, 1989). Such a procedure would be rampant (populist) empiricism rather than theoretical investigation. Rather, it is in the symbolic interactionist (realist) tradition which assumes that if people perceive things as real they will be real in their effects (Thomas, 1951). Taking seriously women's views of their lawbreaking might lead to: political demands for a diminution of the oppressive conditions in which much of women's lawbreaking is committed; the democratic construction of feasible interventionary programmes in relation to the drug-taking, thieving and other crimes which often cause misery to women other than the offender, as well as aggravating the existing problems of the woman lawbreaker herself; and the democratic management of housing and other schemes for women in trouble.

The limits to left realism and the need for feminist and socialist ideals

Although left realists have specified a number of theoretical tenets concerning the left realist approach to thinking about crime, it is often difficult to work out exactly why they have termed their programme 'realist'. One difficulty stems from their conflation of a political programme with a set of theoretical assumptions which do not emanate from either the philosophical realism of, say, Karl Popper or the sociological realism of, for instance, Emile Durkheim. Another results from their juxtaposition of their own left 'realist' theories to those which they call left 'idealist' and where 'idealist' is not being used in its usual sense to refer to theories which *explain* the present by reference to some not yet realized ideal, but merely to condemn theories which would not, according to the realists, lead to any realizable programmes of crime control.

And it may be because they do not clearly define and distinguish 'realism as theory' and 'realism as politics' that left realists produce theoretical propositions which appear positivistic and essentialist as well as a penal politics which can appear to be marred by opportunism, populism and moralism.

Realism, idealism and common sense

Whereas the realism of Durkheim (1964) and Popper (1972) was aimed at subverting common sense, left realists appear to call for a theory of crime that will fit the facts of crime as popularly conceived of in common sense (cf. Jones et al., 1986: 3–4). Hence the often uncritical use of the victim survey.

The essentialism of crime as a unifier

One of the strongest attacks on left realism has been that it is essentialist (Hogg, 1988: 32), that it attributes to the commonsense phenomenon 'crime' – a phenomenon that consists of many different types of lawbreaking and many different modes of criminalization – a unitary existence known to all people of good will and common sense. In other words, there is an easily recognizable reality 'out there', known as crime, that can be understood through empirical investigation and in its own terms.

In answer to the foregoing criticisms Young (1987) has claimed that far from being essentialist, left realists aim to 'deconstruct' the crime phenomenon. However, it turns out that by 'deconstruct' he means that the commonsense 'crime' is broken down into small substantive dimensions for analysis – but not an analysis which might subvert the commonsense meaning. Indeed, once the commonsense meaning is denied it is unlikely that the new explanation will have popular appeal!

The essentialism of criminology as a unifier

Because they portray crime as a unitary concept it follows that left realists idealize 'criminology' as a unitary discipline rather than as an organizational site for the investigation of lawbreaking and criminalization. Linked with this thrust towards the unification of theory and politics is the left realist criticism that other theories are 'partial' – that explanations fail insofar as they are not symmetrical, that is, insofar as they do not provide the same explanations for social action and reaction. Yet one of the greatest contributions of 1960s interactionism was the insistence that lawbreaking and criminalization are two separate processes, each requiring entirely different explanations (Kitsuse and Cicourel, 1963). Furthermore, and as I have argued elsewhere (Carlen, 1980) a deconstructionist position assumes that:

> the theoretical relationships between the criminal law, juridical relations, criminalization processes and lawbreaking are embedded in asymmetrical practices and discourses. These discourses are 'neither mirror images of each other nor reducible one to the other'. 'Today' as Foucault points out, 'criminal justice functions and justifies itself ... only by perpetual reference to something other than itself, by its unceasing reinscription in non-judicial systems' (Foucault, 1977: 22) ... [the preconditions and effects of] criminal law, juridical relationships and criminalization processes are asymmetrical to each other. Once they are inscribed within and around notions like morality, freedom, guilt and retribution ... they fragment into ironic icons of juridical relations. ... [the] effect [of which] is dispersed *not* in criminological but in economic, religious or political discourse. (Carlen, 1980: 16)

Deconstructionist approaches to questions of women and crime can no more be confined within the parameters of a populist criminology than they can be solely and indissolubly tied to the concerns of feminism or the concepts of a 'feminist' theory. For deconstructionism – whether in 'criminology' or in 'feminism' – has constantly to say 'No' to the conditions of its own existence.

Left realists' idealistic and moralistic notions of responsibility

Seeing all previous explanations of crime as being deterministic, left realists insist that individuals must take responsibility for their crimes, they operate within the simplistic free will versus determinism dichotomy. In reply to the crude 'social conditions cause crime' claim, they answer that individuals choose to commit crime. They appear to think that deterministic (sociological?) explanations of lawbreaking alienate from a leftist politics those working-class people who, though living in less-than-ideal conditions, do *not* commit crime. Yet can such a simplistic dichotomy be justified on either theoretical or political grounds? Of course *'people choose to act, sometimes criminally, [but] they do not do so under conditions of their own choosing.* Their choice makes them responsible, but the conditions make the choice comprehensible. These conditions, social and economic, contribute to crime because they constrain, limit or narrow the choices available' (Box, 1987: 29, emphasis in original).

Furthermore, is it either logical or justifiable for left realists to use an anti-social rhetoric of individualism in the furtherance of socialist political ends? I think not. And this crude invocation of free will seems to me to be the worst example of the theoretical bad faith which results from attempting to fashion a theory in the service of a politics. By attempting to appeal to an electorate via populist and individualist conceptions of criminality, left realism loses an opportunity to show how individualized problems of criminal justice are also problems of social justice in general. To follow their example when posing questions of women and crime would be to make it impossible to assume that the experiences of 'women as a status group' have any ideological, economic and political preconditions which are distinctly different to the experiences of 'men as a status group'.

The need for a principled idealism to counter the impossibilism of left idealism and the opportunistic tendency of left realism

A major concern of left realism (and one which I totally support) has been to counter the 'impossibilism' of left idealist theories which claim that nothing can be done about crime until there is a fundamental change in the present exploitative class relations constitutive of capitalism. Yet a refusal to abandon the space of politics should not also entail an abandonment of a principled theoretical commitment to calling into question all already-known explanations of crime, including those developed under the auspices of socialism, feminism and/or left realism. The task of theory is to produce new knowledge; a task of politics is to calculate how, when and if new knowledge can be used to change balances of power and induce desired social change. Principled commitment to an open-ended deconstructionist theoretical programme, plus political commitment to sets of collectivist (feminist and/or socialist) ideals or aspirations is required to help ensure that theoretical production and political practice are neither opportunistically conflated nor opportunistically reduced, the one to serve the other. Which is why I am reluctant to endorse the more conflationary and/or reductionist theoretical and political claims of both feminism and left realism when they invoke either a politics to justify their theories or, conversely, a theoretical position to guarantee the rectitude of their politics and/or policy interventions.

Against theoreticist, libertarian, separatist and gender-centric tendencies in recent feminist writings on women's lawbreaking and criminal justice

Given my very strong reservations about certain aspects of left realist theorizing, it may seem perverse of me now to state that at the time of writing (August 1990) I feel, on balance, more sympathetic towards the general political project of left realist criminologists than I do towards the theoreticist, libertarian, separatist and gender-centric tendencies inherent (sometimes separately and sometimes combined) in some recent feminist writings on women, crime and criminology. In particular, I take issue with the anti-criminology stance of Smart (1990) and the implication that anyone taking a policy-oriented approach is at worst engaged in social 'engineering' or, at best, a committed do-gooding fool unaware of the risk-taking involved in working on the contradictions between theoretical knowledge and political strategy (Smart, 1990; Frigon, 1990). I will now, therefore, make a few observations as to why I believe that certain tendencies in the writings of some feminists on women and crime are neither particularly original nor in the interests of either the minority of women who break the law or that even smaller minority who are imprisoned.

The theoreticist tendency
The theoreticist tendency (which is anti-policy, anti-problem orientation) in the prescriptions of feminist anti-criminologists is most marked in the work of Smart (1989a, 1990). It seems to stem from two major fears: one, that to focus on an empirical referent like crime

which has pre-given ideological and institutional meaning entails an essentialist trap from which there is no escape; second, that radical ideas or strategies used in the service of the state are necessarily subverted by administrators whose aims are far from those of the women's movement.

First I will address the problem of the empirical referent. As I pointed out earlier, fear of the ideological and already institutionalized meanings of the empirical referent is not new among social scientists or political theorists attempting radical critique. Yet the very task of theory is to engage in a struggle for power over the 'meaning of things' (including all material and ideological constructs). The purpose is to produce new meanings which will empower. Now certainly there is no reason why theoretical work should not be valuable *in itself* and certainly no reason why any theorist should *also* engage in political intervention. Yet I would not have expected theorists with an explicit political orientation such as 'feminist' or 'socialist' to inveigh against the suggestion that the theoretical product might at least in part both inform their analyses and empower their own political programme. Of course, there is usually a loss of theoretical rigour (and virtue?) when theories are put at the service of politics. But so what? The non-stop self-conscious elaboration of theoretical 'positions' unrelated to their possible analytic usefulness is in my opinion a peculiarly sterile practice, and a surprising one for those committed to the openness of deconstructionism. The purpose of deconstructing a logic (or anything else) is to find out what makes it work – and then to create new knowledge from the bricolage of the old.

The second fear – of the incorporation and subversion of radical critique and product – is related to the first and has likewise perennially exercised the minds of radical political groups. Yet unless one believes in the possibility of an end to ideology (and, incidentally, to knowledge) such incorporation and subversion needs to be recognized as a necessary part of political struggle without which there would be ideological closure. At the political level, too, it should be remembered that the state is not monolithic, that feminists also work in state agencies (cf. Cain, 1990) and that they continually ruminate about the meanings of their jobs. Furthermore, and as left realists repeatedly remind us, too great a fear of 'incorporation' can eventually lead to a paralysis of action, marginalization and, ultimately a state of powerlessness whence it is difficult to regain ground lost to the enemy.

The 'libertarian' tendency

The libertarian tendency of some feminist writing on crime also repeats the libertarian tendencies of the left idealists of the early 1970s. It implies that women's lawbreaking should not be treated as being problematic either for the lawbreakers themselves or their victims (Smart, 1989b, 1990; Frigon, 1990); that feminist theorists should not put forward policy proposals on the grounds that they might reduce crime as such proposals smack of 'social engineering' (Smart, 1989b); and that women lawbreakers should alone have privileged audience concerning the meaning of their crimes and the appropriate social response to them (Frigon, 1990).

First let me give an example which illustrates both the 'privileging' of subjects' understanding and the fear of 'social engineering'. In reviewing *Women, Crime and Poverty* (Carlen, 1988), Frigon wrote: 'Since 20 out of 39 women have committed drug-related offences, Carlen devotes some time to the subject. Her discussion is interesting but when she talks about the "expensive demands of *destructive* lifestyles involving heroin . . ." (emphasis added, p. 44), the reader can feel uncomfortable with this kind of language that can suggest a judgement' (Frigon, 1990: 226). Sadly, the language in this context was intended as literal description. Women with drink or drug addictions often choke to death on their own vomit, commit suicide or die of a drugs overdose. Others have Aids as a result of either sharing needles or engaging in prostitution to fund their habits. Sleeping rough, nursing bleeding sores and suffering withdrawal symptoms are not particularly life-enhancing processes either. Not one woman of the many I have known with addictions has celebrated her addictive state; many have themselves referred to 'destructive lifestyles', 'abusing my body' and 'killing myself'.

Yet what if the language had intentionally conveyed a judgement? I myself can see no reason whatsoever why a theorist should not also make judgements, as to more or less desirable states of affairs – so long as she does not conflate her analyses with her judgements and imply that there is a one-to-one relationship between the two. Certainly in *Women, Crime and Poverty* I make several judgements (on the state of women's prisons, on recent welfare legislation, on Mrs Thatcher, etc). An academic squeamishness concerning the real problems of women in crime and on drugs is a return to one of the less acceptable faces of 1960s romanticism and idealism. It certainly is not helpful to the development of progressive policies aimed at reducing the further suffering incurred by women in trouble who turn to drugs or drink to relieve their pain and misery.

A second facet of what I have called the 'libertarian tendency' is the glorification by some writers of the notion that feminists should 'let women speak for themselves' or that researchers should 'listen to women'. Now I have no objection to the injunction that social researchers should take seriously people's understanding of their own situations. But what is distinctly 'feminist' about this, and why should such a strategy only involve women? The really difficult question is to decide what status and space to attribute to subjects' understandings of their own situation. My own solution is to quote people verbatim to such an extent that their own voices *are* heard. At the same time I also make my own (usually different) theoretical perspective sufficiently explicit to alert readers to the fact that these extracts have been *chosen* by me to illustrate a particular point. Ultimately, of course, everybody and nobody speaks for herself. The tendency towards an empiricist realism which is immanent in some of the writings of both left realist criminologists and libertarian feminists is not a progressive one.

The separatist tendency

The separatist tendency in feminist writings on crime is usually signalled by the lavish use of 'malestream' (instead of mainstream) and other cryptologically unsatisfying neologisms or puns. Again, Frigon (1990) provides a good example when she complains that control theory is a 'mainstream and/or malestream theory in criminology. To fit women, or more correctly gender, in that mould is therefore problematic.' Now, gender isn't a custard or jelly and theory is not a mould. But positivistic notions that words and theories are like custard *do* ignore all of the more sophisticated theoretical advances that have been made this century concerning the attribution of meanings to words and statements. Given the revolutionary work of Saussure, Foucault and Derrida it is a pity that separatist feminists continue to imply that words, theories and concepts are forever tied to their sites of origin and essentially engendered by their authors. The repeated implication by some feminists that concepts are always already-gendered should offend theoretical, political and even what (in the tradition of the genre) Maureen Cain (1989, 1990) would call 'co-man' (!) sense.

The gender-centric tendency

In fact, Cain's recent writings (1989, 1990) actually eschew separatism. They do, however, contain a tendency towards gender-centrism, as do the works of Smart (1989a, 1989b). My own perspective inclines towards a political realism similar to that of the left realists and, as I have repeatedly said, is not shaken by fear of any essential power of the empirical referent.

Women (as a group) in the penal system are a striking example of what Laffargue and Godefroy (1989) have referred to as the '"hard core" of repression' whose criminalization has been overdetermined by the threefold effects of sexism, racism and the class injustices of an increasingly repressive state. Because explanations of racism, class structure and gender structure are not reducible one to another (cf.

Cain, 1986, on gender and class structures) it is likely that people wishing to engage in criminological work which may have some theoretical, policy or campaigning pay-off in relation to women's crimes and women's imprisonment, will not wish to rely solely on the insights of feminism into gender structure when mounting their investigations. This is not to assert that there is no need for studies and theories which privilege gender as the major explanatory concept – indeed the need for such studies is urgent. It is to warn against a theoretical imperialism which might result in the theoretical closure which self-styled 'transgressive' (Cain, 1989, 1990) and anti-criminologists (Smart, 1990) fear.

An agenda for the realization of some attainable ideals both in the deconstruction and theorization of 'women and crime' questions; and in the development of policies aimed at righting some of the wrongs encountered by women lawbreakers in the criminal justice and penal systems

Academic agenda
Detailed empirical investigation of both the context (that is, economic, ideological and political conditions) in which women break the law and of their subsequent careers through the welfare criminal justice and penal systems (cf. Carlen, 1988). Detailed empirical investigation of the ideological discourses within which women's lawbreaking is known (cf. Carlen, 1983; Allen, 1987; Worrall, 1990). Deconstruction of what is 'already known' about women lawbreakers via a 'bricolage' of concepts appropriated from a variety of theoretical discourses to inform answers to questions about the four main features of women's lawbreaking and imprisonment in Britain, the United States and Canada, namely:

1   that women's crimes are predominantly the crimes of the powerless;
2   that disproportionate numbers of women from ethnic minority groups are imprisoned;
3   that typifications of conventional femininity play a major role in the decision whether or not to imprison women;
4   that the majority of women appear to be law-abiding and when in trouble are much more likely to be in receipt of medical, psychiatric or welfare regulation than caught up in the machinery of criminal justice.

The construction of a feminist jurisprudence which in assuming (and empirically documenting the ways in which) (a) women's experiences are different from men's and (b) the criminal law affects and protects women differently from men, might be advocated as one jurisprudential paradigm (among others) which could inform campaigning strategies and policy recommendations. The establishment of women's law as a special area of study not just as an optional subject but as a component of all compulsory subjects. (See Stang-Dahl, 1986, for an account of the lead in this direction given by the Institute of Women's Law at the University of Oslo where women's law has already been fully integrated into the degree scheme of the Faculty of Law.)

The dissolution of 'women and criminal justice' questions within an interrogation of women and social justice in general. The development of more sophisticated models of the relationships between culpability, responsibility and accountability in societies where class relationships, racism and gender discrimination call into question the very general concept of social justice which must underpin the more specific concept of criminal justice.

Campaigning and policy agenda

Any campaigning and policy agenda might (ideally) be comprised of: (a) fundamental aims; (b) general strategies; (c) short-term achievable goals for the relief of women presently bearing the brunt of both gender-discrimination and racist gender-discrimination in the criminal justice and penal systems; and (d) long-term programmes that, although not achievable under present political conditions, can be argued for on the basis of a deconstructionist analysis of present penal discourses and practices.

Fundamental aims   To ensure that the penal regulation of female lawbreakers does not increase their oppression as unconventional women, as black people and as poverty-stricken defendants still further; and to ensure that the penal regulation of lawbreaking men is not such that it brutalizes them and makes them behave even more violently or oppressively towards women in the future.

General strategies   *Remedial action* to redress the present wrongs of women in the criminal justice and penal systems; *resistance* to penal or other regulatory measures based on essentialized stereotypes of gender; and *democratic exploration* of the many different possible modes of living and learning in a variety of all-female (and, for women who want them, mixed) half-way houses, accommodation schemes and self-help groups (Carlen, 1990).

Short-term achievable goals   The monitoring and (remedying) of sexist and racist–sexist practices within the welfare, criminal justice and penal systems; development of feasible non-custodial programmes for women which recognize that women's social responsibilities and resources are usually different from men's; proper medical provision (especially well-women clinics) for physically and mentally ill women in trouble or in custody; the setting of minimum standards for all prison establishments and the closure of all institutions not conforming to those standards; and rejection of any justification for the discriminatory treatment of women in the penal system which invokes the relatively few numbers of women prisoners as just cause of their less favourable treatment.

Long-term programmes which, though idealistic, need to be adhered to and worked on, to counter the conservative compromises based on pragmatism and opportunism which usually have to be made in order to achieve short-term goals Whatever compromises are made in the name of realist politics, campaigners should not abandon the pursuit of long-term goals (even if, under present political arrangements they are idealistic – for example, the virtual abolition of women's imprisonment, Carlen, 1990). Nor should theorists abdicate (in the name of democracy) their responsibility perpetually to question existent forms of knowledge (including 'feminism' and 'realism'). Of course campaigners will have to be prepared to live with, and work on, the contradictions between the actions required for attainment of short-term goals and the principles to be held to in the construction of new forms of justice. Likewise, theorists will have to work on the contradiction that ideological knowledge (or the already-known) is a necessary constituent of new knowledge. But these tensions are essential elements of any politics or theory which is against closure and committed to being open-ended. The concomitant implication for theorists is that they should forever be intent on seeking that loss of authorship which, in the production and recognition of new knowledge, would render the *politically* important significance of 'feminist' and 'realist' irrelevant.

References

Adelberg, E. and Currie, C. (1987) *Too Few to Count: Canadian Women in Conflict with the Law*. Vancouver: Press Gang Publishers.

Adler, F. (1975) *Sisters in Crime*. New York: McGraw-Hill.

Allen, H. (1987) *Justice Unbalanced*. Milton Keynes: Open University Press.

Allen, J. (1988) 'The "masculinity" of criminality and criminology: interrogating some impasses', in M. Findlay and R. Hogg (eds), *Understanding Crime and Criminal Justice*. Sydney: The Law Book Company. pp. 1–23.

Bachelard, G. (1940) *The Philosophy of No* (trans. G.C. Waterson). London: Orion Press.

Box, S. (1987) *Recession, Crime and Punishment*. London: Tavistock.

Boyle, C., Bertrand, M.A., Lacerte-Lamontagne, C. and Shamai, R. (1985) *A Feminist Review of Criminal Law*. Canada: Minister of Supply and Services.

Brown, B. (1986) 'Women and crime: the dark figures of criminology', *Economy and Society*, 15(3): 355–402.

Burton, F. and Carlen, P. (1979) *Official Discourse*. London: Routledge & Kegan Paul.

Cain, M. (1989) *Growing Up Good*. London: Sage.

Cain, M. (1990) 'Towards transgression: new directions in feminist criminology', in *International Journal of the Sociology of Law*, 18(1): 1–18.

Carlen P. (1980) 'Radical criminology, penal politics and the rule of law', in P. Carlen and M. Collison (eds), *Radical Issues in Criminology*. Oxford: Martin Robertson.

Carlen, P. (1983) *Women's Imprisonment: A Study in Social Control*. London: Routledge & Kegan Paul.

Carlen, P. (1988) *Women, Crime and Poverty*. Milton Keynes: Open University Press.

Carlen, P. (1990) *Alternatives to Women's Imprisonment*. Buckingham: Open University Press.

Carlen, P., Christina, D., Hicks, J., O'Dwyer, J. and Tchaikowsky, C. (1985) *Criminal Women*. Oxford: Polity Press.

Carlen, P. and Worrall, A. (1987) *Gender, Crime and Justice*. Milton Keynes: Open University Press.

Casale, S. (1989) *Women Inside*. London: Civil Liberties Trust.

Cousins, M. (1978) 'Material arguments and feminism', *m/f*, No. 2.

Cousins, M. (1980) 'Men's rea: a note on sexual difference, criminology and the law', in P. Carlen and M. Collison (eds), *Radical Issues in Criminology*. Oxford: Martin Robertson.

Dahl, T.S. (1987) *Women's Law: An Introduction to Feminist Jurisprudence*. Oslo: Norwegian University Press.

Derrida, J. (1976) *Of Grammatology* (trans. Gayatri Chakrovorty Spivak). London: Johns Hopkins University Press.

Durkheim, E. (1964) *Rules of Sociological Method*. New York: Free Press.

Eaton, M. (1986) *Justice for Women?* Milton Keynes: Open University Press.

Edwards, S. (1984) *Women on Trial*. Manchester: Manchester University Press.

Foucault, M. (1977) *Discipline and Punish*. London: Allen Lane.

Frigon, S. (1990) 'Review of P. Carlen, *Women, Crime and Poverty*', *International Journal of the Sociology of Law*, 18(2): 225–9.

Heidensohn, F. (1985) *Women and Crime*. London: Macmillan.

Hogg, R. (1988) 'Taking crime seriously: left realism and Australian criminology', in M. Findlay and R. Hogg (eds), *Understanding Crime and Criminal Justice*. Sydney: The Law Book Company. pp. 24–51.

Jones, T., MacLean, B. and Young, J. (1986) *The Islington Crime Survey*. Aldershot: Gower.

Jupp, V. (1989) *Methods of Criminological Research*. London: Unwin Hyman.

Kinsey, R., Lea, J. and Young, J. (1986) *Losing the Fight against Crime*. Oxford: Blackwell.

Kitsuse, J. and Cicourel, A. (1963) 'A note on the use of official statistics', *Social Problems*, 11: 131–9.

Laffargue, B. and Godefroy, T. (1989) 'Economic cycles and punishment: unemployment and imprisonment. A time series study. France, 1920–1985', *Contemporary Crises*, 13(4): 371–404.

Lea, J. (1987) 'Left realism: a defence', *Contemporary Crises*, 11(4): 357–70.

Lea, J. and Young, J. (1984) *What is to be Done about Law and Order?* Harmondsworth: Penguin.

MacKinnon, C. (1987) 'Feminism, Marxism, method and the state: toward feminist jurisprudence', in S. Harding (ed.), *Feminism and Methodology*. Milton Keynes: Open University Press.

Matthews, R. (1987) 'Taking realist criminology seriously', *Contemporary Crises*, 11: 371–401.

Messerschmidt, J. (1986) *Capitalism, Patriarchy and Crime: Towards a Sociologist Feminist Criminology*. Totowa, NJ: Rowan and Littlefield.

Middlesex Polytechnic (1989) *Realism: A Select Bibliography*. London: Middlesex Polytechnic Centre for Criminology.

Naffine, N. (1987) *Female Crime*. Sydney: Allen & Unwin.

Padell, U. and Stevenson, P. (1988) *Insiders*. London: Virago.

Popper, K. (1972) *Objective Knowledge*. Oxford: Oxford University Press.

Saussure, F. (1974) *Course in General Linguistics*. London: Fontana.

Seear, N. and Player, E. (1986) *Women in the Penal System*. London: Howard League for Penal Reform.

Simon, R. (1975) *Women and Crime*. Massachusetts: Lexington Books.

Smart, B. and Smart, C. (1978) *Women, Sexuality and Social Control*. London: Routledge & Kegan Paul.

Smart, C. (1976) *Women, Crime and Criminology*. London: Routledge & Kegan Paul.

Smart, C. (1989a) *Feminism and the Power of Law*. London: Routledge.

Smart, C. (1989b) 'Review of *Women, Crime and Poverty* by Pat Carlen', *Journal of Law and Society*, 16(4): 521–4.

Smart, C. (1990) 'Feminist approaches to criminology, or postmodern woman meets atavistic man', in L. Gelsthorpe and A. Morris, *Feminist Perspectives in Criminology*. London: Routledge & Kegan Paul.

Stang-Dahl, T. (1986) *Women's Law: Methods, Problems, Values*. Norway: University of Oslo.

Thomas, W.I. (1951) *Social Behaviour and Personality*. New York: Social Science Research Council.

Wilson, J. (1975) *Thinking about Crime*. New York: Basic Books.

Worrall, A. (1990) *Offending Women*. London: Routledge.

Young, J. (1986) 'The failure of criminology: the need for a radical realism', in R. Matthews and J. Young (eds), *Confronting Crime*. London: Sage Publications.

Young, J. (1987) 'The tasks of a realist criminology', *Contemporary Crises*, II(4): 337–56.

4 Realism and corporate crime

Frank Pearce and Steve Tombs

Realists have shown some recognition of the importance of white-collar and corporate crime (Matthews, 1987; Young, 1986, 1987), and have provided an examination of the relative impact of corporate crime and street crime on people's lives. In a discussion of some depth and subtlety of the similarities and differences between these two kinds of crime, Lea and Young (1984) argue that while both display 'the same ethos of individualism, competitiveness and machismo', the former

> ... is the most transparent of all injustices. It is a starting point for a double thrust against crime on all levels. If we concentrate on it alone, as the political right would wish, we are actively engaged in a diversion from the crimes of the powerful. If we concentrate solely on the latter, as many on the left would have us do, we are omitting what are real and pressing problems for working class people, and lose the ability to move from the immediate to encompass the more hidden, and thus demonstrate the intrinsic similarity of crime at all levels of our society. (Lea and Young, 1984: 75)

Undoubtedly many on the left invoke the category of corporate crime as an alibi for downplaying the impact of street crime. They fail to explore it in any depth; nor do they unpack it, nor isolate causal sequences, nor specify the kinds of non-reformist reforms that could limit its occurrence now, and which may have a transformative potential (Gorz, 1980). In truth, much of the recent empirical and theoretical work on the crimes of the powerful has been undertaken by social democrats and liberals rather than by Marxists (Clinard and Yeager, 1980; Braithwaite, 1984; Box, 1983, 1987; for some exceptions see Snider, 1989; Barnett, 1983; Pearce and Tombs, 1989, 1990, 1991). Yet despite the attempts of realism to take crime seriously, there are significant problems with the way that realists have dealt with both street crime and with the crimes of the powerful.

Realism and corporate crime

Unfortunately, some of the references in the realist literature to corporate and white-collar crime are as gestural as those made by 'left idealists'. Matthews (1987: 376), for example, may make reference to these, but when he analyses the relationship between criminal offenders and the victims of crime he restricts his analysis to street crime (1987: 387–8). This inconsistency is not surprising because in practice realism has tended to focus on the more immediate interpersonal anti-social conduct – that is, *on crimes between subjects.*

'Crime is a social relationship. It is institutionalised; it is imbued with meaning; both offenders and victims are predictable, and above all *they relate to one another*' (Young, 1987: 344, emphasis added). Young's characterization of the nature of crime does not adequately describe the anonymous relationship between a manufacturer and a consumer using a faulty or dangerous product. It does not capture the extent to which acts of omission are what cause harm in many such cases or in those involving dangerous pollution, nor that it is the failure of employers to fulfil their statutory managerial duties that lead to many workplace injuries and deaths. *Corporate crime is poorly described or understood if we stay within a conceptual framework restricted to interpersonal relations between subjects; moreover, within this framework it is equally unlikely that methods will be found to control it.* This leads one to wonder if, in analysing subjects like murder realists would routinely include an examination of the statistics for deaths caused by workplace accidents and occupationally caused diseases (Boyd, 1988). Would a realist analysis of the violence and harassment suffered by women at work include a discussion of corporate violence and the particular forms it takes against women?

Realism in its present state of development fails to engage in such analyses – yet we do not want to argue that it cannot do so. Rather, taking corporate crime seriously requires a modification of realism's conceptual categories and a broadening of its field of interest. Such analyses might thus very easily draw upon some of realism's strengths. For example, it is possible to adapt some of its research methods to explore aspects of 'commercial crime'. The *Second Islington Crime Survey* included questions relating to commercial crime, health and safety and pollution. Although these results will be discussed in detail elsewhere (Pearce, 1990b), it is worth noting here that they do indeed indicate a great deal of criminal activity by some of the more 'respectable classes'. For example, of those respondents giving definite answers about their experience of buying goods and services during the previous 12 months: approximately 11 percent had been given misleading information, 21 percent believed that they had been deliberately overcharged and 24 percent had paid for what turned out to be defective goods or services. This indicates that the incidence of commercial crime is high both relatively and absolutely: during the same period, approximately 4 percent of respondents giving definite answers had had a car stolen, 7 percent suffered from a burglary and 7 percent from an actual or attempted theft from their person.

'Left realism', the police and regulatory agencies

Important for the focus of this chapter is the belief that we can build upon some 'left realist' arguments on policing to interrogate the conduct of those agencies entrusted, at least symbolically, with the regulation of commerce, health and safety and pollution. 'Left realist' analysis of the agencies of social control has been developed by studying the nature of and determinants of the modus operandi of the police and by questioning the extent to which they are responsive and democratically accountable to local communities (Kinsey et al., 1986). Very similar questions can be raised about the agencies which regulate the conduct of businesses in relationship to each other, to investors, customers, employees and the local community. These agencies tend to try and achieve 'compliance' through persuasion rather than a 'policing' strategy which uses legal sanctions against businesses and executives found to be in breach of the law. For some this is not a problem; for many others, such as ourselves, it is a major reason why they are in practice so ineffective.

The most fundamental principle of new left realism is that crime really is a problem. Arguing that realism 'must neither succumb to hysteria nor relapse into a critical denial of the severity of crime as a problem' (Young, 1986: 25), the realists state that 'the major task of a radical criminology is to seek a solution to the problem of crime and that of a socialist policy is to substantially reduce the crime rate' (p. 28). This, then, requires that they engage in an analysis of both the formal organization and the modus operandi of the police, to consider ways in which this institution might better address 'the problem of crime'.

Reference to the 'problem' of crime is important. Realists do not believe that increasing crime rates are simply a function of increased police activity, as some 'left idealists' would have it, but rather that these rates reflect reality: that is, the problem of crime has been, and continues to be, a growing one. Moreover, it is one that the police, despite continual (almost exponential) increases in resources, have proved hopelessly inept at tackling.

Lea and his colleagues (1987), for example, note that in the period 1961–1985, the number of police officers serving in England and Wales increased from 75,800 to 120,700, while the numbers of crimes reported to the police rose from 871,000 to 3,612,000. That is, the number of crimes per police officer rose from 12 to 30 (Lea et al., 1987: 32). Focusing on a more recent period, 1979–86, when 'there has been a considerable increase in police resources at every level', the number of crimes cleared has risen by 18 percent – but the increse in crimes reported to the police has been 52 percent (Lea et al., 1987: 34).

This relative decline in clear-up rates is at the heart of realism's focus on police resourcing and practice. Rejecting arguments for even greater resources for the police, the realists state that such increases tend only to 'disappear into an ever expanding bureaucracy' (Lea et al., 1987: 39). More importantly the key problem is not one of the police themselves, but of police–public cooperation. Thus,

> The typical crime is reported to the police by the public and is solved through public cooperation...Over 90% of serious crime in Britain is reported by the public to the police; this rises to over 95% in inner-city areas. The information usually consists of the facts of the crime and a very good indication of who did it. (Lea et al., 1987:40)

For these reasons, realists conclude that: 'the flow of information from the public to the police is crucial. Where the public support the police, they will maintain the flow. When that flow of information dries up, successful policing becomes tremendously difficult' (Lea et al., 1987: 40).

In an explicitly prescriptive section on 'The theory and practice of democratic policing', Kinsey et al. (1986: 186–215) develop a number of proposals which are based on the earlier argument that the police are hopelessly inefficient in dealing with a rapidly rising crime rate, and thus that the inadequate flow of information from the public to the police gives substance to police claims that they can in fact do little about this crime rate. Their proposals focus around two guiding principles, namely 'maximum public initiation' and 'minimum necessary coercion', these principles protecting the rights of individuals and thus providing 'effective guarantees of an *efficient* and socially *just* system of policing' (Kinsey et al., 1986: 193).

'Maximum public initiation' of police action is urged at both the collective and individual level. In this way, it is hoped to minimize the autonomy of police occupational culture and political attitudes in the drawing up of criteria for deciding when to intervene and when not to. 'Minimum necessary coercion' by the police requires a strict limit on police powers. The premise of police work is thus that it is for the police to cooperate with and respond to the demands of the public, rather than vice versa. The realists then go on to set out the legislative framework of minimal policing, which would seek:

1　to define the limits of minimum necessary coercion;
2　to define the precise limits of police powers of intervention and interference in private lives and liberty, and to reduce the scope of police discretion;

3   to minimize the role of police-initiated activity while maximizing that of public-initiated activity.

For the realists, then, minimal policing appears to offer the basis for a 'radical reorganisation of the police and a limitation on their powers, while providing for an efficient and effective system of policing in line with public needs' (Kinsey et al., 1986: 207). We should be clear about the status of these reforms. Following Ryan, we would argue that these policy proposals are liberal rather than socialist in nature: 'Young et al. have increasingly – though, in fairness, not exclusively – justified their law and order policies as socialist ones on the basis of making sure that the police are responsive to the needs of working-class communities. This *responsiveness*, is, primarily, what makes their policies *socialist*' (Ryan, 1986: 30).

We agree with Ryan that 'such a restrictive emphasis is hardly sufficient. Moreover, it is possible that the practical effects of such arguments might be, in certain contexts, profoundly anti-democratic. Nevertheless, to preview the argument to be set out below, it is important to recognize the differential effect of implementing realist-type reforms in the context of safety, health and environmental regulation. For *such an implementation would entail empowering workers and local communities against capital*, and thus these reforms may have a transformative potential, thereby being 'non-reformist reforms' rather than 'mere' or 'liberal' reforms.

To begin to consider the relevance of realist arguments for the enforcement of regulatory law in the spheres of safety, health and the environment, we need to note the objective differences between this context and that with which the realists are concerned, namely street crime.

The regulation of safety, health and the environment

Police officers police local communities. Thus there is no a priori distinction between those to whom 'protection' is being offered (potential victims) and those who might be the object of police action (potential offenders). Indeed, in some of the areas focused on in the realists' crime surveys, the existence of very blurred boundaries between victims and offenders, particularly among the young, is likely. This is very different from the relationship between many regulatory agencies and the groups with whom they interact. While some health, safety and environmental law obviously places duties and obligations upon workers and members of local communities, it is clear that the object of regulation is business. Moreover, it is equally clear that those in whose interests the regulations exist, and for whose protection they should be enforced, are workers and local communities.

This key difference leads us on to a very closely related point. Regulatory law will need to be enforced less 'minimally' than the kinds of law with which the realists are concerned, precisely because of the immense inequalities in power between the regulated – business – and those whom the regulations exist to protect – workers and local communities. (A recognition and full understanding of this imbalance of power also necessitates academic work, in terms of an adequate theorization of the nature of the offenders under regulatory law, namely corporations). When the realists discuss 'public initiation of police action', we not only endorse this with respect to worker and local community initiation of regulatory inspectorate action, but would add that the imbalance of power in this latter sphere requires the development of much more formal mechanisms to encourage, facilitate and render effective such initiation. Just as the realists constantly argue for more democratic means of controlling policing, this need is more urgent with respect to the activities of regulatory agencies. (This, after all, has been a central concern of the 'capture' literature of the last two decades within social science literature on regulation.)

Thus, while realism urges that policing become much more reactive and much less proactive, we would resist this exigence in the sphere of regulatory law. One reason for this is simply that there are some differences between the types of offence that fall within the ambit of the police, on the one hand, and regulatory agencies on the other (though this should not be overemphasized – see below). Regulatory violations are often easily observable, ongoing states of affairs, rather than discrete often concealed acts. For these reasons, a proactive presence by the factory or pollution inspectorate can be more productive in that the chances of an inspector uncovering violations on a site visit are clearly much greater than a police officer happening across an assault, burglary, car theft, and so on (although, of course, this does occur).

Two points follow from this. One is that in the sphere of regulatory law, to the extent that workers and local communities are presented with the formal mechanisms whereby they can initiate inspectorate attention/action, to the extent that they develop trust in those inspectorates, and as far as they themselves develop confidence and expertise, then the need for a proactive inspectorial commitment may decline. But this is to take a very long-term view. Moreover, the need for a proactive presence will never disappear completely – those in unorganized workplaces, for example, will continue to be particularly vulnerable, while the lack of a subjective perception of harm on the part of a local community from a local site/company may be less a consequence of the absence of objective harm, more a consequence of 'unpolitics' (Blowers, 1984; Crenson, 1971; Smith, 1989; Lukes, 1974). The second point that follows is that demands for an increase in numbers of inspectors are perfectly legitimate in a way that, as realists argue, demands for increased police resources are not. In contrast to the increase in the numbers of police officers in England and Wales over the past decade, the same period has witnessed a considerable decline in the numbers of factory inspectors in particular (the same is true of the US), while at the same time the number of workplaces to be inspected has risen dramatically and (European Community-inspired) legislation has meant a significant increase in the range (and, indeed, nature) of laws to be overseen by the Health and Safety Executive in general (Tombs, 1990a).

Thus the central thrust of the above is that while we wish to adopt the realist argument for democratization and maximum public initiation of action in the context of reforming the organization and activities of regulatory agencies, the different circumstances within which these and the police operate mean that arguments for 'minimal coercion', to the extent that this implies strict limitations on agency powers, are wholly inappropriate within the context with which we are concerned.

Before we go on to consider at length the modus operandi of the regulatory agencies in the sphere of health, safety and environmental laws, one further point, as yet unmentioned, needs to be emphasized from realist writing on police work. Realist work on the police has addressed directly the 'problem' of discretion. Many writers on police work have wrestled with the question of how to minimize the exercise of police discretion. But the realists have adopted a slightly, but significantly, different position on this issue. Thus they have emphasized that *policing not only is, but must be, inherently political. The exercise of discretion is not only inevitable but desirable*, allowing the ends in the name of which the police exist to be explicitly considered. This might be one way in which realist proposals can be developed in a socialist rather than simply liberal direction:

> Discretion is thus not to be seen as a failure, nor as inevitably prejudicial to the powerless, nor – precisely because of this – as a matter for the police to determine as they will. Discretion, by definition, cannot be limited by law. At the moment, however, the politics of the police are buried within their existing organisational structures, and ideologically denied in the rhetoric of police professionalism. We have argued that a politics of the police is inevitable, and a certain politics desirable. Changes demand a recognition of these facts and a radical institutional reorganisation which would allow the inevitable to accord with the desirable. (Kinsey et al., 1986: 168)

Again, in the context of debates on health, safety and environment, a recognition of the political nature of the questions involved is important. But so often it is precisely this fact which is at best understated, at worst denied. Questions of how safe is safe enough, what are acceptable costs and benefits of industrial activity, what determines 'reasonable practicability', and so on, are explicitly political issues; they are certainly not technical questions. A recognition of this must be progressive, and indeed is a precondition of the transcendence of a technocratic rationality which pervades much of industry and serves as a barrier to the kind of 'maximum public initiation' which was spoken about above.

Theories of regulation

The first question that must be dealt with is whether regulatory violations should even be considered to be equivalent to street crimes. Capitalists and corporate executives, many judges and regulators, some economists and political scientists and, indeed, many legal theorists and criminologists have argued that regulatory and white-collar offences are inherently different from such activities. James Q. Wilson, appropriately, has claimed 'predatory street crime to be a far more serious matter than consumer fraud, anti-trust violations, etc . . . because predatory crime makes difficult or impossible the maintenance of meaningful human communities' (1975: xx). More recently, in his book with Richard Herrnstein, *Crime and Human Nature*, he has retained a focus on street crime because – 'Robbery, stealing, incest and factory pollution were condemned by overwhelming majorities in every society' (1986: 22). What is bizarre about this work is that in it, he studiously and with no explanation, avoids any discussion of the last and ultimately potentially expansive category of 'factory pollution'.

Proponents of a 'compliance' (as opposed to a 'policing') regulatory strategy argue that the nature of corporate illegalities calls for different forms of regulation than is the case for other kinds of lawbreaking. Businesses and particularly corporations are not, as many would have it, typically 'amoral calculators', but rather 'political citizens' who may indeed sometimes err but more because of 'organizational in-competence' than deliberate wrongdoing. Thus they need advice rather than chastisement: regulatory agencies should act as consultants rather than 'policemen' (Kagan and Scholz, 1984: 68). Although some corporations sometimes act as if they are 'amoral calculators', this is neither necessary nor typical; where regulations are violated, this is usually the result of factors other than pure economic calculation. Corporations can and do have a primary commitment to act in a socially responsible fashion, are not essentially criminogenic, and will not cease to commit violations because of attempts at deterrence (Kagan and Scholz, 1984: 67–8; see also Hawkins, 1984: 110; Hutter, 1988: 45–7, 80; Richardson et al., 1983: 125–49). To accept a view of the corporation as an amoral calculator entails a corresponding view of the most appropriate regulatory response to such corporations, namely, 'strict enforcement of uniform and high specific standards, backed by severe penalties', with regulatory officials acting quite literally as 'policemen' (Kagan and Scholz, 1984: 72).

In their view, this is quite wrong, because legal infractions by business are unsuitable for criminalization. In the case of pollution there is a need 'to preserve a fragile balance between the interests of economic activity on the one hand and the public welfare on the other' (Hawkins, 1984: 9), and, relatedly, it is 'the inherent nature and circumstances of factory "crime"' that 'necessarily engender a compliance response' (Jamieson, 1985: i). Not only is *mens rea* inapplicable in most cases of regulatory violations, particularly since such deviance occurs within an organizational framework (Richardson et al., 1983: 56–7), but there is an inherent injustice in the use of a standard of strict liability, and, anyway, many regulatory offences involve acts or omissions, which are *mala prohibita* rather than *mala in se*. Regulatory violations differ from 'traditional' or 'consensual' crimes in that the former are 'morally problematic' (Hawkins, 1984: 11), lack 'self-evident moral blameworthiness' (Jamieson, 1985: 30) or are characterized by 'moral ambivalence' (Hutter, 1988: 10–11).

These controversies, of course, are not new. In the 1940s Sutherland and Tappan debated the status of the concept of 'white-collar crime' (Sutherland, 1940, 1941; Tappan, 1947) and recently Blum-West and Carter (1983) have vindicated many of Sutherland's arguments by showing that there are no substantive differences between torts and crimes. Glasbeek and Rowland have convincingly developed detailed legal arguments as to why killing and injuring at work should be treated as typical crimes of violence (Glasbeek, 1984, 1988; Glasbeek and Rowland, 1979) and, elsewhere, we have addressed the issue of the status of such regulatory offences by drawing out an analogy between such health and safety violations and motoring offences (Pearce and Tombs, 1990). It is clear that these activities can be criminalized, particularly, as we show below, with some relatively minor changes in company law.

Let us then, for the moment, turn to the argument that corporations are not amoral calculators. In our view the claim that corporations can do anything other than attempt to maximize long-term profitability is theoretically untenable. It is the basic rationale for, indeed constitutive of, their very existence. For any corporation to have a primary commitment to social responsibility would entail ignoring both its rationale and the nature of the existing economic system. This is *not* to argue that such rational calculation necessarily means that all regulations are ignored by corporations, nor that any particular corporation will in practice succeed in either a correct interpretation of what is rational, nor be able to act in accordance with that interpretation. Clearly, then, corporations will, at times, act 'irrationally' – what the 'compliance school' calls incompetence and political citizenship are both perfectly compatible with a concept of corporations as amoral calculators. Nor is it to imply that business firms or the individuals who hold positions of power and take decisions within them will all act criminally. It is simply to recognize that, as Box has argued, the nature of the capitalist mode of production forces corporations to attempt to exert as much control as possible over their operating environments, this pushing them into violating those regulations which seek to prevent individual corporations from using their corporate power to exert certain forms of control over consumers, workers, governments, other corporations, and so on (Box, 1983).

A more plausible view, then, is that of Edwin Sutherland (1983) who argued that corporations are 'rationalistic, amoral and nonsentimental':

> The corporation probably comes closer to the 'economic man' and to 'pure reason' than any person or any other organization. The executives and directors not only have explicit and consistent objectives of maximum pecuniary gain but also have research and accountancy departments by which precise determination of results is facilitated ...
>
> ... the corporation selects crimes which involve the smallest danger of detection and identification and against which victims are least likely to fight.... The corporations attempt to prevent the implementation of the law and to create general goodwill.... (Sutherland, 1983: 236–8)

Indeed, although recent theorists differ somewhat about the appropriate models for describing business organizations, few, if any, give any credibility to the notion of the 'soulful corporation' (Pearce and Tombs, 1989, 1991).

In the view of economists of the Chicago school, for example, everybody's pursuit of self-interest in the free market produces an efficient allocation of resources, enhances individual self-satisfaction and promotes liberty and freedom of choice. Such self-interest, they argue, is much more likely to produce a satisfactory social order than is the invocation of such vague goals as social responsibility: 'If businesses do have a social responsibility other than making maximum profits for share holders, how are they to know what it is? Can self selected private individuals decide ... how great a burden they are justified in placing on themselves of their stockholders to serve the social interest?' (Friedman, 1962: note 26, pp. 133–4). In their view, management's desire to take account of social interests – the community, consumers, employees – would be merely a ploy to give them some autonomy from shareholders. (For examples see the debate about 'corporate responsibility' in the Sunday *New York Times* during March 1990).

Although, as we will show, such economists tend to agree with the compliance school about the appropriate status of regulatory offences, they raise some interesting questions. In their view in the relationship between economic activity and the state there are tremendous dangers to the working of market rationality and efficiency. Since all economic actors, including corporations and state agents, are motivated by self-interest although state activities are justified because they are alleged to correct allocative problems due to market failure, in fact, they primarily function to redistribute resources by interfering with the normal working of the market. The major beneficiaries are usually small groups of highly motivated and well-organized economic actors – iron triangles of established companies, regulators and politicians. Control is achieved through the regulatory apparatus favouring such companies directly or by imposing prohibitive costs on potential competitors by, for example, demanding expensive safety standards. Consumers also suffer because they have to pay higher prices. In other words, they are very cynical about the autonomy of regulatory agencies and their utility for achieving any kind of social goals (cf. Stigler, 1971; Peltzman, 1976).

Thus, in their view, 'social regulation' is something best achieved by a combination of market forces and litigation rather than by governmental regulation. Optimum realizable health and safety standards, for example, are likely to be reached when employers find the level of expenditure on safety which is just marginally less than the expenditure incurred by accidents made up of the damage to property, of training new workers, of increased insurance premiums, of workmen's compensation, of litigation and of paying workers increased wages because they know that they are engaging in relatively dangerous work. The most that regulatory agencies can realistically do is to set performance hazard standards or develop injury taxes (Oi, 1977). First, let us note that the very idea that one can distinguish between 'social regulation' and 'economic regulation' is ideological. For example, the 'regulation of hazardous products is the soft underbelly of economic regulation, precisely because it deals ultimately with who will bear the hidden costs of new products and production processes' (Doern, 1977: 17). Then, for insurance and workmen's compensation to have any effect compensation levels must be high. For an injury tax to work, the tariff must be significant. For litigation to be effective courts must be sympathetic to those who are injured, resources must be made available to equalize them and employers in the competition for legal help, and settlements must be substantial. For workers to know about injury rates and for them to be able to demand higher wages it is essential that they have access to accurate information about company affairs. All of these require a combination of substantial legal aid, the coercive power of regulatory agencies and strong trade unions – exactly what such theorists wish to avoid!

Wilson is sympathetic to the arguments of these economists but he is also critical of them for certain oversimplifications. He suggests that not all regulatory agencies are captured by those that they are meant to regulate, and therefore a more complex model is required of the relationship between state agencies and the different social groups competing to influence them. First there are not one, but four, political situations. He redefines as *client politics* the situation where costs are widely distributed and benefits concentrated (as in state licensing laws). *Majoritarian politics* occur when both costs and benefits are widespread (as in the Social Security and Sherman Acts). *Interest group politics* exist when both costs and benefits are narrowly distributed and hence negotiation and compromise can occur (as in the labour laws). Finally, *entrepreneurial politics* occur when benefits are widely distributed and costs are highly concentrated (as in environmental and motor safety regulation). Secondly, while it is true that some regulatory officials are politicians ambitious for higher appointive or elective office, others are careerists motivated by organizational bureaucratic concerns, and yet others are professionals responsive to the norms and interests of their wider occupational community. Thirdly, although in economics what is relevant is not what individuals want or why but only consumers 'revealed preferences' known through market conduct; in politics values often only emerge in the course of the political process and efforts are continuously made to change people's wants so that they are in accord with the emerging political programme:

> Both economics and politics deal with problems of scarcity and conflicting preferences. Both deal with persons who ordinarily act rationally. But politics differs from economics in that it manages conflict by forming heterogeneous coalitions out of persons with changeable and incommensurable preferences in order to make binding decisions for everyone. (Wilson, 1980: 363)

This, in Wilson's view, had become a serious problem in the 1970s since unqualified, irrational political actors – trade unionists and 'bureaucrats, professionals, academics, the media, those whose political position depends upon controlling resources other than wealth and whose motivations are more complex than wealth maximization' – sometimes interfere with both market forces and the internal workings of the professionally run corporation. Unreasonable laws can be passed, excessive damages awarded, unworkable regulations promulgated, and product certification unfairly denied. Such individuals and attitudes – a belief in a risk-free society, for example – can gain excessive influence within democratic assemblies, in the courts, in juries and can capture regulatory agencies. There can be another iron triangle of regulatory entrepreneurs, regulatory agencies and, for example, environmentalist politicians (Wilson, 1980; Weaver, 1978).

Although some of the specific points made by Wilson, about the different kinds of regulatory political situations for example, are not without value, it is clear that he fails to attend to the wider structural context of the situations that he explores or to examine long-term outcomes. There is a need to examine the significance of both the Social Security Act of 1935 and the 1890 Sherman Act, and ask why the former presaged such a minimal welfare state in the US (the development of which has been subject to such tremendous vagaries and extraordinary resistance – cf. Block et al., 1987) and why the latter, and subsequent legislation, have not stopped the economic system becoming increasingly oligopolistic (Coleman, 1989: 14; Jones, 1982). He provides no explanation of why environmentalists and trade unionists advocating a healthy and safe environment within and without the workplace were successful in developing effective regulation for only three or four years in the mid-1970s. In fact, *contra* Wilson and David Vogel (cf. Vogel, 1989), their short-term victory – as a result of heightened social conflict and a profound but temporary crisis in the legitimacy of the American political and economic order (Donnelly, 1981) – but speedy defeat, is testimony, not to the plural nature of the US political system, but rather to the resources, resilience and power of business which was able to launch the massive counterattack associated with deregulation (Calavita, 1983; Szasz, 1984, 1986a, 1986b).

One can reinterpret some of the arguments of compliance theorists to make this point, albeit after making some pretty fundamental criticisms. Bardach and Kagan, for example, make two objections to the 'regulator-as-policeman' strategy. First, it engenders rigidity and/or legalism, which in turn generates 'regulatory unreasonableness' and 'unresponsiveness' (Bardach and Kagan, 1982: 58). Here the regulatory inspector is seen as something akin to an automaton, compelled towards the prosecution of each and every violation detected. Such a representation is not only stereotypical, echoing Thatcherite and Reaganite 'anti-statist' rhetoric, but is based upon a misconception of what the police actually do. Because of the necessarily wide range of laws that they exist to enforce and for operational/practical reasons, police officers regularly and routinely exercise discretion, as an indispensable (Lustgarten, 1987), and even desirable (Kinsey et al., 1986), part of their work. Their second, and more telling, objection is that this strategy stimulates 'opposition and the destruction of cooperation' (Kagan and Scholz, 1984: 73). Business may resort to legalistic counter-measures, organize politically and attack the agency at the legislative level, jeopardizing 'the agency's legal mandate, its funding, and its very existence' (Kagan and Scholz, 1984: 74).

On the one hand, they imply that if regulators were only more reasonable – both British and US occupational health and safety inspectors were instructed in being more polite when visiting businesses, and business executives were asked to comment on their conduct to the inspectors' superiors (Wilson, 1985) – then compliance would be the normal outcome. On the other hand, they argue, and themselves find it a reasonable state of affairs that: regulation is viable only when it prevents the *avoidable* harmful side-effects of wealth creation and an inspectorate's mandate would be withdrawn if it were seen to be overzealous; regulations are only passed which do not pose a fundamental challenge to an industry's economic viability and industry is powerful enough to resist the enactment or enforcement of over-restrictive regulations. *The legitimacy of a capitalist economic system and the illegitimacy of its being policed are in fact starting-points for such analyses.* There is, however, no reason for us to endorse any such view. Their own analysis suggests that there are two distinct inequalities of power – those that derive from an imbalance in resources, including knowledge and expertise, and those that derive from corporate ideological hegemony. As we have shown elsewhere (Pearce and Tombs, 1990), while 'compliance theorists' recognize that the enforcement realities/necessities they describe are defined and limited by the 'needs of business' they consistently fail even to attempt to transcend or subvert the limitations placed upon 'realistic' possibilities by this de facto dominance. Dominance, of course, implies struggle and resistance and it is important to recognize deregulation and other Reaganite policies, for example in relation to welfare, as a recuperative counterattack against some real historical gains (Block et al., 1987). Ironically, recently, a contingent event, the Bhopal disaster, has made it possible to reopen the debate about these issues. Indeed, if the workings of the capitalist system and its empowering of the major corporate actors is the omnipresent context of all political situations this does not mean that it is in total control of its own destiny. It does not automatically secure its economic, political or ideological conditions of existence. It is the unpredictability and uncontrollability of the US economy, rather than the nature and function of regulatory agencies, that has been the major focus of Kolko's work for the last 20 or so years (Kolko, 1962, 1963, 1984).

Kolko's work is relatively compatible with a conception of regulatory bodies as more hegemonic apparatuses than captive agents. In this view a stable capitalist social order depends upon one fraction of capital achieving leadership – in both the state and civil society – over both other fractions of capital and the subordinate classes. In order to do this it does all that it can to disarm these other groups while winning their consent through (limited) compromises with their interests. In the 'relatively autonomous' state there is established an 'unequal equilibrium of compromises' and an 'unequal structure of representation'. Regulatory agencies always involve representation of fractions of capital, of the wider state and, sometimes, of other social interests: 'Like other parts of the state apparatus, these institutions represent the interests of a specific fraction [of capital] – but in a particular way, as they are effectively combined with the long term interests of the hegemonic fraction. That is, they simultaneously represent and regulate (Mahon, 1979: 155).

This means that such apparatuses may give *some* privileges to businesses already operating in an area and may give partial recognition to the interests of subordinate groups. However, the overall control exercised over the state and civil society by the hegemonic fraction means that such concessions are likely to be strictly circumscribed, at least in the long run. Rianne Mahon has shown how this can be achieved through the medium of the hierarchical relationship that exists between the different state apparatuses – specialist regulatory agencies can be located in relatively weak government departments and/or their activities can be subject to the review of other state agencies which more closely reflect the interests or rationales of the hegemonic fractions of capital. In the US the Office of Management and Budget fulfilled this latter function in the 1980s (Horwitz, 1989: 208–11). Mahon's work (1977, 1979, 1984), which we have only been able to sketch here, represents the beginnings of an alternative and more sophisticated analysis of regulatory agencies.

For Wilson, however, it is bureaucratization and inefficiency that are characteristic of state activities. Thus the fewer the demands that are made on the state – and the less political activity there is – the better. There is little point in trying to change anything because 'the relationship between electoral needs and policy outcome is problematic' (1980: 390). He produced a similar argument with somewhat different conclusions, of course, in the case of street crime, since here he argues that nothing can be done about the social causes of crime, which anyway are unknowable, but deterrence remains very much on the agenda (Wilson, 1975: xiv–xv; Young, 1986: 9–12). Yet, while usually he claims that the less regulation the better, in his article with Rachal (1977), he argued that regulation can in fact be very effective but only if it is private enterprise that is being regulated and not government bureaucracies. He makes unfavourable comparisons between the effective and ineffective regulation of private and public housing, hospitals and utilities, respectively. Although there are indeed *difficulties* in regulating state activities (cf. Hirst, 1986), generally what

Wilson claims are that examples of the *impossibility* of such regulation are due rather to a failure to supply governmental agencies with sufficient funds and adequate guidelines – for example, to maintain public housing and both to provide cheap electricity *and* control pollution. It is conservative hostility to public enterprise that is the problem, not public enterprise itself. It is also worth noting that it is impossible adequately to regulate some markets because adequate regulation makes them economically unviable for private enterprise, and conversely they can only be viable if they are inadequately regulated. Szasz's (1986b) discussion of the regulation of hazardous waste disposal and Campbell's (1987) of the state and nuclear waste are instructive in this regard. Indeed, overall it is only too clear that:

> In the end, the politics of regulation turns less on the dynamics of coalition formation, the behavior of regulatory officials, or the rulings of the courts, important as these are, than on the dominant vision of the larger society in which nationally organized interests, policy entrepreneurs, bureaucrats, and courts are merely highly specialized, and unrepresentative manifestations. That vision encompasses a conception of the good society and of the place of the citizen in that society, a notion of the proper boundaries between public and private, and of the appropriate domains of community norms and individual decision. That vision, whatever its content, ultimately prescribes the tolerance within which conventional regulatory politics can be conducted. (Schuck, 1981: 723)

Different kinds of economics and different forms of analyses are also forms of politics. While claiming objectivity they are tied to particular interests, while guiding and justifying actions they can also obscure what is occurring.

Amoral calculators: some empirical evidence

That most corporations are not amoral calculators, and thus that their adherence to regulations is not conditional upon their short-term or longer-term self-interest, is, as we have seen, a central tenet of the arguments of those advocating compliance strategies. Bardach and Kagan (1982) even attempt to quantify the proportion of all corporations which are amoral calculators, or 'bad apples'. They assume, 'for analytical purposes', that at most they 'make up about 20 per cent of the average population of regulated enterprises in most regulatory programs' (Bardach and Kagan, 1982: 65). If the theoretical argument for viewing corporations as amoral calculators is unconvincing, the empirical evidence as to the spread of illegalities among all types of corporations seems, *contra* Bardach and Kagan, in favour of a view which sees the commitment of corporations to regulations as essentially contingent.

We will illustrate these points by a brief analysis of the state of occupational health and safety in the UK. This is not because there exist no useful analyses of the state of health and safety in the US (Coleman, 1989) or Canada (Glasbeek, 1988; Goff and Reasons, 1986) but for reasons of space. Currently in the UK more than 600 people die in work-related accidents every year, and in excess of another 18,000 suffer major injuries from work-related incidents. Moreover, after a long period of decline in the numbers injured at work in Britain, the 1980s have seen dramatic increases in major injuries in certain industrial sectors (HSE, 1987). About 750 people each year are officially recorded as dying per year from occupational diseases, but these are based upon very narrowly drawn categories. Trades unions have estimated that 20,000 people die each year partly as a result of work-related ill-health (Work Hazards Group, 1987), and this figure is given significant support by the Royal Commission on Civil Liability (1978) which estimated that what are recorded as occupationally related illnesses may be only 20 percent of the true figure of such illnesses.

Moreover, in report after report, the Health and Safety Executive and its Inspectorates state that management bears primary responsibility for these accidents, for example: 75 percent of maintenance accidents in the chemical industry (HSE, 1987), '2 out of 3 deaths in general manufacturing' (HSE, 1983), '3 out of 5 farm deaths' (HSE, 1986), 78 percent of fatal maintenance accidents in manufacturing (HSE, 1985b), 70 percent of deaths in the construction industry (HSE, 1988), and so on. *In other words, in more than three out of five cases of fatal accidents, managements were (fatally) in violation of the Health and Safety at Work Act 1974 in terms of their General Duties to employees (Sections 2 and 3).*

Further, *contra* Bardach and Kagan, existing empirical evidence suggests that regulatory deviance is not confined to a tiny proportion of firms. Carson's (1970) work on the Factory Inspectorate found that whatever their size every one of the 200 firms visited in the course of his research violated health and safety laws at least twice, and the average number of violations per firm was 19. Few however were legally sanctioned. Recent HSE industry 'blitzes' have also revealed widespread regulatory violations. One recent blitz on the textile industry, for example, found that *191 of 300 premises inspected were not even registered with local regulatory agencies, as required by law* (Health and Safety Executive, 1985a). Similarly, when, in the summer of 1987, the work of about 4500 contractors on construction sites was inspected, 868 prohibition notices were issued to stop work immediately because of dangerous conditions. In other words, as a result of one set of inspections conditions on one in five building sites visited were so bad that work had to be stopped immediately (*Occupational Safety and*

Health, December 1987). Moreover it is not only small and 'fly-by-night' firms that engage in such violations. Violations are widespread among companies of all sizes and in all sectors of the economy (Pearce, 1990a; Pearce and Tombs, 1991; Clinard and Yeager, 1980: 130; Carson, 1982). Although these data are not conclusive as to the common-place and routine nature of regulatory deviance with respect to health and safety law, they are surely enough to call into question empirically that which we had earlier questioned theoretically – namely, the claim that only a minority of corporations should be treated as if they are amoral calculators.

Corporate illegalities, corporate organization and corporate responsibilities

We have argued that the distinction between 'traditional' criminals and corporate offenders contains both real and ideological aspects. It describes certain aspects of reality in that business is an activity which has certain socially useful consequences. But it remains largely ideological in that it implies that the corporation can have a primary commitment to act in a socially responsible manner; it is ideological in that illegalities are currently considered to form a marginal element of business activity; and it is ideological in its acceptance of business's own definitions as to what constitute 'reasonable' regulations.

Once these assumptions which underpin the distinction between 'traditional' and 'regulatory' offenders, and the different regulatory responses engendered by this distinction, are problematized, then both the distinction itself and the arguments against the 'policing' of industry are greatly weakened. This allows us to reopen the question of the most 'appropriate' regulatory strategy for dealing with corporate violations of health and safety laws, to transcend at least some of the ideological 'understandings' within which both the questions we may pose and the answers we can find are presupposed.

On this basis, we have been able to consider eminently practicable strategies for controlling corporate activities, including the use of automatic penalty points as one among a wider range of sanctions available to regulatory agencies, and the application of the principles of licensing in this sphere (which has in fact become a reality recently in a number of US states – this for explicitly political reasons) (Pearce and Tombs, 1990). Thus the transcendence of the assumption that corporations cannot be policed allows serious consideration to be given to the practicalities of such a strategy – and many of the practical problems are, indeed, attested to usefully in the work of the 'Compliance school'. Yet there is no need to conflate the immediately practicable with either the once-and-for-all possible or desirable forms of regulation. Avoiding this conflation is indeed crucial once it is recognized that what is 'feasible' is in fact a political issue, and thus subject to change.

Let us consider one of the allegedly key practical difficulties in 'criminalizing' regulatory deviance. Because regulatory deviance occurs within an organizational framework, it has been alleged that there are overwhelming practical difficulties in prosecuting businesses (Richardson et al., 1983: 56-7), so we need to show that it is or could be feasible to prosecute corporate offenders. Certainly, until very recently, it has been the case in the UK that where a company is prosecuted for regulatory violations it is the corporate entity that is charged – rather than particular individuals such as senior executives – with the company being represented in the court by the company secretary, usually to face a fine which in practice is little more than a tax. Company law, while increasingly specific about financial responsibilities (and with a possibility of criminal prosecution for negligence as in Section 89 of the 1986 Insolvency Act), is extremely vague about those concerned with occupational safety and environmental damage, thus creating problems in determining individual and collective responsibility for disasters and accidents. Nevertheless, there are possibilities both in current law, and in relatively minor law reform, to make directors and chief executives legally as well as morally responsible for accidents and disasters while still providing them with a reasonable defence if they are not in fact to blame. This will also make prosecution easier and hence a more rational option for the Inspectorates.

The problem of establishing corporate culpability in the UK context is exemplified by the important Appeal Court Decision on the Zeebrugge disaster. The court found that a Corporation can be indicted for manslaughter, when the *mens rea* and *actus reus* of manslaughter can be established against those who are identified as the embodiment of the corporation itself. The court determined, however, that the evidence (available to the coroner) did not support a prosecution in this case (Law Report, *The Guardian*, 15 October 1987). However, the DPP eventually issued eight summonses for manslaughter, arising out of the Zeebruggge tragedy. These included two issued against company directors and one issued against P&O European Ferries (Dover) Ltd (formerly Townsend Car Ferries). With this latter summons is raised again the issue of corporate manslaughter. A company may well be held liable through the doctrine of identification, on the grounds that the acts and omissions of certain 'controlling individuals' may be seen as the acts and omissions of the company itself. Thus a company is held personally liable. The crucial issue here, as yet unresolved, is whether the corporate guilt of a company can be established by 'aggregating the actions of various different officers which on their own do not amount to manslaughter' (James, 1989: 4). Of equal importance is the fact that 'the notion of corporate man-slaughter is now entering the popular vocabulary' (Wells, 1988), opening the possibility of reforming how corporations are organized and behave. Both the law and sentencing could be used to force companies to improve their organizational structure, their manage-ment of health and safety and to attend to 'total quality control' in these kind of activities as well as with respect to finished products.

In the US many companies have developed sophisticated systems that monitor safety and clearly define the responsibilities of mana-gerial personnel (Braithwaite and Fisse, 1987) and it is surely no coincidence that some have also been successfully prosecuted for manslaughter and murder (Coleman, 1989). Moreover, and *contra* Braithwaite (1985), even rigorous self-regulation will only ever work if there is an effective external inspectorate. Since there is no reason to believe that companies would be rigorous about recording incidents and accidents (Di Mento, 1986: 56; Tombs, 1990b) independent monitoring is essential. It is only the fear of effective legal sanctions that will begin to make management genuinely safety-conscious.

On the basis of the preceding, and our work presented elsewhere, we believe that a punitive policing strategy is necessary, desirable and practicable. Such policies obviously will be resisted by capital and its allies (Snider, 1989) and will only be forced upon corporations by other social groupings, such as workforces, local communities and con-sumers. Although the parameters of capitalist social relations place real limits on how far such reforms can proceed, that some reforms can proceed should now be clear enough. In the next section, we aim to show that one important means of bringing pressure to bear on capital is by challenging corporations to justify their claim that they are responsible political citizens.

Calling the corporate bluff

When large corporations claim to be socially responsible they rarely spell out the conditions that, given their primary goal of profit, would be necessary for them to consistently act in a responsible way. How realistic, for example, would it be for them to show genuine concern about the impact of their operation on occupational and community health and safety if their competitors did not do the same? Even in this limited area they could only act responsibly if they accepted signifi-cant changes in their own and their competitors' forms of organization and operating environments; if they acknowledged the importance of environmental impact assessment and social accounting; and if they accepted the public's right to know. Let us look at corporate arguments to see how they often both proclaim social concern and at the same time avoid what it would really mean.

Corporate executives claim to do everything reasonably practicable to make a profit by using safe and efficient production processes to make safe and useful products which are then sold in highly competitive markets. Essentially they can be trusted to be self-regulating although they will work with regulatory agencies. These agencies are useful when they are responsive to government, industry and other legitimate interest groups and when they impose appropriate standards on a minority of, usually small, incompetent or dubious businesses. Although the typical corporation accepts reasonable state intervention, unfortunately unreasonable laws can be passed, excessive damages awarded, unworkable regulations promulgated, and product certification unfairly denied. Less external regulation, then, is usually the preferred and more reasonable option. Corporations, after all, are responsible political citizens.

Thus, we find that in 1988, the chairman and chief executive of Monsanto announced that his company 'abandoned a possible substitute product for asbestos ... because a whole generation of lawyers had been schooled in asbestos liability theories that could possibly be turned against the substitute' (Mahoney, 1988). In the 1970s, the chemical industry had opposed a proposed federal PVC standard because it would cost two million jobs and $65 billion. It 'was simply beyond the compliance capacity of the industry' (Rattner, 1975). Pro-business analysts calculated that in 1976 the overall administrative cost of regulation in the US was $3.2 billion and the compliance cost $62.9 billion – a total of $66.1 billion. In 1975 federal regulations had increased the average price of a car by $449.41 forcing the car industry and consumers to spend an additional $3.025 billion on cars, money that both industry and consumers could have spent more productively elsewhere (Weidenbaum and de Fina, 1978). However, if we look more closely at these examples we can draw quite different conclusions. First, one reason for high settlements in asbestos cases – Johns-Mansville had to pay approximately $2.5 billion to 60,000 claimants (*Los Angeles Times*, 22 February 1989) – is that, from the 1920s onwards, the major companies concealed from their workers and the public a mass of accumulating evidence of the dangers of asbestos (Brodeur, 1985). Secondly, when an approximately equivalent PVC standard was eventually adopted industry developed new technology, continued to flourish, without job losses and at only 5 percent of the expected cost (Wilson, 1985: 15–16). Thirdly, although health and safety and environmental regulations are expensive to implement they also cut down on the destruction of property and on the cost of deaths and injuries to individuals, their families and the community as a whole – air pollution control saved something like 13,900 lives per annum and reduced property damage by nearly $6 billion (Freeman, 1979; see also Wilson, 1985). Similarly, making cars less dangerous may simply be an additional cost for car manufacturers but this is not true for the community as a whole. The additional $3.025 billion spent on the purchase of cars helped save $2.5 billion through exhaust fume control, and over £5.5 billion from reductions in accidents even if we restrict ourselves to insurance and litigation-based estimates of the value of life and limb. From the point of view of the rest of the community – including some corporate executives – then there was a net benefit from this regulation of about $5 billion.

Expenditure on pollution control may simply be a cost for polluting industries but it may often stimulate economic growth. In the US in the 1970s 'some 20,000 employees were put out of work because of plant closings, but over 600,000 were employed in various pollution related activities' (Marcus, 1980). The absence of pollution control may inhibit development. Recently, William Waldegrave admitted that 'Inferior environmental regulations and a lack of government support is undermining the £2 billion plus [British pollution control] industry' (*The Guardian*, 2 May 1987). In the US where industries have been forced to monitor and register emissions of dangerous chemicals, 'savings from controlling waste and improving processes efficiencies often more than outweigh the costs' (Elkins, 1989: 3).

But this is by no means necessarily true. Many pollution control and some health and safety measures *will* involve industry in significant additional expense. For example in 1975 and 1976 the US chemical industry spent approximately 9 and 12 percent of capital expenditure on pollution control equipment and although it was expected to decrease subsequently it remained nearly double the expected expenditure overseas (Castleman, 1979; and see Wilson 1985). A key political issue, then, is who will bear the costs of safe production? Furthermore, there are a number of situations where profits and safety are necessarily at odds with each other. One is where there is a declining market, and hence fixed costs may be cut to maintain profitability. Another is where companies keep extending the life of plant and machinery by replacing parts, even when they have already received a good return on their investment. Yet another is when in an expanding market a relatively undercapitalized corporation, wishing to maintain its market share, may dangerously overutilize both plant and personnel. Bhopal serves as an example of the first situation, US airline passenger services of the second and Boeing aircraft production of the third (Pearce and Tombs, 1989; *The Guardian*, 27 and 31 January 1989). What may be economically rational behaviour from the point of view of the corporation certainly is not from the point of view of workers, consumers, the community or even from the point of view of a market economy as a whole – if it is truly competitive, that is. It is only a countervailing ethical commitment of the corporation to act in another way or the threat of sanctions that under these circumstances would lead a corporation to act in a socially responsible manner.

The previous discussion shows that whereas corporations are usually reluctant to submit themselves to effective regulation, it is sometimes possible to pressurize them to do so and that at times their resistance may be weakened by appealing to the long-term self-interest of both corporate executives and their major shareholders. This suggests the necessity and feasibility of developing strategies to challenge the corporations to live up to their self-representation as 'responsible political citizens'. We should stress, however, that any victories won through such strategies may well be temporary. Corporate capital will fight back – industry can emigrate, laws can be changed, regulatory agencies can be captured, starved of funds, or disbanded. As long as corporations and capitalistic social relations remain there will be a continuous struggle. This is no reason to despair but rather to develop ever-new strategies. Pressure can be brought on corporations both externally and internally – corporations are not themselves internally homogeneous.

In some ways the rational actor model of the corporation is an oversimplification. First it leaves unresolved the issue of the relationship between short-term and long-term profitability. Corporate raiding is intimately connected with the demand by some shareholders that short-term profitability should be maximized even if this involves the selling of assets which are essential to long-term profitability. An example would be land (owned by a corporation) which has increased in value and hence could be sold at a substantial profit, but is earmarked as the prime site for new plant when a new product goes into volume production a few years down the line. Here there is a conflict of interest between those – both management and certain key investors – concerned with the long-term viability of a corporation and those merely concerned with the turnover of their money. To make matters even more complicated most large companies themselves now engage in speculative investments in money markets, in addition to actually producing and selling commodities. Whatever, these different pressures tend to strengthen the power of the accounting and purely financial departments of corporations over and above sales or production. Furthermore, this dominance is perfectly compatible with the trend in recent years, noted by Kreisberg (1976), for many corporations to decentralize decision making and goal setting away from head office to local management while specifying standard operating procedures. What Kreisberg does not mention, however, is that this is often accompanied by the setting of strict financial targets by the head office. This, incidentally, is an inherently criminogenic relation. First, it demands certain levels of profit independently of the specific difficulties in operating safely and legally in particular operating environments. Secondly, it is very easy for the chief executives to avoid knowing or at least to refuse to acknowledge how profits are actually made and thus avoid liability for any wrongdoings. The events at Bhopal can be read as a tragic outcome of just such an arrangement (Pearce and Tombs, 1989) and on a more mundane level the Tesco judgment implicitly encourages higher management to be 'wilfully blind' about what happens at lower levels (Fife and Machin, 1982; Wilson, 1979).

Both the 'rational actor' and this 'organizational process' model of corporate structure can be viewed as sub-types of 'bureaucratic politics' in which the corporation is viewed as a site of struggle between different groups (Kreisberg, 1976). These groups can be defined by, for example, the ownership or non-ownership of capital, by sectoral employment or by professional affiliation. Any resolution of this struggle is dependent upon the relative resources available to different groups and the operating environment of the organization. This means that although certain groups or alliances of groups become dominant this is not necessarily a stable arrangement, and there are always compromises since all groups have some power (cf. Foucault, 1982). If currently accountants and major shareholders dominate the corporation, professional engineers, *qua* professional engineers, can still have some influence. It may be possible to mobilize these in conjunction with organized labour and citizens' groups to demand that corporations attain certain environmental and health and safety standards.

So, for our purposes, a number of questions need to be addressed. First, given capitalistic social relations, what kind of legal framework could be set up to pressurize corporations, corporate executives and engineers to be responsible citizens while still engaging in productive business activity? Secondly, how could engineers and other employees, committed to high standards of health and safety and pollution control, press the board of their companies to act responsibly and how would they in turn persuade their shareholders? We know that because of the demand for high immediate returns on investments, the threat from corporate raiders and so on, many executives are finding any kind of long-term planning and investment problematic, never mind those associated with health and safety and pollution control. Thirdly, how could other corporations and corporate executives who wished to act unethically (and often thereby steal a competitive advantage) be stopped from doing so? In other words, how could the ethical be empowered to be responsible without being disadvantaged vis-a-vis

irresponsible (albeit 'instrumentally rational') competitors and colleagues?

To be a genuine political citizen whether of the world community or
more local ones such as a common market, nation state or locality,
means to be committed to the continued viability of this community, to
bring immediate (net) benefits and to help secure its future. The major
transnational corporations are all based in democratic countries. To
prove that this is not merely a happenstance, corporations, as members
of democratic political communities, should be challenged to recognize that workers, consumers, etc, have a right to participate freely in
the political process and to know to what dangers they are being
exposed. Corporations should accept responsibility for the dangerous
side-effects of their productive processes, products and waste, and they
should recognize that calculations of cost and benefit also include the
costs and benefits to present and future members of communities.

Industry must be challenged to acknowledge that the community
has a right to call all its members to account, whether by market
mechanisms, litigation or regulatory agencies. This necessitates readily
available detailed information about the nature of corporate activities
and products and about the decisions and decision-making processes
of corporations. There must exist the capacity effectively to bring
corporations and their executives to account for their actions. Industry
must be forced to accept the need for effective external regulation.

There is good evidence that when corporations organize production
safely it is not primarily because of a commitment to safe production
for its own sake but also because a safe firm is often an efficient firm and
vice versa. Braithwaite's analysis of the 'organizational characteristics'
that 'make for safe mining' apply equally well to all large-scale
manufacturing, namely, 'clout for the safety department, clearly defined accountability for safety imposed on line managers, top management commitment to and monitoring of safety performance, programs
for guaranteeing safety training/supervision, effective communication
and, most important of all, effective plans to cope with hazards'
(Braithwaite, 1985: 71).

Yet if, as we have seen, there are some situations where there will be
financial advantages in engaging in less than safe production, then if a
corporation puts safety first it needs to know that competing and
potentially less scrupulous corporations are unlikely to risk cutting
corners. The only way that a corporation could routinely behave
ethically and not be disadvantaged would be for irresponsible corporations to be publicly sanctioned. The issue was put clearly by an
executive vice-president of Dow when he pointed out that by resisting
expenditure on air pollution control, some companies are able 'to
establish a margin of advantage over their competitors. Such conduct

is hurting the rest of industry and should not be defended or tolerated' (cited in Brown, 1987: 242). It is thus quite understandable that in her study of pollution control Brittan found that firms whose discharges complied with water control standards 'favoured a hard line on enforcement' (1984: 79).

Regulatory agencies that have effective powers and adequate financing can, however, equalize the market conditions to which all are subject. This is the rationale informing the support by the Chemical Manufacturers' Association of the USA, of 'the adoption and enforcement of the hazardous materials regulations by State and Local governments' (Smith, 1986: 83). They may also raise the cost of engaging in a particular business to the advantage of the well-resourced larger corporations. Perhaps this is part of the reason why 'Britain's biggest waste tip operator...dismissed regulations...covering the passage of dangerous wastes across national frontiers as a "dramatic failure" to control hazardous waste imports...[and] called for a US-style environmental protection agency to take over all aspects of policy-making, legislation, and enforcement of regulations' (*The Guardian*, 9 September 1988). This is one situation where if private enterprise is used it can be to the advantage of the public that it is a large corporation.

Moreover, to be cynical, if something does go wrong corporations will try to shift blame – on to employees and on to regulators. This has been no more clearly demonstrated than when Union Carbide, having sought out a weakly regulated country, attempted to blame Sikh extremists, employees and the Indian government for the Bhopal disaster. They alleged that the latter may have granted 'a licence for the Bhopal plant without adequate checks on the plant'; the 'agencies responsible for the plant were grossly understaffed, lacked powers and had little impact on conditions in the field'; 'the Bhopal department of labour office had only two inspectors, neither of whom had any knowledge of chemical hazards' (Muchlinski, 1987: 575). However inadequate the regulation, as we have argued elsewhere, the major responsibility for the disaster clearly remains with Union Carbide (Pearce and Tombs, 1989).

This reminds us that it is only if we have effective regulation nationally and internationally, thus equalizing the conditions under which corporations compete, that the same safety standards might apply throughout the world. This could generate new markets, force technological development and help sustain and enhance the quality of life. In the context of the current development of large trading blocs there exists the possibility of producing adequate regulatory frameworks which will have some binding effect on the major corporations if they wish to produce for and sell in their major markets. The safety-conscious public is not without leverage.

If is no coincidence that in its eagerness to gain access to the profitable French agricultural producer markets Union Carbide agreed to French trade union demands that in its pesticide plant at Béziers expenditure on safety would increase to 20 percent from the usual 3.5 percent (Dinham et al., 1986). Thus if corporations are serious about their social responsibilities they will accept the kinds of changes that have been advocated in this chapter. They would not be painless or cost-free. But if corporations do not accept the need for change then we can only assume that their self-representation as socially responsible organizations and as 'political citizens' committed to the long-term interests of the communities in which they operate is little more than a public relations ploy. The suggestions in this chapter, then, should be construed as both a set of practical measures and as a challenge.

Conclusion

In this chapter we first explored, challenged and then modified some of the arguments of left realism as a prelude to exploring the phenomenon of corporate crime and to developing strategies to combat it, or at least to regulate it more effectively. We were critical of the individual-centred nature of much left realist writing and showed how this inhibited their study of 'crime in the suites'. We then referred briefly to an example of left realist empirical work on commercial crime, namely the *Second Islington Crime Survey*, before turning to the topic of corporate crime. That section of the chapter provided an extensive criticism of those who write on corporate crime from the point of view of the compliance school and entailed a refutation of their view that corporate illegalities are not 'real crimes' and that corporations should be assisted rather than policed. We then provided detailed examples of what this could mean in practice; in doing so, we attempted to develop elements of the realist arguments for the reform of the policing of street crime, which we had considered earlier. Finally we explored the conditions under which those corporations that represent themselves as responsible could be forced actually to behave in a responsible manner. This entailed both challenging them to live up to their self-portrayals and exploring the unacknowledged conditions that make this more likely. The most important of these is that 'responsible corporations' need strong independent regulatory agencies to police their own and their competitors' conduct in order to equalize the conditions of competition. Even if corporations refuse to accept these suggestions they have the great advantage that by taking the corporations at their word and by accepting the existence of a competitive capitalist economy they challenge the corporations on their own terrain. Furthermore, since they involve the restructuring of corporations, the empowering of different groups and the assertion of collective rights over those of private property they could be the basis of non-reformist reforms.

Despite some of our reservations concerning the descriptive and prescriptive work of the realists on crime and policing, the spirit underlying the argument developed here for the policing of corporations is strictly congruent with the realist exigence that crime be taken seriously. In attempting to indicate the extent of the commonplace victimization from corporate crimes, and to develop practical strategies for ways in which workers and local communities may both be protected and be empowered to protect themselves from such illegalities, we hope that we have at least begun to stimulate realist work in a further, much neglected and often inadequately treated, area of crime.

Note

The research upon which this chapter is based was made possible in part by grants from both Queen's University and Wolverhampton Polytechnic.

References

Bardach, E. and Kagan, R. (1982) *Going by the Book: The Problem of Regulatory Unreasonableness.* Philadelphia: Temple University Press.

Barnett, Harold (1982) 'The production of corporate crime in corporate capitalism', in Peter Wickman and Timothy Dailey (eds), *White Collar and Economic Crime.* Lexington, MA: Lexington Books.

Block, Fred, Cloward, Richard A., Ehrenreich, Barbara and Piven, Frances Fox (1987) *The Mean Season.* New York: Pantheon.

Blowers, A. (1984) *Something in the Air. Corporate Power and the Environment.* London: Harper and Row.

Blum-West, S. and Carter, T.J. (1983) 'Bringing white-collar crime back in: an examination of crimes and torts', *Social Problems,* 30(5): 545–54.

Box, S. (1983) *Power, Crime and Mystification.* London: Tavistock.

Box, S. (1987) *Recession, Crime and Punishment.* London: Tavistock.

Boyd, Neil (1988) *The Last Dance: Murder in Canada.* Scarborough: Prentice-Hall Canada.

Braithwaite, J. (1984) *Corporate Crime in the Pharmaceutical Industry.* London: Routledge & Kegan Paul.

Braithwaite, J. (1985) *To Punish or Persuade: Enforcement of Coal Mine Safety.* Albany: State University of New York Press.

Braithwaite, J. and Fisse, B. (1987) 'Self-regulation and corporate crime', in C.D. Shearing and P.C. Stenning (eds), *Private Policing.* London: Sage.

Brittan, Y. (1984) *The Impact of Water Pollution Control on Industry: A Case Study of 50 Discharges.* Oxford: Centre for Socio-Legal Studies.

Brodeur, Paul (1985) *Outrageous Misconduct: The Asbestos Industry on Trial.* New York: Pantheon.

Brown, Michael (1987) *The Toxic Cloud.* New York: Harper and Row.

Calavita, K. (1983) 'The demise of the Occupational Health and Safety Administration:

a case study in symbolic action', *Social Problems*, 30(4).

Campbell, John L. (1987) 'The state and the nuclear waste crisis: an institutional analysis of policy constraints', *Social Problems*, 34(1).

Carson, W.G. (1970) 'White-collar crime and the enforcement of factory legislation', *British Journal of Criminology*, 10.

Carson, W.G. (1982) *The Other Price of Britain's Oil*. Oxford: Martin Robertson.

Castleman, Barry I. (1979) 'The export of hazardous factories to developing nations', *International Journal of Health Services*, 9(4).

Clinard, M.B. and Yeager, P.C. (1980) *Corporate Crime*. New York: Free Press.

Coleman, J.W. (1989) *The Criminal Elite*. New York: St Martin's Press.

Crenson, M. (1971) *The Un-politics of Air Pollution: A Study of Non-decisionmaking in the Cities*. Baltimore: Johns Hopkins Press.

Di Mento, Joseph F. (1986) *Environmental Law and American Business: Dilemmas of Compliance*. New York: Plenum Press.

Dinham, B., Dixon, B. and Saghal, G. (1986) *The Bhopal Papers*. London: The Transnational Information Centre.

Doern, Bruce (1977) *Regulatory Processes and Jurisdictional Issues in the Regulation of Hazardous Products in Canada*. Ottawa: Ministry of Supply and Services, Canada.

Donnelly, Patrick (1981) 'The origins of the Occupational Safety and Health Act of 1970', *Social Problems*, 30(1).

Elkins, Charles (1989) (director of the Office of Toxic Substances at the Environmental Protection Agency), 'Corporate citizenship – toxic chemicals, the right response', *New York Times*, 13 November.

Fife, I. and Machin, E.A. (1982) *Redgrave's Health and Safety in Factories* (2nd ed.). London: Butterworth.

Foucault, Michel (1982) 'The subject and power', an afterword to Hubert Dreyfus and Paul Rabinow (eds), *Michel Foucault: Beyond Structuralism and Hermeneutics*. Chicago: University of Chicago Press.

Freeman, A. Myrick (1979) 'The benefits of air and water pollution control: a review and synthesis of recent estimates'. A report prepared for the Council on Environmental Quality.

Friedman, M. (1962) *Capitalism and Freedom*. Chicago: University of Chicago Press.

Glasbeek, H.J. (1984) 'Why corporate deviance is not treated as a crime – the need to make profits a dirty word', *Osgoode Hall Law Journal*, 22(3): 393–439.

Glasbeek, H.J. (1988) 'A role for criminal sanctions in occupational health and safety', *Meredith Memorial Lectures*.

Glasbeek, H.J. and Rowland, S. (1979) 'Are injuring and killing at work crimes?', *Osgoode Hall Law Journal*, 17: 507–94.

Goff, Colin and Reasons, Charles E. (1986) 'Organizational crimes against employees, consumers and the public', in Brian Maclean (ed.), *The Political Economy of Crime*. Toronto: Prentice-Hall Canada.

Gorz, A. (1980) *Ecology as Politics*. London: Pluto.

Hawkins, Keith (1984) *Environment and Enforcement*. Oxford: Clarendon Press.

Health and Safety Executive (1983) *Annual Report of the Chief Inspector of Factories, 1982*. London: HMSO.

Health and Safety Executive (1985a) 'Measuring the effectiveness of HSE field activities', *HSE Occasional Paper 11*. London: HMSO.

Health and Safety Executive (1985b) *Deadly Maintenance. Plant and Machinery. A Study of Fatal Accidents at Work*. London: HMSO.

Health and Safety Executive (1986) *Annual Report of the Chief Inspector of Agriculture*. London: HMSO.

Health and Safety Executive (1987) *Statistics 1984-5*. London: HMSO.

Health and Safety Executive (1988) *HM Chief Inspector of Factories 'Health and Safety at Work': Report 1986-87*. London: HMSO.

Hirst, Paul (1986) *Law, Socialism and Democracy*. London: Unwin Hyman.

Horwitz, Robert B. (1989) *The Irony of Regulatory Reform*. New York: Oxford University Press.

Hutter, B. (1988) *The Reasonable Arm of the Law?* Oxford: Clarendon.

James, P. (1989) 'Manslaughter: a new liability?', *Health and Safety Information Bulletin*, 164: 2-5.

Jamieson, M. (1985) *Persuasion or Punishment – The Enforcement of Health and Safety at Work Legislation by the British Factory Inspectorate*. Oxford: Unpublished MPhil thesis.

Jones, Kelvin (1982) Law and Economy: the Legal Regulation of Corporate Capital. London: Academic Press.

Kagan, R. and Scholz, J. (1984) 'The criminology of the corporation and regulatory enforcement strategies', in K. Hawkins and J. Thomas (eds), *Enforcing Regulation*. Boston: Kluwer-Nijhoff.

Kinsey, R., Lea, J. and Young, J. (1986) *Losing the Fight against Crime*. Oxford: Blackwell.

Kolko, Gabriel (1962) *Railroads and Regulations: 1877-1916*. Princeton: Princeton University Press.

Kolko, Gabriel (1963) *The Triumph of Conservatism*. New York: Free Press.

Kolko, Gabriel (1984) *Main Currents in Modern American History*. New York: Pantheon.

Kreisberg, Simeon M. (1976) 'Decision making models and the control of corporate crime', *Yale Law Journal*, 85: 1091-1129.

Lea, J., Matthews, R. and Young, J. (1987) *Law and Order. Five Years On*. Centre for Criminology, Middlesex Polytechnic.

Lea, John and Young, Jock (1984) *What is to be Done about Law and Order?* London: Academic Press.

Lukes, S. (1974) *Power: A Radical View*. London: Macmillan.

Lustgarten, L. (1987) 'The governance of the police'. Paper presented at the Annual Conference of the Socio-Legal Group, Sheffield, 23-6 March.

Mahon, Rianne (1977) 'Canadian public policy: the unequal structure of representation', in Leo Panitch (ed.), *The Canadian State: Political Economy and Political Power*. Toronto: University of Toronto Press.

Mahon, Rianne (1979) 'Regulatory agencies: captive agents or hegemonic apparatuses', *Studies in Political Economy*, 1(1).

Mahon, Rianne (1984) *The Politics of Industrial Restructuring*. Toronto: University of Toronto Press.

Mahoney, Richard (1988) 'Punitive damages: the costs are curbing creativity', *New York Times*, 11 December.

Marcus, A. (1980) 'Environmental protection agency', in J.Q. Wilson (ed.), *The Politics of Regulation*. New York: Basic.

Matthews, R. (1987) 'Taking realist criminology seriously', *Contemporary Crises*, 11: 371-401.

Muchlinski, Peter T. (1987) 'The Bhopal case: controlling ultra-hazardous activities undertaken by foreign investors', *The Modern Law Review*, 50(5).

Oi, Walter (1977) 'On socially acceptable risks', in J. Phillipps (ed.), *Safety at Work*. Oxford: Centre for Socio-Legal Studies and Social Science Research Council.

Pearce, Frank (1990a) ' "Responsible corporations" and regulatory agencies', *Political Quarterly*, (October–November).

Pearce, Frank (1990b) 'The contribution of "left realism" to the empirical study of commercial crime'. Paper presented at a conference on Realist Criminology, Vancouver.

Pearce, Frank and Tombs, Steve (1989) 'Union Carbide, Bhopal, and the hubris of a capitalist technocracy', *Crime and Justice*, June.

Pearce, Frank and Tombs, Steve (1990) 'Ideology, hegemony and empiricism: compliance theories of regulation', *British Journal of Criminology*, (Autumn): 423–43.

Pearce, Frank and Tombs, Steve (1992) *Crimes of Capital*. London: Sage.

Peltzman, Sam (1976) 'Toward a more general theory of regulation', *The Journal of Law and Economics*, 19.

Rattner, Steve (1975) 'Did industry cry wolf?', *New York Times* 28 December.

Richardson, G., with Ogus, A. and Burrows, P. (1983) *Policing Pollution*. Oxford: Clarendon.

Royal Commission on Civil Liability (1978) *Statistics and Costings*, Vol. 2. Cmnd. 7054, London: HMSO.

Ryan, M. (1986) 'Law and order: left realism against the rest', *The Abolitionist*, 22: 29–33.

Schuck, Peter (1981) 'Review of James Q. Wilson, *The Politics of Regulation*', *Yale Law Journal*, 9: 702–25.

Smith, D. (1989) 'The un-politics of major hazards'. Paper presented at the Second International Conference on Industrial Crisis Management, New York University, 3–4 November.

Smith, M.H. (1986) *The Chemical Industry after Bhopal: An International Symposium held in London*. London: IBC Technical Services.

Snider, Laureen (1989) 'Models to control corporate crime: decriminalization, re-criminalization and deterrence'. Mimeo. Department of Sociology, Queen's University, Kingston, Ontario.

Stigler, George J. (1971) 'The theory of economic regulation', *Bell Journal of Economics and Managerial Science*, 2.

Sutherland, Edwin (1940) 'White-collar criminality', *American Sociological Review*, 5.

Sutherland, Edwin (1941) 'Crime and business', *Annals of the American Academy of Political and Social Science*, 217.

Sutherland, Edwin H. (1983) *White Collar Crime: The Uncut Version*. New Haven: Yale University Press.

Szasz, Andrew (1984) 'Industrial resistance to occupational safety and health legislation: 1971–1981', *Social Problems*, 32(2).

Szasz, Andrew (1986a) 'The reversal of federal policy toward worker safety and health: a critical examination of alternative explanations', *Science and Society*, 50: 25–51.

Szasz, Andrew (1986b) 'The process and significance of political scandals: a comparison of Watergate and the "Sewergate" episode at the environmental protection agency', *Social Problems*, 33(3).

Tappan, Paul (1947) 'Who is the criminal?', *American Sociological Review*, 12.

Tombs, Steve (1990a) 'Industrial injuries in British manufacturing', *Sociological Review*, May, 38(2): 324–43.

Tombs, Steve (1990b) 'Managing safety: how the chemical industry's best is not good enough', *Occasional Papers in Crisis and Risk Management, No. 2*. Leicester: Leicester Polytechnic Business School.

Vogel, David (1989) *Fluctuating Fortunes: The Political Power of Business in America*. New York: Basic Books.

Weaver, Paul (1978) 'Regulation, social policy and class conflict', in Donald P. Jacobs (ed.), *Regulating Business: The Search for an Optimum*. San Francisco: Institute for Contemporary Studies.

Weidenbaum, Murray and de Fina, Robert (1978) *The Costs of Federal Regulation of Economic Activity*. AEI Reprint no. 88, Washington, DC: American Enterprise Institute.

Wells, Celia (1988) 'What can we do if the guilty parties are corporations?', *The Guardian*, 26 August.

Wilson, Graham K. (1985) *The Politics of Safety and Health: Occupational Safety and Health in the United States and Britain*. Oxford: Clarendon Press.

Wilson, James Q. (1975) *Thinking About Crime*. New York: Basic Books.

Wilson, James Q. (1980) (ed.) *The Politics of Regulation*. New York: Basic Books.

Wilson, James Q. and Rachal, Pat (1977) 'Can the government regulate itself?', *The Public Interest*. Reprinted in David M. Ermann and Richard J. Lundberg (eds) (1978), *Corporate and Governmental Deviance*. New York: Oxford University Press.

Wilson, James Q. and Herrnstein, Richard J. (1986) *Crime and Human Nature*. New York: Touchstone, Simon and Schuster.

Wilson, Larry C. (1979) 'The doctrine of willful blindness', *University of New Brunswick Law Journal*, 28: 175–94.

Work Hazards Group (1987) *Death at Work*. London: WEA.

Young, J. (1986) 'The failure of criminology: the need for a radical realism', in R. Matthews and J. Young (eds), *Confronting Crime*. London: Sage.

Young, J. (1987) 'The tasks facing a realist criminology', *Contemporary Crises*, 11: 337–56.

5 Appreciating the victim: conventional, realist or critical victimology?

Sandra Walklate

> While criminology used to be about crime and criminals, modern research has elevated victims to primary status, as if to exorcise the spectre of 60's deviancy theory with its 'appreciative' stance towards offenders. The successors to those deviancy theorists are now earnestly scouring residential areas for people's views on crime constructing real rates of victimization and lobbying for victims' rights. (Grimshaw, 1989: 13–14)

Observations like Grimshaw's are now almost commonplace. The purpose of this chapter is to construct a closer examination of this interest in victims of crime and to set that interest within a broader political context. To facilitate this process a framework of 'victim appreciation' will be constructed, namely that of conventional, realist and critical victimology.

Historical roots of victimology

What might be understood as conventional victimology is to be historically located in the work of von Hentig and Mendelsohn. Von Hentig's book, *The Criminal and His Victim* (1948), intended as a textbook in criminology, introduced 13 classes of victim who were considered to be, either psychologically or socially, more prone to victimization. Mendelsohn's work (quoted in Schafer, 1976) introduced a sixfold typology of victims classified according to their culpability for a crime. Both of these writers left a considerable historical legacy for victimology, particularly in the way in which they encouraged a focusing of attention on the characteristics of individual victims as a means whereby criminal activity might be understood. This focus, particularly in the form of the notion of the culpable victim, underpins the influential concept of 'victim precipitation'.

This concept was most precisely formulated by Wolfgang (1958) in his *Patterns of Criminal Homicide*. In that empirical investigation he classified 26 percent of the cases of criminal homicide recorded by the police as being victim-precipitated. While several writers attempted to develop this concept and apply it to different circumstances, the study conducted by Amir (1971) must be considered one of the most controversial in its impact. This study used a very broadly defined notion of victim-precipitation and applied it to officially recorded cases of rape. (This is not the place to enter into a specific critique of Amir's study, but see, for example, Morris, 1987.) The feminist critique of the victim-blaming view of rape constituted in the Amir vein has, in more recent years, done much to disabuse the academic community (if not a wider public) of the validity of such a view of rape. But, as shall be seen, the roots of this concept and the concomitant notion of victim-blaming run deep.

A range of work has illustrated this from the observations made by Mawby and Gill (1987) concerning the Criminal Injuries Compensation Board, to the comments by Morris (1987) and Kitzinger (1988) on child abuse to Jeffreys and Radford's (1984) analysis of the 'car rapist case' and the judicial response to it. An understanding of the persistence of this concept is to be located in an appreciation of the political purposes it serves (to be seen to be doing something for victims of crime who have a legitimate claim to that status, see Miers, 1978, on the emergence of the CICB) and the deeper ideological processes sustained by it (in the context of the position of women and children, for example). The persistence of these themes will be returned to.

One of the key problems associated with the concept of victim precipitation is that it confines an explanation of victimization to individual events and their individual precipitative characteristics. Reliance on such a concept does not facilitate an understanding of the patterning of criminal victimization. The introduction of the concept of 'lifestyle' by Hindelang et al. (1978) overcomes this problem and constitutes the emergence of what might be called conventional victimology.

Conventional victimology

Hindelang and his colleagues (1978) constructed a model of personal victimization, grounded in victimization data, which introduced the concept of lifestyle defined as: 'routine daily activities, both vocational activities (work, school, keeping house, etc) and leisure activities' (1978: 241). This model proposes that any individual in society is constrained by both role expectations and structural characteristics, the nature of which are to be connected to demographic variables: age, sex, race, etc. The authors argue that individuals adapt to these constraints and that these adaptations are reflected in their daily routines: their lifestyle. This general framework is detailed in a series of eight hypotheses (Hindelang et al., 1978: 250–66) to which Garofalo (1986) has suggested several modifications. This work postdates the emergence of the use of the criminal victimization survey in the United States and is empirically grounded in that methodological approach. This constitutes an advance on the work of Wolfgang (1958) for example, since its concepts and propositions are derived from criminal victimization survey data rather than official statistics, and can be (and have been) used to inform further data-gathering processes.

It is clear that the data from the *British Crime Surveys* is informed in some respects by the lifestyle-exposure model. This has served to challenge 'commonsense' thinking on victimization (victims of street crime are most frequently young men who go out drinking two or three times a week, not elderly frail females) and is supportive of Hindelang et al.'s (1978) fourth proposition; that the chances of personal victimization are related to the extent to which the victim shares the same demographic characteristics with the offender. Although criminal victimization surveys themselves are not without their problems, (for a summary of the relative advantages and disadvantages of the criminal victimization survey, see Walklate, 1989: ch. 2), this approach does avoid the more obvious pitfalls associated with the work of Wolfgang (1958) and Amir (1971).

An additional advantage associated with the work of Hindelang and his colleagues is its ability to frame an explanation of victimization which draws on variables lying beyond the control of individual participants. The lifestyle-exposure model does postulate the existence of structural constraints which act as precursors to an individual being in a particular place at a particular time. It is clear that the model also postulates an individual's *adaptation* to these constraints. It is at this point that it is useful to reflect on this model's weaknesses.

First, the concept of lifestyle, particularly in the way in which it has been researched, clearly places an emphasis on aspects of lifestyle which can be articulated and measured in criminal victimization surveys. Lifestyle appears to be conceived of as a measurable, objective entity. As a consequence this excludes that which cannot be articulated, that which is a part of our routine, everyday activities but is very much taken for granted. This is a crucial question for victimology if that victimology is to focus on, for example, the routine criminal victimization of children; on women whose lives are routinely structured in fear of male violence in public and private (Stanko, 1989) and for black people who are so used to being subjected to racial harassment that they would not think it worth articulating to an interviewer even if such events were recognized and defined by them as criminal.

While there are structural characteristics identifiable in all the examples given (age, gender, ethnicity), they also exemplify a range of circumstances in which lifestyle is constituted and reconstituted through activities which are shared, commonly understood, and commonly taken for granted by individual participants within a family (child abuse) or by collectivities (women, people who belong to ethnic minorities). The lifestyle-exposure model fails to tap these commonly held and taken for granted aspects of lifestyle.

This first weakness leads into a second. This model sets itself up as a model of personal victimization and yet its first proposition states that the probability of suffering personal victimization is related to the amount of time a person spends in public places. It thus excludes from consideration the extent to which the world of the private, the home, the family, is an arena for personal victimization. This exclusion is further endorsed by proposition six which suggests that the more time an individual spends outside the family the greater the chances of personal victimization. Feminist research has revealed the extent to which such an exclusion does little justice to the real incidence of personal victimization in the form of child abuse (particularly sexual) and domestic violence. This weakness also highlights the focus given in the lifestyle-exposure approach to a conventional understanding of crime; a focus which is sharpened when the underlying theoretical presuppositions of the model are outlined.

This model of victimization implicitly reflects a functionalist sociology, which is displayed in two ways; first in its image of the human being. This is most clearly observed in the notion of adaptation. Individuals might engage in daily routines, but that engagement has to be seen as a product of individual adaptations to role expectations and structural constraints. Thus the individual is seen as being a passive actor within, as opposed to an active resister, or questioner of, those expectations and constraints. In this sense they are victims of events rather than survivors of them, but also their routines (lifestyles) are not seen as actively constructed and reconstructed on a daily basis. Hence this image encourages a static rather than a dynamic interpretation of the concept of lifestyle (see above).

A further display of functionalism is derived from the way in which the structural constraints are themselves conceived. They are identified, within the model, as being legal, economic, educational and familial. The demographic variables which are connected to these are seen as being descriptive: race, age, sex, income, marital status, education, occupation. These are not conceived as ageism, sexism, racism, etc. In other words, they are not constructed in such a way as to be seen to be critically implicated in sustaining a particular power structure. This, alongside the focus on public rather than private victimization, significantly limits our thinking about the victimization process.

The way in which power relationships are conceived within the lifestyle-exposure model not only matters in terms of how the model addresses what is conventionally understood as personal victimization (violence in the street rather than violence in the home), but also fails to include corporate crime as personal victimization. The work of Hindelang et al. (1978) then constitutes a conventional approach to victimology, not only in its reliance on rather conventional research techniques but more importantly in its failure, conceptually, to challenge that which is conventionally understood as criminal victimization. It explicitly excludes the private as a domain of personal victimization, alongside a failure to conceptualize corporate crime as a source of such victimization.

In the development of conventional victimology, the work of Sparks (1982) comes closest to defining the relevant concepts for this framework. He states that:

> variations in proneness to victimization among different types of persons, places, organisations, situations etc., where proneness in turn is defined in terms of differences in the a priori probability of victimization or a crime taking place. Thus precipitation, facilitation, vulnerability, opportunity, attractiveness, and impunity all imply the probabilities of crime or victimization are higher with some situations than with others. (Sparks, 1982: 33)

Thus Sparks offers us six concepts which he considers to be theoretically important for victimology. It is clear that he employs these concepts in a flexible fashion, for example, 'a woman's husband repeatedly brutalizes her over a long period of time; terrified and distraught, she kills him in his sleep. It does not seem unnatural to regard this as a case of precipitation' (1982: 27). Though while this constitutes a more flexible use of the concept of precipitation than has been historically the case, the explanation for the behaviour so precipitated lies within a further concept, namely: 'In part, this is a matter of opportunity; persons who never encounter one another cannot (logically) be involved in victim-precipitated crime, or indeed, any other kind of crime' (Sparks, 1982).

And while the notion of opportunity is then broadly conceived (there can be no cheque card frauds without cheque cards), it does little to advance the explanation of the event beyond correlating particular incidents with particular variables. Potential explanations couched in these terms constrains this vision of victimology in much the same way as that offered by the lifestyle-exposure model. The failure to appreciate the nature and impact of the structuring features of individual acts, places, situations, is a failure to appreciate those features of the social process which exist above and beyond those individual acts. Individuals (places, situations) are somehow envisaged as being structurally neutral and subsequently similar (equal) in their capacity to respond to or resist victimization. This again results in a distorted vision of what might be understood as criminal; victimization by corporations or the processes which potentially result in the criminal victimization of sections of the population, with or without the knowledge of individuals, is largely ignored.

Setting the explanatory potential of victimizing events within this framework, however, lends any empirical findings generated by these concepts to policy-oriented initiatives. Policy initiatives are easy to construct if assumptions are made concerning the role of the individual in the victimizing process. Thus, those who fail to protect themselves when they know, for example, that burglary rates in an area are high, increase, through their own behaviour, the chances of being burgled (facilitation). The attractiveness of a property can be evaluated, hardened and thus modified. Policies focused in this way move attention away from the crime-inducing process to the victim-creation process. The inherent dangers of such a focus commented on by Antilla (1974) result in a form of victim blaming in which the victim and/or potential victim are expected to modify and change their behaviour to prevent any further victimization.

Conventional victimology and its conceptual relationship with national criminal victimization surveys has produced evidence which supports a general patterning of criminal victimization not dissimilar to that discernible from official criminal statistics (Reiss, 1986) and while the lifestyle model itself is not conclusively supported (Clarke et al., 1985, report a low victimization rate for the elderly even when lifestyle is controlled for), the evidence from the Home Office-sponsored *British Crime Surveys* has lent credence to the view that crime is a pretty rare occurrence (Hough and Mayhew, 1983) and its impact when it happens is not substantial (Hough and Mayhew, 1985). If this is the case there is no need for massive state intervention to alleviate the plight of victims of crime, though this does not mean that individualistic and voluntary responses to criminal victimization should not be encouraged (see Phipps, 1988, for a discussion of the political parties' response to victims of crime). Hence the financial support which was forthcoming to the National Association of Victim Support Schemes and the political encouragement given to 'active citizenship' and 'social responsibility'. It is this conservative view of citizenship, which both implicitly and explicitly builds upon an unquestioned view of women, children, the elderly, people from ethnic minorities, and is more about obligations than rights (Plant, 1988), which is sustained by conventional victimology.

These comments are not intended to imply that the data from these surveys cannot be used in a more radical way. The work of Worrall and Pease (1986), Mawby and Gill (1987) and Mawby (1988) illustrate how that data can be worked to uncover more detail about the differential incidence and impact of personal crime. There are, however, limitations to how far data constructed in this way can be read. Those on the left have addressed the academic and political issues raised by some of these problems through the construction of 'left realism' within criminology. It is to that approach which we now turn.

Realist victimology

The work constructed by radical left realism can legitimately be considered within the framework of victimology since despite the argument that realist criminology embraces the reality of the criminal process, the offender, the victim, informal social control, and the state (Jones et al., 1986), to date, much has been heard about the necessity for an 'accurate victimology' (Young, 1986: 23), from 'problems as people experience them' (p. 24). This new left realism has thus placed the victim at the centre of the stage and the primary purpose here is to focus on the differences and similarities between this and what has been outlined above.

There are a number of places one might begin to develop an appreciation of left realism. Given some of the concerns of this chapter an interesting and useful starting point is the claim made by the new realists to have embraced the questions concerning criminal victimization raised by the feminist movement.

There are a range of questions raised by feminist work for victimology. Two questions of interest at this point are conceptual and methodological; do the concepts employed by victim-oriented research adequately convey women's experiences, and can the measurement techniques chosen adequately uncover the essential nature of women's everyday lives? Stanko (1988) talks in detail of the way in which much of the violence against women is hidden from view; from official agencies and crime surveys alike. She concludes by stating that: 'Unless policing and crime survey researchers lend credence to the concept and reality of gender stratification, violence against women will, on many levels, remain a hidden, but all too real a part of women's lives' (1988: 46).

Young (1988) claims that the local crime survey approach adopted by the new realists takes to heart the questions raised by the feminist movement and at the same time places the victim in their material context (p. 173). How is this achieved? The answer offered by Young (1988) is both conceptual and methodological. He argues, in discussing risk from and fear of crime, that the extent to which criminal victimization survey figures reveal anything about the real incidence of these is a function of a number of mechanisms. He illustrates these using the example of the victimization of women. First, he argues, it must be recognized that much of the actual impact of crime on women is trivialized and hence *concealed*. This concealment is then *compounded* by the levels of sexual harassment which women experience on a day-to-day basis, which, given the relative powerlessness of women, makes them more unequal victims and therefore *vulnerable*. All of these processes are framed by the way in which crime is ultimately constructed within a particular set of social relationships: *patriarchy*. Thus, concealment, compounding, vulnerability and patriarchy are the mechanisms underpinning the victimization of women which the new left realist is committed to uncovering by using the local crime survey.

The use of the local crime survey is constructed on a different basis from the national crime survey. Designed to be explanatory rather than descriptive, the local survey builds on existing knowledge concerning the patterning of criminal victimization; in other words it takes the variables of age, gender and ethnicity as crucial to informing the sampling process. Such surveys are also geographically focused. The *Islington Crime Survey*, for example, focuses on an inner-city area, thus explicitly espousing a concern with the class base of victimization. The analysis of data generated in this way is also important. Sampling procedures which facilitate analysis by sub-group enables the differences in experiences of crime to be more precisely highlighted (Young, 1988: 3). This method is intended not only to be the means whereby left realism embraces the concerns of feminism but also the means whereby the left can address the thorny issues of intra-class and intra-racial crime.

It is clear that the evidence produced by the local crime survey approach has done much to document in greater detail the extent of criminal victimization within local communities on gender, ethnic and class dimensions (see for example, Kinsey, 1984; Jones et al., 1986). In this respect the approach has certainly paid dividends confirming the view that for particular sections of society crime is by no means a rare occurrence. A number of difficulties remain, however.

The first is methodological. Although the local crime survey approach does seem to have been successful in revealing more incidents of crime as they relate to specified groups within a population, the question still remains as to whether this success is equal to the claim of having embraced the concerns raised by the work of feminism. Galtung (1967) discusses the individual and democratic bias inherent in the sample survey, long recognized by feminist researchers. Such a bias inevitably militates against the ability to fully understand and document the impact of the material constraints which structure the incidents uncovered (a point acknowledged by Jones et al., 1986: 183). To understand this it is necessary to construct an in-depth understanding of women's everyday lives in relation to men. Much more is learned in this respect, for example, from the work of Stanko (1989). Expressed in a slightly different way, but perhaps concerned with the same general problem, Cain (1989) states that, 'the criminological gaze cannot see gender' (1989: 4). Translated in this way with an emphasis on the survey method, neither can realist victimology.

The second difficulty is rather more theoretical but not unconnected to the first. The theoretical difficulty emerges in two ways: from the left realist conception of material conditions and from their conception of how this relates to consciousness. Young (1988) states that: 'victimization research commonly *trivializes that which is important and makes important that which is trivial*' (p. 173, emphasis in the original). Here Young is exhorting us to take what human beings consider to be important as our yardstick for appreciating the impact of crime while simultaneously recognizing that some groups experience more criminal victimization than others. So we have to take seriously what people define as real as well as taking seriously the material conditions which frame that reality; in particular, race, class, age, gender. The tension here lies between those features of criminal victimization which people define as real (which may or may not be accurate; see the discussion of 'stop and search' from the viewpoint of the young as compared with the views of most of his sample on Merseyside, in Kinsey, 1984, 1986, and Brogden et al., 1988: 187–8); and those features of the criminal victimization process which they do not define as real and yet, nevertheless, still have an impact on them.

This latter comment implies material conditions of which we may not be aware; and of which realism has, as yet, said very little; the activities of business corporations, for example. This is also a theoretical problem since it reflects a tendency to 'reduce agents to the "bearers" of structures' (Outhwaite, 1987: 111). Cain (1989) expresses the problem in this way: 'the linking spaces between people in terms of which these people are constituted, can exist independently of anyone's consciousness, either that of the people constituting the relationship, other people in their society, or social researchers. And any one of these may recognise a relationship without others doing so' (p. 15). Ultimately left realism has not as yet fully articulated a view of the relationship between agency and structure, but leaves us with the impression that it is sufficient to take agents seriously and espouse a theoretical commitment to structure. Unfortunately this results in a position where it is possible to be distracted by the articulations of agents (from an eminently laudable political viewpoint) and consequently fail to complete the picture of their experience of criminal victimization.

This discussion is not intended to suggest that one level of analysis should be abandoned in favour of another, but is intended, at the simplest level, to highlight the importance of inserting into the criminal victimization equation those processes which go on behind our backs as well as those of which we are aware. At a more complex level it demands a fuller consideration of both theoretical and philosophical issues. Despite these problems left realism clearly suggests an agenda for policy formation.

Challenging the view that criminal victimization was either a pretty rare occurrence or greatly exaggerated by the media, the data from the local crime survey approach has clearly permitted a construction of a socialist-based response to the crime problem. Putting much of their faith in harnessing the democratic process (see, for example, Lea, 1987) left realists have constructed specific policy initiatives around the notions of 'demarginalization', 'pre-emptive deterrence', democratic control of the police, and community participation in crime prevention and policy development (Lea and Young, 1984) and a re-evaluation of informalism within the criminal justice system (Matthews, 1988: 1-25). It is within these socialist-inspired responses to criminal victimization that some of the theoretical and methodological tensions re-emerge.

An example of these tensions is to be found in the argument for minimal policing based on what the community wants (Kinsey et al., 1986). The issue here is the way in which an exception is made for 'domestic disputes' (p. 205). The argument, quite rightly, presumes a material base for the victimization of women; the question is, however, whether that material base is a reality for 'the community'. In other words, if a policy response, in this case a strategy of minimal policing, is to be constructed on the basis of what the community wants, there is no guarantee that the community, made up of men and women, will recognize, define, and make an exception of domestic violence and argue for more police intervention in these cases (an argument developed by Dekeseredy and Schwartz, 1991). This is the tangle which results from a viewpoint which wants to take feminist issues seriously, but at the end of the day, because of theoretical and methodological tensions, does not have the capacity to do so. Expressed in a somewhat different manner, it is possible to argue that this is a problem of 'standpoint' (Cain, 1986: 259). The commitment to the view that crime is a problem for the working class and therefore should be taken seriously as people define it, makes it difficult for left realism 'to see or know from two different sites at once' (Cain, 1986: 261), that is, also to see gender.

Addressing the policy implications of left realism, Stenson and

Brearly argue that the 'theoretical bias towards methodological individualism creates the risk that it will be increasingly drawn into the methodologically individualistic, utilitarian discourses which have long dominated state sponsored criminology and crime control policy' (Stenson and Brearly, 1989: 3). Sim et al. (1987), in their critique of left realism state that the policies which flow from the realist position 'accept rather than challenge the terrain of the powerful. It remains politically conservative in its conclusions about what can be done about the state' (p. 59), leading Downes and Rock (1988, quoted by Stenson and Brearly, 1989) to observe that many of their suggestions are not that far from those emanating from the more liberal sections of the Home Office (Downes and Rock, 1988: 309–10). Perhaps the question here is that the position, insofar as it has been outlined in policy terms, has a limited theoretical capacity to have more than a narrow understanding of who the powerful are, and how that power is mediated and hidden from individuals.

In some ways there are a number of similarities between conventional and realist victimology. They both rely on the criminal victimization survey as a key source of data, though the left realists would argue that their use is more sensitively deployed and theoretically informed. Both focus on crime as it is commonly understood; that is neither tackles the question of victimization by corporations or by implication the victimization of children (though left realism has commented on the statutory response to this, see Lea et al., 1987). The left realist would again point to their greater success in tapping incidents of racial harassment and domestic violence. A key difference between these two positions lies not so much along these dimensions as in the political connections to be made from them.

Conventional victimology lends itself to notions of active citizenship. Realist victimology has entered the political debate on citizenship by emphasizing social rights and social obligations (Corrigan et al., 1989). One of the problems with this conception of citizenship is that it presumes a harnessing of the democratic process as the means whereby the community participates in and makes decisions on the questions of rights and obligations. There are a number of general difficulties with this position (Hall and Held, 1989) and with respect to the issues addressed in this chapter it presumes that participation can be achieved (the difficulties associated with this are discussed by Jefferson et al., 1988, with respect to police monitoring groups), and that communities have all the available knowledge on which to base their decision making (what about what goes on behind our backs?). The ultimate problem is, however, that Corrigan et al. (1989), echoing some of the ideas of Plant (1988), locate their image of the citizen within an individualistic framework: 'It would be impossible to defend the social individualism of a person who was registered as looking for work but refused both work and training' (Corrigan et al., 1989: 17).

This 'social individualism' appears still to be tainted with liberal principles: the right to labour as opposed to the right to property, but nevertheless an individual right and obligation. This raises moral questions. For example, for the victim of crime, is their social individualism also indefensible if they refuse to participate in community-defined crime prevention schemes? Even if all the funds were made available for the most sophisticated equipment to be provided for every householder to protect themselves against household burglary this may just as likely lead to a 'fortress mentality' and add to the victimization process as necessarily constitute a move towards the 'common good'. The notion of the common good being at the end of the day a key but problematic issue, particularly if the commitment to feminism and subsequently other collective movements is to bear political fruit.

Given the theoretical and methodological tensions highlighted earlier, it is perhaps no great surprise that this version of victimology is able to construct this kind of argument around the question of citizenship, locating it increasingly in 'the middle ground of analysis and policy formation' (Stenson and Brearly, 1989). If, then, both conventional and radical victimology end by contesting the middle ground politically, is there an alternative?

Conclusion: the need for a critical victimology

The proposal for a critical victimology (not necessarily a mirror image of critical criminology) stems from a number of concerns which have been highlighted by the foregoing discussion: theoretical, methodological, and political.

At a theoretical level, it can be seen that whereas current conventional and realist victimologies have both advantages and limitations neither to date has fully incorporated an understanding of power relationships into their theoretical frameworks. Although each of these positions obviously connects more easily with right-wing views on the one hand and left-wing views on the other, their view of the individual (victim) varies somewhat; one passively adapting, the other consciously aware and to be taken seriously. Both images have been constructed within a structurally defined framework, but one is descriptive and the other more explanatory. Neither of these understandings of structure, however, facilitates an understanding of how individuals actively resist or campaign against their structural conditions. Neither do they fully articulate how those structural conditions have real effects on individual lives of which they may not be aware. In constructing a critical victimology both of these questions (among others) would need to be addressed.

There is a good deal of evidence to support the argument that individuals do actively resist or campaign against their structural powerlessness. Much of the in-depth work produced by the feminist movement with and for women illustrates this and has seen the parallel emergence of support networks for survivors of domestic violence, incest and rape. These responses to structural powerlessness are defined collectively and challenge patriarchy. 'Consumer revolts', from the drug thalidomide to the unavailability of the *Sun* on Merseyside in the aftermath of Hillsborough, 1989, are collective responses and constitute active resistance to structural powerlessness. Such strategies are becoming more and more clearly displayed in the effects of the Green movement as victories are won over farmers and chemical companies in reducing the exposure of individuals to harmful pesticides (perhaps more effectively organized in the United States than in the UK) but to an extent reflected in the 'greening' of the electorate.

So it can be seen that individuals do organize and resist collectively for the common good despite their structural position. It is also clear that opposite tendencies are present. The readiness with which Piper Alpha was defined as a 'disaster' is a clear illustration of how much more comfortable people are with the idea of an event occurring as a result of unforeseen circumstances rather than as an inherent feature of the business (see Carson's discussion of the *Alexander Kielland*, 1982, for a comparative analysis of such processes). There are many other examples of this sort which would be cited to suggest that we need a much clearer understanding of how and why some issues become 'consumer issues' and others not. Their relevance for victimology is clear. Fattah (1986) states that:

> Victim movements have focused their attention on, and directed their action to, the so-called conventional crimes. This is understandable. Homicide, rape, robbery, assault, burglary, have visible, identifiable victims. This is not always the case with corporate and business crimes which may victimize millions and millions of people and still go largely unreported and unprosecuted .... And so are other socially harmful acts such as pollution of the environment, the production of hazardous substances, the manufacture and sale of unsafe products, and so on, although they cause more death and injury and harm than all violent crimes combined. (Fattah, 1986: 5)

It is perhaps more usual to associate such statements with the work of Reiman (1979) or Box (1983), but the point is nonetheless relevant. Victimology needs to keep sight of these processes; the levels of awareness of them and resistance to them.

This, however, demands a more sophisticated theoretical and methodological construction for victimology, one which allows for an understanding of individual action which is constructed and reconstructed within unacknowledged material conditions and which may have both intended and unintended consequences (Giddens, 1984). The 'duality of structure' in which human action is constructed emphasizes not only the constraining influence of structure but also its enabling effects. This means that, as Cain (1989) points out, while women may have had the physical marks of domestic violence, until the work of Erin Pizzey they only had a male discourse with which to understand it. The feminist movement has contributed significantly to our understanding of such issues and emphasizes not only the constraining structure of patriarchy, but in the recognition of its effects, the enabling practices of resistance (an unintended consequence of the material circumstances).

The development of such a theoretical position demands a more thoroughgoing examination of the usefulness of realist philosophy in this context. This requires that social scientists do not reduce one level of analysis to another; in the space between agency and structure there is struggle. It also means developing an understanding of the processes of change and transmission between generations; that is setting our explanations in an historical context (Abrams, 1982). (What do you do with a seven-year-old who asks why you have mahogany window frames and are thereby contributing to the destruction of hardwood forests?). This position requires a methodology which does not suffer from 'fetishism' of method (Cain, 1986: 262) and is clear on the site from which it is speaking.

Such a view moves empirical work towards a methodology which is pluralistic in technique and clear in its standpoint. In this way it may be possible to connect different empirical findings, gathered from different standpoints, with one another. For example, an examination of child abuse requires an understanding not only from the standpoint of gender but also from a viewpoint which takes seriously the social construction of age. These two positions interconnect at significant points but the one viewpoint does not necessarily entail the other. Empirically speaking, a number of research techniques are required to uncover the layers of reality which structure both the experience of and response to this particular form of victimization. The studies which have been done in the area of corporate crime illustrate this. A critical victimology would also be concerned to document the interconnections between corporate crime, commonsense understandings of being a victim, and the slippage between these two.

This theoretical position would connect, politically, with a view of citizenship which avoids the trap of talking about rights and obligations as if they were the possession of individuals per se. It would allow an appreciation of the ongoing role of historical and social processes in which a collective and pluralistic notion of citizenship might be constructed in response to the demands of a variety of social movements (feminism, the gay movement, Greens, etc; see Mouffe, 1988). In addition it implies that policy initiatives cannot be constructed solely on the basis of what people think they want, though this may inform us better about how people view their material conditions. But that: 'capitalism has changed at least partly as a result of popular working class conflict and continues to change as a result of social struggles of a variety of social movements which are not class based' (Turner, 1986: 142).

There may be, therefore, more political mileage, for those on the left, in tackling the question of citizenship, not with the same conceptual apparatus as those on the right (that is talking about consumer rights, etc) but by embracing a conceptual apparatus which recognizes that taking individuals seriously means taking the social construction of their actions seriously both synchronically and diachronically (consumer rights do not mean very much if people are not aware of them or are not aware of the material circumstances which affect the common good).

Final comment

Although realist victimology has certainly contributed much to encouraging taking issues as victims define them seriously, it carries with it inherent theoretical and methodological confusions which severely limit its further contribution to a full understanding of the processes of criminal victimization. The point has now been reached where it is perhaps time to stand back from the actor's viewpoint and to relocate that view in an enabling as well as a constraining structural context. A critical victimology might facilitate a process whereby ideal type constructions of victims in which: 'A minimum strength is a precondition to being listened to, but sufficient strength to threaten others would not be a good base for creating the type of general public sympathy that is associated with the status of being a victim' (Christie, 1986: 21) could be challenged.

References

Abrams, P. (1982) *Historical Sociology*. Shepton Mallett: Open Books.
Amir, M. (1971) *Patterns of Forcible Rape*. Chicago: University of Chicago Press.
Antilla, I. (1974) 'Victimology – a new territory in criminology', in N. Christie (ed.), *Scandinavian Studies in Criminology* Volume 5. London: Martin Robertson. pp. 3–7.
Box, S. (1983) *Power, Crime and Mystification*. London: Tavistock.

Brogden, M., Jefferson, T. and Walklate, S. (1988) *Introducing Policework*. London: Unwin Hyman.

Cain, M. (1986) 'Realism, feminism, methodology and law', *International Journal of the Sociology of Law*, 14: 255–67.

Cain, M. (1989) 'Feminists transgress criminology', in M. Cain (ed.), *Growing up Good: Policing the Behaviour of Girls in Europe*. London: Sage. pp. 1–18.

Carson, W.G. (1982) *The Other Price of Britain's Oil*. Oxford: Martin Robertson.

Christie, N. (1986) 'The ideal victim', in E.A. Fattah (ed.), *From Crime Policy to Victim Policy*. London: Macmillan. pp. 17–30.

Clarke, R., Ekblom, P., Hough, M. and Mayhew, P. (1985) 'Elderly victims of crime and exposure to risk', *The Howard Journal of Criminal Justice*, 24(1): 1–9.

Corrigan, P., Jones T. and Young, J. (1989) 'Rights and obligations', *New Socialist*, February–March: 16–17.

Dekeseredy, W.S. and Schwartz, M.D. (1991) 'British left realism and the abuse of women: a critical appraisal', in R. Quinney and H. Pepinsky (eds), *Criminology as Peacemaking*. Indiana: Indiana University Press.

Downes, D. and Rock, P. (1988) *Understanding Deviance*. Oxford: Oxford University Press.

Fattah, E.A. (1986) 'Prologue: on some visible and hidden dangers of the victims' movement', in E.A. Fattah (ed.), *From Crime Policy to Victim Policy*. London: Macmillan. pp. 1–16.

Galtung, J. (1967) *Theory and Method of Social Research*. London: George Allen and Unwin.

Garofalo, J. (1986) 'Lifestyle and victimization: an update', in E.A. Fattah (ed.), *From Crime Policy to Victim Policy*. London: Macmillan. pp. 135–55.

Giddens, A. (1984) *The Constitution of Society*. Cambridge: Polity Press.

Grimshaw, R. (1989) 'Booktalk: policing', *Network*, (BSA Newsletter) January: 13–14.

Hall, S. and Held, D. (1989) 'Left and rights', *Marxism Today*, June: 16–23.

Hindelang, M.J., Gottfredson, M.R. and Garofalo, J. (1978) *Victims of Crime: An Empirical Foundation for a Theory of Personal Victimization*. Cambridge, Mass: Ballinger.

Hough, M. and Mayhew, P. (1983) *The British Crime Survey: First Report*. Home Office Research Study no. 76. London: HMSO.

Hough, M. and Mayhew, P. (1985) *Taking Account of Crime: Key Findings from the Second British Crime Survey*. Home Office Research Study no. 85. London: HMSO.

Jefferson, T., McClaughlin, E. and Robertson, L. (1988) 'Monitoring the monitors: accountability, democracy and policewatching in Britain', *Contemporary Crises*, 12: 91–106.

Jeffreys, S. and Radford, J. (1984) 'Contributory negligence or being a woman? The car rapist case', in P. Scraton and P. Gordon (eds), *Causes for Concern*. Harmondsworth: Penguin. pp. 154–83.

Jones, T., MacLean, B. and Young, J. (1986) *The Islington Crime Survey*. Aldershot: Gower.

Kinsey, R. (1984) *Merseyside Crime Survey: First Report*. Liverpool: Merseyside County Council.

Kinsey, R. (1986) 'Crime in the inner city', *Marxism Today*, May: 6–10.

Kinsey, R., Lea, J. and Young, J. (1986) *Losing the Fight against Crime*. Oxford: Blackwell.

Kitzinger, J. (1988) 'Defending innocence: ideologies of childhood', *Feminist Review*, no. 28: 77–86.

Lea, J. (1987) 'Left realism; a defence', *Contemporary Crises*, 11: 357–70.

Lea, J., Matthews, R. and Young, J. (1987) *Law and Order Five Years On*. Centre for Criminology: Middlesex Polytechnic.

Lea, J. and Young, J. (1984) *What is to be Done about Law and Order?* Harmondsworth: Penguin.

Matthews, R. (1988) *Informal Justice*. London: Sage.

Mawby, R.I. (1988) 'Women and crime: from victimization rates to the crime experience'. Paper presented to tenth International Congress on Criminology, Hamburg. Also *Plymouth Polytechnic, Dept of Social and Political Studies, Occasional Paper no. 5*.

Mawby, R.I. and Gill, M. (1987) *Crime Victims: Needs, Services and the Voluntary Sector*. London: Tavistock.

Miers, D. (1978) *Responses to Victimization*. Abingdon: Professional Books.

Mouffe, C., (1988) 'The civics lesson', *New Statesman and Society*, 7 October: 28–31.

Morris, A. (1987) *Women, Crime and Criminal Justice*. Oxford: Blackwell.

Outhwaite, W. (1987) *New Philosophies of Social Science: Realism, Hermeneutics and Critical Theory*. London: Macmillan.

Phipps, A. (1988) 'Ideologies, political parties, and victims of crime', in M. Maguire and J. Pointing (eds), *Victims of Crime: A New Deal*. Milton Keynes: Open University Press. pp. 177–86.

Plant, R. (1988) 'Citizenship and society', *New Socialist*, December: 7–9.

Reiman, J.H. (1979) *The Rich Get Rich and the Poor Get Prison*. New York: John Wiley.

Reiss, A. (1986) 'Official statistics and survey statistics', in E.A. Fattah (ed.), *From Crime Policy to Victim Policy*. London: Macmillan. pp. 53–79.

Schafer, S. (1976) *Introduction to Criminology*. Virginia: Reston.

Sim, J., Scraton, P. and Gordon, P. (1987) 'Introduction: crime, the state, and critical analysis', in P. Scraton (ed.), *Law, Order, and the Authoritarian State*. Milton Keynes: Open University Press. pp. 1–70.

Sparks, R.F. (1982) *Research on Victims of Crime: Accomplishments, Issues and New Directions*. Rockville, Maryland: US Dept of Health and Human Services.

Stanko, E.A. (1988) 'Hidden violence against women', in M. Maguire and J. Pointing (eds), *Victims of Crime: A New Deal*. Milton Keynes: Open University Press. pp. 40–46.

Stanko, E.A. (1989) 'Fear of crime in public and private'. Paper presented to ALSISS, London, May.

Stenson, K. and Brearly, N. (1989) 'Realism, crime and ethics'. Paper presented to the BSA Annual Conference, Polytechnic South West, March.

Turner, B. (1986) *Citizenship and Capitalism*. London: Allen and Unwin.

von Hentig, H. (1948) *The Criminal and his Victim*. New Haven, Conn: Yale University Press.

Walklate, S. (1989) *Victimology: The Victim and the Criminal Justice Process*. London: Unwin Hyman.

Wolfgang, M.E. (1958) *Patterns of Criminal Homicide*. Philadelphia: University of Pennsylvania Press.

Worrall, A. and Pease, K. (1986) 'Personal crime against women', *Howard Journal of Criminal Justice*, 25(2): 118–24.

Young, J. (1986) 'The failure of criminology: the need for a radical realism', in R. Matthews and J. Young (eds), *Confronting Crime*. London: Sage. pp. 4–30.

Young, J. (1988) 'Risk of crime and fear of crime: a realist critique of survey based assumptions', in M. Maguire and J. Pointing (eds), *Victims of Crime: A New Deal*. Milton Keynes: Open University Press. pp. 164–76.

6 Reason and unreason in 'left realism': some problems in the constitution of the fear of crime

Richard Sparks

The fear of crime has occupied an important place in recent criminological debates. It is not only the subject of increasingly extensive and sophisticated research attention in its own right but also a dimension along which differing theoretical positions, and their associated policy diagnoses, are ranged. Simply put, one of the ways in which 'realist' criminology has come to be defined as a movement has lain in its conscious attempt to differentiate its attitude towards the fear of crime from those of either antecedent radical criminologies on the one hand or 'administrative criminology' on the other. Insofar as some such triangular argument has existed, the fear of crime has become more than simply a focus of empirical disagreements and has assumed a heavy polemical charge in theoretical and political disputes.

In this chapter I will explore some of the reasons for the contentious role of the problem of fear in recent criminological discourse. I want to show that 'realism' has performed an important service in reinstating the question of fear as a central one for sociological criminology. In asserting the 'real' basis of fearfulness and the 'rationality' of risk perception in inner urban communities it has also provided an important corrective to earlier conventional wisdom. However, it is also necessary to recognize that, in this insistence on the 'reality' and 'rationality' of fear, 'realism' has been wielding some blunt theoretical instruments. The terms which 'realism' has so far devised for talking about fear and risk have not really amounted to an increase in explanatory or interpretative power for locating fear as a dimension of personal and collective experience in contemporary social life. To insist on speaking about the fear 'of crime' as though it was both simply a function of the facts 'of crime' and sharply distinct from other kinds of fear is to impose a limit on the scope, importance and complexity of discussion of the issue of fearfulness in people's lives.

Briefly, I will argue that recent contention about fear of crime resides mainly in competing interpretations of survey data on victimization. Thus, although it has been a topic of fierce argument, fear has also been regarded as in some important senses subsidiary to the main line of enquiry, which has been to determine the extent of victimization and objective measures of risk. To this extent fear has generally come to be treated as predominantly a function of risk, and hence as only requiring any effort of understanding in cases where there seems to be some discrepancy between objective risks and prevalent fears. The main tenor of 'realist' argument has been that these discrepancies are usually more apparent than real and that fear of crime almost always has a 'rational kernel' (Young, 1987: 348). I will argue, on the other hand, that both those who insist that the fear of crime is rational and those who allege that it is frequently not have oversimplified the problems involved in deciding when and under what circumstances it would be rational to be afraid. Analysts of risk perception and rational choice in other fields no longer make such simple attributions. I will argue that, having once broken down the false choice between rational and irrational fears, it is unnecessary for 'realists' to insist that fear is simply an adjunct of victimization, and that they can modify this view without jeopardizing any of their primary arguments. Indeed, if the larger project of 'realism' is a serious sociology of the impact of crime in particular locales and communities then a more grounded and contextual understanding of the nature of fear is essential to the further development of a 'realist' paradigm.

'Realism', the 'great denial' and the problem of fear

Young (1987) provides a rather peremptory characterization of 'left idealism' and its influence on criminological thought. As is well known, he draws a particular connection between the thesis of 'moral panic', which gradually became a commonplace of radical criminological discourse during the 1970s, and what he terms the 'great denial' of the impact of crime on contemporary urban social life. The 'great denial', Young argues, facilitated both an abstentionist politics of radical pessimism and a concentration on discourse *about* crime and deviance, especially in the mass media, to the detriment of any careful attention to crimes as social facts – as events with consequences. Young thus tends to regard the notion of 'moral panic', as something to which societies 'appear to be subject every now and then' (Cohen, 1972: 28), as explanatorily evasive and misleading. He inveighs against: '...those idealist theories which portray moral panics as media instigated events without any rational basis and against those writers who talk glibly of irrational fears of crime without specifying what a rational fear would look like' (Young, 1987: 338). Among writers participating in the 'great denial', Young holds, any assertion of the real consequences of victimization, including its attendant fears, was regarded as *prima facie* reactionary and as lending weight to the extension of strategies of surveillance and control.

Meanwhile, Young further insists, the radical 'denial' unwittingly colluded with a parallel denial on the part of the 'new administrative criminology' which also claimed to find disproportions between the level of threat and the existence of fear. Fear thus comes to occupy the explanatory space between measures of actual and perceived risks. Such a position sends the investigators off in search of the 'surplus' of fear, whether in the form of 'broken windows' (Wilson and Kelling, 1982) or the existence of 'incivilities' (Maxfield, 1984) or other 'perceptions of neighbourhood change' (Skogan and Maxfield, 1981; cf. the summary provided by Box et al., 1988).[1]

Young and other realists have several objections to these positions. They argue:

1 that they are empirically false and that a more thorough and methodologically adequate understanding of the true extent of victimization reduces the scale of the apparent disparities or dissolves them altogether;
2 that such arguments make it possible to style certain fears, perhaps particularly those of women and elderly people, excessive or undue or fanciful, and that whether or not such fears are based on an empirically precise estimation of risk, this contradicts the realist theoretical premise that they are intelligibly related to 'the day-to-day lives of the fearful' (Young, 1987: 348);
3 that these arguments sustain misleading policy choices by encouraging strategies aimed at 'fear reduction', either by cosmetic improvements in the physical environment or by the heavier policing of incivility, independent of the real problems of risk reduction through effective crime prevention and the provision of more adequate and accountable service delivery by the police and other agencies as such.

Thus, realists contend, the 'idealists' and the administrators have incorporated at least some of one another's assumptions. At bottom each of them asserts that a significant number of fearful citizens are simply mistaken in the way they have interpreted their relation to the social world and their exposure to risk. So far as the question of fear is concerned it is to this that realism fundamentally objects:

> Realism . . . believes that fragments of reality are re-contextualised just as they are in criminological theory itself. To take crime seriously, then, is not to reflect the public images of crime. But it is to say that there is a rational core to public concerns and images. That is, that popular conceptions of

crime and policing are, in the main, constructed out of the material experiences of people rather than fantasies impressed upon them by the mass media or agencies of the State. (Young, 1987: 337)

Realist criminology thus echoes Giddens's account of the embeddedness of the day-to-day knowledge of all social actors in 'practical consciousness' (1984: 41–5), his strictures against the 'derogation of the lay actor' (1979: 71; cf. MacLean, 1989: 13) and his caution against supposing the corrigibility of lay knowledge by social science (1984: 339). Thus, to take only the most important and controversial issue in the area, namely women's fear of crime, 'realist' social surveys indicate that a proper account of women's subjection to domestic, work-related and other peripherally visible forms of victimization, their experience of other harassments and marginally criminal incivilities, their unsatisfactory experience of police protection and the multiplication of each of these problems by factors of race, class and age, entirely dispels the apparent disparity between risk and fear (Jones et al., 1986; Hall, 1985). And so, Young asks, 'Does not a seeming irrationality become transformed when we place it in terms of the real predicaments of the individuals involved?' (Young, 1987: 349).

Realism and the problem of rationality

However, this account of rationality, presented as the playing of a trump card, is in fact one of the weakest features of the realist position. It is, moreover, one of the ways in which realism risks *quite unnecessarily* giving away some part of its 'criminological good sense' (Garland, 1987: 199). Briefly, I will argue that the way in which the notion of rationality functions in realist discourse is to stipulate that a fear is fully 'rational' only if its existence is wholly accounted for by an antecedent level of objective risk. I can see no warrant for this assumption. Moreover, it is such a simplification of processes of social cognition as to constitute precisely the kind of derogation of lay knowledge which the realists are concerned to avoid. Similar, or converse, problems obtain in the use of the concept of rationality (or its cognate terms: warrantability, appropriateness, reasonableness, dueness) throughout the fear of crime literature, including in the publications surrounding the *British Crime Survey* (Hough and Mayhew, 1985; Maxfield, 1984).

Thus, I suggest, in his dismissal of 'those writers who talk glibly about irrational fears', Young (1987) has raised the question of 'what a rational fear would look like', but he has scarcely begun to answer it. Robert Reiner has also alluded to this problem, but recognizes that it is not easily resolved:

When is concern, and public policy directed towards it, to be analyzed as a 'panic', as distinct from a reasonable response to a problem? Hall et al. speak of 'panic' when 'the official reaction to a person, groups of persons or series of events is out of all proportion to the actual threat offered'. But this reference to 'proportion' makes the concept an arbitrary value judgement unless it is solidly anchored in both agreed criteria of proportionality and convincing evidence about the scale of 'the threat'. (Reiner, 1988: 151)

Since the period to which Reiner refers there has been plenty of new information about dimensions of threat and even a good deal about the nature of public responses to threats, but precious little about the 'unanalyzed notion of proportionality' (Reiner, 1988) in the relation between them. The equation between the 'reality' of a risk and the appropriateness or rationality of an emotional or dispositional state called fear (or worry, or anxiety, or concern) is more complicated than research into fear of crime, which has needed some sort of working rule of thumb for making such judgements, has yet admitted. Moreover, in making such attributions criminological debate, including the work of the realists, has unduly simplified its notions of what fear actually is, or is like as a mode of experience and perception. Thus the level of empirical detail which research on fear of crime has furnished has not been matched by parallel conceptual development, and scope has arisen for confusion between questions which can be solved empirically (on the basis of current knowledge or further data gathering) and those which require theoretical elaboration and interpretation.

There is nothing intrinsically anti-realist about entering these caveats, though there seems to be some danger of the realists assuming that there is. The danger lies in the denial of the 'great denial' becoming the main mode of theoretical argument, so that the terrain of debate becomes artificially divided between those who 'deny' and those who assert. Consider, for example, MacLean's tetchy response to certain remarks by Ian Taylor, where Taylor observes that:

... the evidence presented in the various victimization studies conducted by left realists has more to do with patterns of victimization and fear than it has to do with any detailed, careful excavation of popular consciousness with respect to questions of deterrence, coercive punishment and/or social policies as answers to [problems of] crime and social order. There is no really creative attempt in survey work of the left realists to investigate the *range* of sentiments that might be found in the population with respect to the ways and means of combatting crime, or of restoring some sense of order in dislocated inner-city neighbourhoods or in the downtown city centres. (Taylor, 1988: 9)

MacLean is correct in replying that realist crime surveys have been more sophisticated in method and scope than Taylor might seem to imply, and he goes on to detail ways in which crime surveys should proceed towards still more careful definition and sampling in investigating victimization. Yet this seems to misconstrue the drift of Taylor's remarks, which are not mainly directed towards contesting questions of victimization as such. Meanwhile, MacLean grumbles that criticizing surveys for what they do not include is 'akin to criticizing the Pope for not being Jewish' (1989: 15). This is beside the point. Criminological thinking has always moved forward through critiques of incompleteness, just as Young seeks to establish realism's claims through criticizing the partiality of earlier approaches (1987: 339–44). Instead Taylor is proposing (admittedly somewhat speculatively but not necessarily particularly controversially) that the questions of victimization and fear might be seen as having some fairly close connections with wider dimensions of social identity and well-being, and that such possible relations are deserving of closer attention. Victimology is not the whole of criminology. The immediate transactions between the offender, the victim and the police are not the only resources by means of which people construct their views of crime problems or on the basis of which they make personal and political judgements and choices. To argue that this were the case would be to say that citizens were only entitled to hold views on questions of crime, policing and public order in their guise as actual or potential victims (that is, ultimately on grounds of self-interest) and not as mutually responsible participants in a political community in any wider or more substantial sense. This returns us once again to the conceptual difficulties inherent in calibrating levels of risk against 'rational' fear.

Fear of crime and risk perception

It is not difficult to see that in crime surveys, as in other forms of empirical social enquiry, there are logical problems involved in assigning valuations to quantities. MacLean quotes the late R.F. Sparks on the subject:

> Without data on ... risk determining variables, we cannot make sense of victimization rates: we cannot even say if they are in some sense 'low' or 'high' ... it is thus important for future surveys not only to measure victimization more accurately but also to obtain the contextual information which makes it possible to understand victimization rates. (Sparks, 1981: 48–9)

If this is true of relatively 'hard' categories like victimization there is a further order of difficulty in assigning any but the simplest comparative notation (more or less of it) to the incidence of fear. The assignation of any of the currently available polarities (high/low, warranted/ unwarranted, reasonable/unreasonable, appropriate/excessive) is to risk making highly presumptive but theoretically under-justified judgements about the nature of emotions and cognitions: hence indeed the vehemence of the ripostes to approaches which formerly asserted that the fear of crime among women and the elderly was excessive or undue. On the other hand, to insist that the fear of crime, in whatever population, is therefore in any strong sense of the term 'rational' may simply be to invert the logic of the moral panic thesis rather than to correct it.

These difficulties arise even before one embarks on any more thoroughgoing reconsideration of what is meant by the category 'fear'. Ordinary language, as usual, runs ahead of survey method by incorporating a variety of inflections, experiences and modes of perception in its uses of the word. We fear many things: war, accident, illness, death, financial ruin, scandal, estrangement and loneliness, the dark, dentists. It is not immediately apparent that the term 'fear' is being used in precisely the same way in each case, and we might recognize real scope for disagreement about the degree of attention or concern which would be warranted by the dangers which each of them presents.[2]

Two particular analogies which illustrate some problems in determining the rational basis of fears come to mind. First, the fear of flying is widespread. Some people suffer it to a debilitating degree. It attaches to possible events whose occurrence lies outside one's immediate control, which do happen and which have serious consequences when they happen. They happen, moreover, in a way of which the risks are more precisely calculable than are the risks of crime. Yet most of us fly without knowing these calculations precisely. All we know is that we consider them high or low, worth taking or not. Is there a conclusive resolution to the problem of 'rationality' in this case? Many of us, moreover, carry on flying while also still being afraid. A second and closer analogy with the fear of crime is the fear of being bitten by dogs. Dogs sometimes bite people with little provocation and occasionally injure them badly or kill them. Different breeds of dog appear to be more or less dangerous. When people are afraid of all dogs, including small cuddly ones, we often say that they are being irrational. I, on the other hand, quite like dogs on the whole and am disposed to presume that they will like me in return. But from the point of view of someone who is more fearful of them than I am, my approach to dogs looks like a bizarre disregard for my personal safety. None of this tells us prescriptively how afraid it is reasonable to be on any given occasion. Rottweilers are said to be dangerous dogs, but have they also been the object of the canine equivalent of a moral panic?

Researchers interested in fear of crime have responded to problems of this kind by breaking down the category into more refined components. These include fear for self as against fear on behalf of others; fear as distinct from 'worry'; fear of some situations, places or people but not others and, most controversially, fears which might appear to have other antecedent conditions than objective risk as such. However, it is a moot point whether such empirical differentiations have been sufficient to resolve all the most tenacious conceptual problems. I argue that both 'realist' and 'administrative' researchers should reconsider their views on the rational basis of fear of crime in the light of considerations which have been seen as governing risk perception and rational choice in the social sciences more generally, and that progress away from the stalemates in which arguments over the rationality of the fear of crime seem to me to terminate awaits such a consideration.

A number of relevant arguments have been summarized and synthesized by Mary Douglas (1986). Arguments about the reality of fear of crime have been particularly vehement. Logically, however, the kinds of considerations on which they ought to turn are similar to those which apply to the assessment and perception of many other sorts of risk. For instance, one of Young's most trenchant points is to stress that the risk of crime is disproportionately concentrated in certain locales and among certain groups of people. In this respect the risk of crime is very like other risks: the poor risk more from infant and general mortality, accidents at work, pollution, chronic ill-health. To this extent the distribution of risk is one way of thinking about inequality and social justice (Douglas, 1986: 10).

However, none of the usual definitions of risk (for example, that it is the product of the probability of an event multiplied by the severity of the harm which would result (Campbell, 1980)) really settles the question of when it is reasonable to be worried or fearful (Douglas, 1986:20).[3] Indeed, one of the strangest features of fear of crime debates is the extent to which the participants imagine that people *ought* somehow to be able to calculate what risk they run of becoming a victim. What from the point of view of an outside observer looks like an actuarially calculable risk is, from the point of view of any individual (potential victim) more like a problem of *uncertainty*. The notion of risk, strictly speaking, is only really intelligible in a situation 'governed by known probabilities' (Douglas, 1986: 43). At the same time, however, and for a similar reason, those who argue that the fear of crime is 'undue', 'excessive' or 'irrational' (cf. Wright, 1985, for an example) are very premature. Such writers give the impression that people would only deserve to be considered rational if they behaved like bookmakers, laying accurate odds against their own chances of falling victim to crime. As Young makes plain, they speak as though an appropriate level of fear were empirically decidable, when in fact it involves moral and political choices.

It may be the case, therefore, that anxiety about crime is as much a product of uncertainty itself as of risk – or at least that different senses of the term 'fear' are operative for different circumstances and groups of people. In most cases what we mean by fear of crime is not so much a calculation of probabilities as a set of 'intuitions' (Cohen, 1981) grounded in experience. This is also what Giddens has in mind when he distinguishes between 'validity criteria' and 'credibility criteria' in analysing beliefs (1984: 339–40). This much is close to Young's views (Young, 1987: 349). However, since fear is an intuitive mode of perception we cannot restrict *a priori* the set of experiences which may be relevant to it: indeed the more pervasive fear is the more likely it is that its constitution is open to influences which extend beyond induction from first-hand past experience.

Analysts of risk perception have long known that not all risks which are equally probable receive equal attention or concern (cf. von Neumann and Morgenstern, 1953). Rather, the salience for individuals of particular risks is related to the place those risks hold in a given culture; where culture means, according to Douglas, an 'actively invoked conventional wisdom' (1986: 66). The risk of crime, it would appear, is more publicly salient than, say, the risk of domestic accidents: and some crimes are more salient than others. The interest which we generally pay to the reporting of crime, or to its representation in stories, is similar to our attention to rumour and gossip – it reflects both our need for information and for conventions within which to frame and interpret our knowledge. The modes of reporting and talk with which we are familiar are 'heuristics' (Douglas, 1986: 79) for framing bits of information and fragments of experience about things which concern us.[4]

It follows from this that we need not accept a direct opposition between 'realism' (and hence rational choice and perception) and other modes of perception. Fear of crime is not necessarily either unreal or unreasonable simply because the chances of falling victim to crime are not its only determinant, even if most of us might want to reserve the right to see it as excessive or damaging under certain circumstances. Conversely, there is no need to deny that people are subject to definite risks in order to agree that crime and justice carry cultural and political meanings which precede and extend beyond our direct encounters with them. Indeed, one may conjecture, the more fearful people become, whether this is directly in proportion to the risks they run or not, the more urgent and important such meanings are likely to become for them.

An empirical example: Smith on north-central Birmingham

Susan Smith (1986) presents relevant issues in a lucid way by relating the spatial distribution of fear to other features of local social relations, in the context of the economic and political marginalization of an inner urban area. She concludes that if fear of crime is indeed realistic in this setting it is because 'victimised populations and fearful populations (which anyway overlap) are structurally bound together by their shared location in social, economic and physical space'.

Equally, however, Smith is concerned to show that whereas fear and risk do tend to coincide, they do not coincide uniformly. The sense of living in a dangerous place also has to do with awareness of economic and political marginality and of decline. These perceptions may crystallize in imputations of dangerousness across group (especially racial, but also age) boundaries, where the presence of incomers is experienced as an incursion upon previous familiarities and stability (1986: 111). To this extent fear seems to be accentuated by social divisions among the fearful. In a similar way, Maxfield ventures (1984: 25) and Smith is prepared to consider (1986: 129) that fear may result from 'incivilities', where the behavioural improprieties of some groups, which may not be specifically criminal, are viewed by others as indices of social disorganization and of threat.

In these senses diffuse anxieties result from social representations of the social and physical environment, whose sources are broader than the risk of victimization as such. Both Lewis (1980: 22) and Skogan and Maxfield (1981: 127) refer to these environmental features as 'signs' of decay or trouble: yet neither goes any further in elucidating the nature of the *signification* in question.

One problem with a notion like 'incivility', therefore, is that it has been too narrowly conceived. In most usages it is a commonplace which is deployed either as a secondary way of censuring young people's use of public space, or else it is reduced to a simple set of 'cues' from the physical environment: the so-called 'broken window hypothesis' (Wilson and Kelling, 1982). Each of these generates correlative policy stategies directed towards 'fear reduction' (Maxfield, 1984), whether by increased surveillance of working-class youth or by cosmetic improvements to the physical environment. Young's frustration with such measures, to which I have alluded above, is that they constitute knowing manipulations of public perception, predicated on a presumed disparity between fear and risk.

Lewis and Salem (1986) propose a broader and more interesting notion of 'incivility'. For them the term incorporates a more general sense of disorder which in turn undermines any sense of well-being in the relation of specific publics to both their social and physical environments. In this respect 'incivility' also summarizes a problem in the relation of these publics to political authority since it derives from the failure to sustain adequate levels of public provision and participation, or the preconditions for *civility* (1986: 20; see also Taylor,

1988). To this extent the incidence of crime and the fear of crime are not co-extensive but they have the same prior causes. They result from a failure of social organization and a lack of public provision. These broader considerations also raise the question of the representations of crime in television and print, and the degree of attention which is paid to them insofar as these are informed not only by the fear of crime as such but also by the fear of disorder from which the former in part results (Lewis and Salem, 1986: 22). The impact of crime, through the experience of fear, on particular communities thus cannot be understood without attention to the question of what kind of 'communities' they are, and how their members actually go about forming their views of themselves and one another and of their place in the wider world.

Smith shows that whether information circulating about crime is accurate or not the fact of its circulation, the channels it follows and the motivations people have to attend to it remain important. The special significance of local news media, she argues following Garofalo (1980), lies in the opportunity they provide for 'information seeking' consequent on the awareness of risk (1986: 117). The spatial distribution of events reported, as well as the specifically social proximity of the victims, both strongly influence the salience of reports of crime for any one individual (Skogan and Maxfield, 1981: 74).

It is through such reports, and more particularly the networks of rumour and gossip for which, as forms of 'improvised news' (Smith, 1986: 124), they provide the raw materials, that crime is constituted as an aspect of the social experience of a locality. Smith indicates a dual importance for rumour and gossip. At a manifest level rumour is a form of talk which mediates the transmission of crime-related information – on the basis of which strategies for the management of danger may be instituted. More obscurely, rumour is also consequential in defining and continually reproducing local social relations. Crime-related rumours flow most easily between socially and spatially proximate individuals. Insofar as the sharing of a rumour is also a confirmation of this proximity rumours have multiple purposes and dimensions: they intrinsically exceed the information given. Members of particular networks agree on 'maps' (Smith, 1986: 124) which designate both *sites* of danger and origins of danger in other sub-populations. Information about crime is thus integrated into local structures of affiliation and suspicion and the confirmation of their associated norms of propriety and censure. Such 'mapping' necessarily includes the potentiality for the overestimation of danger especially where demand for information exceeds its availability or where rumours refer to spatially or socially distant places or people. It is in these terms that Smith understands the occurrence of 'fantastic rumour', where the ostensible topic of the rumour acts as a surrogate for more diffuse, discursively unavailable or socially unacceptable anxieties. In her own study of north-central Birmingham Smith argues that the operation of fantastic rumour frequently results in mutual misperceptions across group boundaries, tending in this instance towards the exaggeration of race and crime issues (Smith, 1986: 127).

Clearly Smith's analysis is consonant with the widespread finding that, even in high-crime areas where fear is arguably based on accurate estimates of risk, subjects nonetheless tend to overestimate the dangers of other, further removed neighbourhoods and cities (cf. Maxfield, 1984). Even those observers who are most concerned to argue that fear of crime is realistically grounded in the inner cities (for example Kinsey, 1985) may also acknowledge that those who live in areas with a lower incidence of interpersonal violence and robbery may nonetheless overestimate *both* overall dimensions of crime problems as they affect the whole society and, more particularly, the dangerousness of inner urban locales.

The apprehension of danger is, in part and for some people, closely consequent upon real risks. Yet to the extent that fear of crime is both more widely distributed than are risks and is bound up with other sources of social anxiety and stress it is also related to representations across social boundaries. In these dimensions fear is a function of *distance*. For these reasons the vocabulary and imagery in which these representations are encoded, the media through which they are disseminated and the political rhetorics and strategies within which they are subsumed remain important, notwithstanding the 'realist' challenge (Lea and Young, 1984). Smith distinguishes between the levels at which fear impinges upon the experience of living in inner urban environments and at which it is coordinated in a national politics of law-and-order. To the extent that the latter is also 'mapped', as it were by a global rumour, it tends to ratify the surveillance of sites of agreed danger (Jones et al., 1986: 62). Through the dynamics of distance and proximity inner urban residents (objectively exposed to the greatest risks) are doubly marginalized – subject, that is, not only to fearfulness but also to strategies of policing and investigation ulterior to their needs, stemming from the diffusion of anxiety throughout the social formation.

Conclusions

There are a number of implications of these arguments for the modification and development of a 'realist' paradigm.

I have argued that 'rationality' and its cognate terms have been used misleadingly and tendentiously in research and debate about fear of crime. I have introduced arguments about risk perception which derive from theories of rational choice. These suggest that the issue of what constitutes a reasonable fear, if indeed the notion makes sense at all, may not be empirically decidable. This is not just logic-chopping. Rather it draws attention to some complexities in the real-world constitution of social knowledge about risk, some of which are in turn demonstrated in the illustration drawn from Smith's detailed, local ethnographic work.

I conclude, first, that to introduce elements of complexity and unevenness in the relation between risk and fear is not necessarily to gloss over the seriousness of real risks, nor is it inherently non-realist. Rather it is to argue that precisely because crime, anxiety and the sense of threat occupy important places in the lives and awareness of many people, it is unreasonable to foreclose the questions of the range of significances they hold for those people, or the ways in which they find out about them. There is nothing unreal about the embeddedness of social knowledge about crime in communication networks. Indeed, I regard Young's observation about the 'contextualization' of crime (1987: 338) as logically leading towards some conclusion of this kind. To this extent it seems difficult to refute Taylor's propositions (quoted above), however speculatively framed, on the basis of 'realist' assumptions.

Secondly, this has important consequences for understanding the place of crime in public discourse and private feeling. Fear of crime remains inadequately theorized unless it is viewed in relation to the density of social knowledge about crime as a function of the division of social space and the unequal distribution of risks. Again, these topics are raised but insufficiently explored within the 'realist' approach, as when Young introduces the figure of the 'suburban soul' whose direct experience of victimization may be small but whose preoccupation with crime may be great (1987: 338). Maxfield raises a similar problem when he observes that 'A country resident's "very common" may only qualify as "fairly common" to his counterpart in London' (1984: 19), but he seems to regard this issue as unresolvable. However, it seems to me at least plausible that some of the fears of 'suburban souls' may also be intelligible once they too have been properly contextualized and interrogated. Moreover, there are clear senses in which the lives of 'suburban souls' and inner-city dwellers are related. In a complex political society notions of citizenship and responsibility (at least as much as fear per se, or prejudice) may make people feel *required* to hold views of some sort about places and crimes of which they have little direct experience. It would thus be surprising if talk of fear was *not* bound up in a context of meaning and significance, involving the use of metaphors and narratives about social change (cf. Cohen, 1985), over and above calculable considerations of risk. To this extent the fears and other views of crime held by people in low risk areas and groups also need to be independently studied and interpreted.

Thirdly, these arguments have an evident bearing on methodological considerations in future research. 'Realists' already recognize the significance of the fact that particular groups of people attach differing weight and significance to particular offences, for example in determining whether or not they define them as 'violent' (cf. Pease, 1988), and that victimization therefore takes place against a background of expectation, experience and thresholds of tolerance. This encompasses problems of refinement in sampling and definition to which MacLean draws attention (1989: 16–26), but it also broaches the questions of how theoretical inferences and policy choices are arrived at on the basis of research findings. There is thus a need for open and exploratory forms of questioning, which are less presumptive than hitherto about the reasonableness of possible responses.

When it addresses issues of this kind 'realism' begins to break down the reliance of past research into the fear of crime on utilitarian assumptions of rational calculation in risk perception and avoidance. In so doing it can also dispose of the implicit behaviourism of the 'broken windows' hypothesis and return the analysis of the perception of crime to a more 'fully social' footing – that is as a dimension of a whole mode of concrete practice and experience, and as one of the ways in which people define the parameters of what is for them a habitable social environment.

Analysts of risk perception have thus been driven to recognize the non-viability of solving questions of reasonable risk or rational fear in definitive or objective ways. The differences between chronic and catastrophic risks is one important issue, but so are the questions of the degree of control which people feel they can exercise over their exposure to risk and hence the degree of voluntariness or involuntariness in their subjection to it. As Douglas concludes 'the important issues in risk perception can never be analyzed just with an inventory of the physical features of events, their scale of damage, suddenness or duration' (1986: 28). In that fear of crime is embedded in people's 'practical consciousness' (Giddens, 1984) it is always likely to be more than inductive. Hence there is no benefit in condescending to it as 'irrational' when it is found to be so.

Crime presents people with certain dangers of which they must take account as best they may. In taking account of these dangers each of us engages in some version of risk analysis. But the resources available to us in making the necessary judgements are both enormously extensive, varied and complex and inherently incomplete. We are not really reckoning probabilities bounded by known parameters: we are facing up to possibilities surrounded by uncertainty. If we are afraid of a thing we must first have an image or representation of it (cf. Cohen, 1981). Why then should it *not* be the case that the fears which preoccupy us most would not be those which are most likely to come to pass? Rather they are likely to be the most representationally powerful fears – fears which attach to our sense of identity, security and potency in the world and which therefore affect us as whole social beings and not as the risk-accounting ciphers of crude rational choice theories. At the same time what should also be questioned and resisted is the implication in the predominant discourse, through the deployment of the notion of rationality, that people not only can but must engage in risk analysis such that they can be held in part accountable for their own victimization. Women in particular are thus made subject to an expectation of 'reasonable risk-taking' which in turn conditions the kind of redress or blame they can expect in the event of being victimized.

Some people, by reason of gender, age, geography, race and class are not only subjected to risks they should not have to bear but also obliged to live in physical and social environments that are chronically fear-inducing. Fear opposes the sense of 'trust' (Giddens, 1984: 61) in the continuity and reliability of the world and undermines our sense of our place in it. For these reasons the fear of crime cannot be sharply separated from the fear of place.[5] It should be reconsidered as meaning the occupancy of a fearful social position. Under such conditions it can turn out that the recommended remedies for fearful experiences ('avoidance behaviour', staying at home, turning the home into a fortress, tooling up with weapons, being surrounded by Guardian Angels, going to the police, appearing in court) are also in themselves fear-inducing.

In these circumstances it would be no surprise if something like 'moral panics' did indeed occur, not because they have been fabricated in the way that the original formulation of the concept seemed to imply, but simply because fears about crime are inextricably bound up in the tangle of experiences, hopes, worries, preferences and prejudices which compose our relation to the social world.

The relevant political questions thus become sharper, though no easier to answer. They include not only 'how do you prevent crime and reduce risk?' but also 'how do you go about devising social arrangements, buildings, transport systems and subways, public spaces, or indeed seek to recover supports for civility and politeness in dealing with one another, so that the media which people must use in order to act and interact are not also instruments of terror?'

Notes

I would like to thank Ian Taylor, Nigel Walker and Ruth Jamieson for constructive criticism and encouragement on reading a first draft of this chapter. I am also grateful for the insightful comments of my friend Tom Woodhouse on earlier work.

1. Wilson and Kelling in particular are reductive in styling people's perceptions of and reactions to environmental 'signs' of trouble as taking 'cues' from the state of their physical surroundings. These are not explanations. They are conjectures introduced to fill a perceived 'gap' between risk and fear. So far, however, 'realism' has mainly responded by trying to abolish the gap.

2. David Downes comments: 'That the "fear of crime", in itself a growth area for research interest following the *British Crime Surveys*, remains most developed in relation to certain forms of street crime is probably more to do with collective representations of unpredictable violence than that which more frequently occurs within the home, or which is normalised as accidental, or where victimisation is indirect and dispersed as with corporate crime.' (1988: 182)

3. To join battle with the 'new administrative criminology' on the basis of directly disputing calculations of this form, as the realists have so far tended to do, stands in danger of succumbing to the same kind of pseudo-mathematics, just altering the variables. But what on earth does 'multiplied' mean in this context? Risks may be 'multiplied', but why should risk perceptions or fears, and by what factor?

4. As Douglas comments in relation to Fried's (1970) concept of the 'risk pool', out of which we are obliged to draw unequally on 'risk budgets', any social organization must at some point decide to what 'budgets' it is acceptable to expose its members. In so saying, Douglas argues, we must place 'social and physical probability in the same frame', thereby moving from the question 'what level of risk do we accept?' to the question 'what kind of society do we want?' (Douglas, 1986: 16).

5. One currently promising line of research stems from recent work by human geographers into the conditions for well-being or otherwise for people in relation to the significances they attach to particular buildings, places and localities. Some places are held sacred and some are considered disreputable and/or frightening. Yi-Fu Tuan uses the concepts 'topophilia' and 'topophobia' to express these relations and reactions, for example in his *Landscapes of Fear* (1979). These concepts have also recently been used by John Bale (1989) to describe people's varying reactions of pleasure, loyalty, anxiety and alienation regarding football grounds.

References

Bale, J. (1989) 'Football and topophilia: the public and the stadium'. Paper presented to conference on Football and its Public, Florence.

Box, S., Hale, C. and Andrews, G. (1988) 'Explaining fear of crime', *British Journal of Criminology*, 28(3): 338–56.

Campbell, T. (1980) 'Chemical carcinogens and human risk assent', *Federation Proceedings*, 39: 2467–84.

Cohen, J. (1981) *The Probable and the Provable*. Oxford: Clarendon.

Cohen, S. (1972) *Folk Devils and Moral Panics*. London: MacGibbon and Kee.

Cohen, S. (1985) *Visions of Social Control*. Cambridge: Polity Press.

Douglas, M. (1986) *Risk*. London: Routledge & Kegan Paul.

Downes, D. (1988) 'The sociology of crime and social control in Britain: 1960–1987', in P. Rock (ed.), *A History of British Criminology*. Oxford: Clarendon Press.

Fried, C. (1970) *An Anatomy of Values*. Cambridge, Mass.: Harvard.

Garland, D. (1987) 'Review of Kinsey et al., *Losing the Fight Against Crime*', *Contemporary Crises*, 11(2): 198–200.

Garofalo, J. (1980) 'Victimization and the fear of crime', in E. Bittner and S. Messinger (eds), *Criminology Review Yearbook*, Vol 2. London: Sage.

Giddens, A. (1979) *Central Problems in Social Theory*. London: Macmillan.

Giddens, A. (1984) *The Constitution of Society*. Cambridge: Polity Press.

Hall, R. (1985) *Ask any Woman: A London Inquiry into Rape and Sexual Assault*. London: Fallingwall Press.

Hough, M. and Mayhew, P. (1985) *Taking Account of Crime*. London: HMSO.

Jones, T., MacLean, B. and Young, J. (1986) *The Islington Crime Survey*. Aldershot: Gower.

Kinsey, R. (1985) *Merseyside Crime and Police Surveys: Final Report*. Liverpool: Merseyside County Council.

Lea, J. and Young, J. (1984) *What is to be Done about Law and Order?* Harmondsworth: Penguin.

Lewis, D. (1980) *Sociological Theory and the Production of a Social Problem: The Case of Fear of Crime*. Northwestern University Center for Urban Affairs.

Lewis, D. and Salem, G. (1986) *Fear of Crime*. New Brunswick: Transaction Books.

MacLean, B. (1989) 'In partial defence of socialist realism'. Paper presented to the British Criminology Conference, Bristol Polytechnic, July.

Maxfield, M. (1984) *Fear of Crime in England and Wales*. London: HMSO.

Pease, K. (1988) *Judgements of Crime Seriousness*. London: HMSO.

Reiner, R. (1988) 'British criminology and the state', in P. Rock (ed.), *A History of British Criminology*. Oxford: Oxford University Press.

Skogan, W. and Maxfield, M. (1981) *Coping with Crime*. London: Sage.

Smith, S. (1986) *Crime, Space and Society*. Cambridge: Cambridge University Press.

Sparks, R.F. (1981) 'Surveys of victimization: an optimistic assessment', in M. Tonry and N. Morris (eds), *Crime and Justice: An Annual Review*. Chicago: Chicago University Press.

Taylor, I. (1988) 'Left realism, the free market economy and the problem of social order'. Paper presented to the American Society of Criminology Meetings, Chicago.

Tuan, Y. (1979) *Landscapes of Fear*. Oxford: Blackwell.

von Neumann, J. and Morgenstern, O. (1953) *The Theory of Games*. Princeton: Princeton University Press.

Wilson, J. and Kelling, R. (1982) 'Broken windows', *Atlantic Monthly*, March.

Wright, K. (1985) *The Great American Crime Myth*. Westport: Greenwood.

Young, J. (1987) 'The tasks facing a realist criminology', *Contemporary Crises*, 11: 337–56.

7 Law and order politics – left realism and radical criminology: a view from down under

David Brown and Russell Hogg

This chapter is a reflection on recent radical criminology in the Australian and British contexts. The main focus, consonant with the theme of the book, is the project generally known as left realism or radical realism in criminology. Left realism is most clearly represented by a series of publications and activities (Taylor, 1981; Lea and Young, 1984; Kinsey, 1985; Kinsey et al., 1986; Jones et al., 1986; Lea, 1987; Matthews, 1987; Young, 1987; Lea et al., 1987; Jones et al., 1987; Painter et al., 1988; Painter, 1988; Young, 1988; Painter et al., 1989; Crawford et al., 1990) which constitute a theoretical and political intervention in British criminology of considerable significance; an attempt to develop a political criminology on the left which takes crime problems seriously and offers a programme of reforms that are both progressive and realizable in Britain in the 1980s and 1990s.

While there have been left realist resonances within US (Platt and Takagi, 1981; Gross, 1982; Currie, 1985) and Australian (Boehringer et al., 1983; Campaign for Criminal Justice, 1988; Hogg, 1988a, 1988b) criminology, these have been far more muted and partial. The US radical criminology journal, *Crime and Social Justice*, appeared to be sponsoring a 'realist' 'taking crime seriously' current in the early 1980s, but in recent years this seems to have dissipated somewhat, the change in name to *Social Justice* reflecting a shift to more macro concerns, political economy and international politics, or as the subtitle puts it 'Crime, Conflict and World Order'. Elliot Currie's excellent *Confronting Crime* (1985), although not written under a left realist banner, remains the most impressive and programmatic radical US re-evaluation of criminal justice policy. It is not possible to identify a clear-cut left realist 'school' in the Australian context, although the *Bulletins* of the Campaign for Criminal Justice Group in New South Wales (NSW) have adopted a broadly left realist approach and Hogg has 'in a critical though sympathetic vein' (1988a: 47) supported aspects of the realist project. (For a review of post-war Australian criminology see Carson and O'Malley, 1989; Australian sociology of law: O'Malley, 1984; and for an assessment of left realism and Australian criminology see Hogg, 1988a). In as much as we have recently been identified with a 'taking crime seriously' position within Australian radical criminology, this chapter illustrates our qualified support for the realist concern with specific and realizable policies for crime prevention and control and the conditions for their implementation by reform governments and other organizations and movements here and now.

The qualification is however major. We argue that the realist project in its appropriation of the unifying category 'crime' around which to formulate policies and politics which express the true interests of the working class continues elements of the essentialism of past radical criminologies. This argument will be fleshed out at a general level in relation both to radical criminology, left realism and the left critiques of left realism. In the second half of the chapter Australian criminology will be examined by way of a brief outline of post-war developments, the emergence of a radical tendency and suggestions for future directions which include an assessment of the relevance of left realism to the Australian context.

Radical criminology and Marxist essentialism

Debates within radical criminology, like debates within other areas of radical social theory, have to a considerable extent since the 1970s been preoccupied with the problem and effects of economic reductionism or, to use a more inclusive term, theoretical essentialism. Barry Hindess has defined essentialism as: 'Essentialism ... refers to a mode of analysis in which social phenomena are analysed not in terms of their specific conditions of existence and their effects with regard to other social relations and practices but rather as the more or less adequate expression of an essence (Hindess, 1977: 95).

Within variants of Marxist social theory this essence is the capitalist economic structure. Capitalist society is treated as a social totality governed by general principles of organization. To one degree or another, the social relations of capitalism (politics, law, culture, etc) are explained within Marxism as the necessary and essential effects of the capitalist economy. One of the most familiar effects of such a theory is to draw a distinction between political strategies and demands that attack the fundamental structure of capitalist society and those that only seek to reform parts of it while leaving the structure intact. Thus, crime is frequently understood (with varying degrees of sophistication) as an expression of class inequalities and capitalist state control, conditions which can only be remedied through a socialist transformation of society.

Although it is a familiar pastime of anti-Marxists to attack such forms of reductionism, this is hardly a problem that is confined to radical social theory. Less totalizing theories within the social sciences are just as prone to essentialisms of various kinds. The political right, for example, frequently takes crime as a pretext for advancing a whole series of other claims – with regard to inadequate social and moral controls in the family, schooling and legal and penal apparatuses – rather than seriously exploring the causes of particular types of crime problem.

One form of essentialism that has long characterized criminology flows from the legacy of positivism and relates to the taken-for-granted status of the concepts of 'crime' and 'criminality'. 'Crime' has no necessary or essential reference point of a behavioural or other kind. Although it is usually formally considered in terms of the shifting legal definitions of the state, it is fair to say that crime is constituted as an object in a range of discourses – popular, fictional, administrative, psychological, etc, as well as strictly legal. While this is widely accepted now, its implications for criminology are not always so clearly appreciated, for example, that it disrupts any notion of criminology as a unified discipline or discourse or as a vehicle for applying a general body of theory (such as Marxism) to the object 'crime'.

In the late 1960s a self-consciously radical political project in criminology emerged in Britain and the USA (and a little later in Australia), directed against the pragmatic and administrative criminology that had hitherto dominated. It reproduced in varying forms the essentialism of the Marxism which informed it.

Some radical criminologists in the USA appropriated Marxism to produce what is perhaps best thought of as a radical conflict theory of crime (Chambliss, 1976; Quinney, 1974). In the Marxist version of such theories the contradiction between social classes in the economic structure of society is argued to be manifest in a direct way at every level of society. Thus the law, and criminal law in particular, is held to be an instrument of class rule, wielded by the ruling class against the working class as a repressive instrument of social control.

It is difficult to sustain the view, however, that economic classes are polarized around the criminal law and state social control in societies such as North America, Britain and Australia. As Young pointed out in 'Working class criminology', an essay which marked one important step along his path to left realism:

> However much the new deviancy theorists talked of diversity and dissensus in society, the ineluctable reality of a considerable consensus over certain matters could not be wished away. This was particularly noticeable,

moreover, in the widespread and uniform social reaction against various forms of deviancy (and especially, against crimes against the person and certain crimes against property). (1975: 71)

Young went on in that essay both to acknowledge that much crime is intra-class in nature and to demonstrate how the working class does have a real stake in social order. However, such working-class concerns and demands were argued to be organized and mobilized by bourgeois state ideology and practice in such a way as to deflect attention from the 'real' sources of crime and the 'real interests' of the class in a transformation of the social order.

Many of the early appropriations of Marxism in criminology have been subjected to fairly severe attack by other Marxists concerned to defend the conceptual integrity of Marxist theory against pragmatic and empiricist deviations. This assault began with an essay by Paul Hirst (1975), and there have been a variety of further critiques of a similar nature since (Bankowski et al., 1977; Sumner, 1976; O'Malley, 1988). These more rigorous readings of the pertinence of Marxism to the study of crime emphasized that as crime was itself merely an ideological artefact, a product of state legal and policing practices, it had no privileged status within the corpus of Marxist theory, but rather was subsumed within its general concepts – those of forces and relations of production, accumulation, state, ideology, etc. Crime was not an autonomous and unified entity or object within which class contradictions were condensed and expressed in any direct sense, but rather it was dispersed across and within the different levels of the Marxist totality. There could be no Marxist theory of crime as such. Some aspects of the phenomena grouped under the label crime at any given time might relate to economic production and distribution, conditions of wage labour, state practices or ideology. In each case it would be appropriate to conceptualize and analyse the concrete instance in the relevant Marxist terms. Marxism had nothing to say about crime-in-general though. The most sophisticated example of such a concrete analysis of crime-related issues and events in which the object 'crime' is reconceptualized in Marxist terms is the study of mugging in Britain by Stuart Hall and others and published as *Policing the Crisis* (1978).

In recent times much socialist theoretical work has emphasized the limitations of orthodox Marxism as a political theory which of itself is adequate to address the conditions of modern capitalism and serve as a guide to socialist politics (cf. Cutler et al., 1977, 1978; Laclau and Mouffe, 1985). These engagements with Marxism by no means share a common theoretical position, but throw into doubt different aspects of Marxist theory. What they do share is a rejection of totalizing theory of all kinds, be it Marxist or not, as necessarily essentialist. Politics and the theories appropriate to informing it are conceived in more pluralistic terms – as consisting of a diversity of overlapping projects with no necessary unity, manifest or latent; with no privileged sites of struggle (production); with no vanguard elements (party or working class). Political strategy and effects are consequently unable to be read off from some general theory of capitalist society.

This does not involve abandoning general social objectives or principles, but it does require that social analysis always consider them alongside other considerations and objectives which encompass a recognition of the real constraints imposed by prevailing conditions (cf. Hindess, 1987). It entails a recognition that such conditions, and society itself, are only 'finitely modifiable' at any given time. On the other hand, if society is not to be understood in terms of a necessary structure, governed by the capitalist economy, '... then the options facing socialist politics can no longer be reduced to a matter of confronting this essential structure or else refusing to do so' (Cutler et al., 1977: 317). Reforms of various kinds cannot be assigned a fixed and necessary place in any overall conception of capitalist society and its transformation.

This might be regarded as especially evident at the present time given the diversity in the political issues and forces in contention in societies such as Britain and Australia. Politically the project of socialist politics associated with the Marxist tradition, and indeed the social democratic tradition as well, has fragmented and a proliferation of social antagonisms have come to mark the politics of late twentieth century capitalist societies. Marxism and social democracy have both adhered to conceptions of politics organized around the centrality of the working class as the vehicle of social change. Of course, in practice it has never been the *class* which has functioned as the agent of change, but only ever political parties, trade unions, factions, movements and so on. And as Hindess points out, it could never be otherwise: classes are not political actors, but are definable only by reference to economic relations of production (Hindess, 1987). Attempts to posit some necessary relationship between the two levels have dogged left politics since the last century.

These traditions of theorizing, whatever their substantial differences and variants, entail the assumption that economic classes share in common certain necessary and objective interests which exist prior to, and independently of, their representation in particular political organizations, movements, etc. The performance of such organizations can then be assessed in relation to the supposed interests of the class. Within such a scheme political analysis and evaluation has often tended to degenerate into a familiar pattern: of accusations of treachery or reformism on the part of the leadership or party and endless debates about whether parties, such as the Australian Labor Party, are socialist or not, that is, whether they do or can ever represent 'the true interests' of the working class. This serves to reduce political analysis to sloganizing and a constant competition on the part of parties and individuals to out-credential each other in terms of criteria which are ultimately indeterminate. Policy debate and formation ceases to be organized around political calculation as to desirable and realizable goals in the light of prevailing conditions and the means of their realization and becomes an exercise in expressing 'the correct line'.

The other assumption present in left politics is that despite what the available evidence (voting, public opinion polling, etc) suggests about the (diverse) attitudes of those who compose the working class to a variety of issues, there is a latent socialist consciousness lurking within the class waiting to be aroused and crystallized around a radical programme. This is another expression of the notion that classes share certain necessary and objectively identifiable interests which are in a sense a more real, more fundamental, basis for conducting political analysis regardless of whether there is any evidence that these interests are actually recognized by persons composing the relevant classes. This serves to insulate socialists from the real problems of confronting popular resistance to socialist and even liberal progressive ideas and it ultimately also leads to political arrogance, elitism and substitutionism. The crime issue might be regarded as a prime illustration of this problem.

Some of these problems have been highlighted by the emergence of new political movements – of women, gays, ethnic and racial minorities, students, environmentalists, tenants, welfare claimants, prisoners, mental patients, urban social movements, etc. Such movements emerged and organized around a variety of issues which were not straightforwardly definable in class terms, which were more focused in their concerns and which often cut across the assumed allegiances and shared interests bounded by class position. Attempts to construe them in class terms run up against the problems of positing a necessary relationship between economic relations and politics discussed above, only more obviously. Such attempts have tended to be elaborated politically in terms of the potential for a system of alliances involving such movements and traditional political organizations. This has similarly often taken the form of attributing common and necessary (anti-capitalist) interests to such movements and hence a latent unity among them which is also shared by the working class. Again this obscures the precise nature of the political objectives and differences that are at issue across this broad array of people and movements.

Left realism in Britain

Left realism in Britain emerged at least in part as a response to the general shift to the right on British politics since the mid-1970s. It seeks to offer an alternative programme for the reconstruction of social order to that of the British Conservative government and their right-wing intellectual supporters. It has developed as more than simply a theoretical enterprise. The local victim survey has been embraced as the most appropriate method of enquiry and analysis and several major local victim surveys have been carried out to date, in Merseyside, Islington, Broadwater Farm, North London, Hilldrop, West Kensington, and Hammersmith and Fulham (see earlier references). Half have been funded by local councils, indicating the growing political alliance between left realist criminologists and sections of the British Labour Party.

Among the most important tenets of the new realism in Britain are the following:

1   crime is a major social problem, especially personal violence and property crime, and it is a problem of growing proportions;
2   official crime statistics considerably understate the problem due to the levels of unreported crime, which is in large part a result of public alienation and frustration with the ineffectiveness of criminal justice agencies, especially the police (Jones et al., 1986);
3   most personal crime (robbery, assault, burglary, etc) is intra-class and disproportionately afflicts the poor and their neighbourhoods, thus compounding the inequalities and exploitation they already experience;
4   the police are both extremely inefficient at dealing with inner-city crime and endemically hostile and discriminatory with regard to the inner-city populace (especially youth and ethnic minorities);
5   the mutual antagonism between police and local communities sets in train a vicious circle of non-cooperation whereby alienated communities do not report crimes to the police and do not pass on much-needed information to them, thus forcing police into more proactive and discriminatory strategies of crime control (such as systematic stop and search and targeting of whole social categories of people thought to be crime-prone), which in turn alienates the community even further, who respond by further withholding co-operation, and so it goes on;
6   the inner-city working-class communities are deeply concerned about local crime, want effective policies to control it and see the police as central to crime control;
7   effective policing requires that the police concentrate on those crimes that the public sees as most serious, that they relinquish

those heavy proactive policing methods that alienate their most important resource, the local community itself, and that they are placed under local democratic control through elected local police authorities.

Many of these propositions find empirical support in the surveys carried out to date. They confirm in far more concrete, localized and detailed terms the findings of many other surveys of opinion which indicate that crime is an issue of deep concern among the general public. This appears to be no less the case in Australia.

On the one hand, many of the arguments of the left realists appear to be important advances on the traditional abstentionism of left and liberal commentators and organizations on issues of crime and law and order. However, on the other, many may be left wondering, with Geoff Mungham, why it was necessary for radical criminology to spend nearly two decades travelling a route that seems to have led back to something like the orthodoxy of post-war liberal criminology in Britain, which has its Australian equivalents in the work of people like Gordon Hawkins and Duncan Chappell, the current director of the Australian Institute of Criminology (Mungham, 1984: 372).

What, if anything, is different about left realism and why should we take any notice of it in Australia? Liberal criminology has always tended to see itself as engaged in an essentially scientific exercise, largely value-free and dictated by the authoritative specification of social problems, primarily by agencies of state and other political elites. Popular feeling about crime has been taken-for-granted as the consensual backdrop to the work of criminology. It has not been romanticized or rationalized away as it has by many radicals, but nor has it really been taken seriously as a variable factor in the essentially political processes and struggles that fashion debates, attitudes and responses around crime issues. Defining and responding to crime was essentially something to be left to the experts and the relevant specialist bureaucracies.

Abandoning the radical tendency to simply invert this picture, left realists have argued that popular experiences of and attitudes to crime must be taken seriously as an arena of political practice with far-reaching implications for the organization of the state. Central to this is a socialist strategy which places the democratization of state apparatuses, and other areas of social and economic life, at the forefront. Responding to crime becomes not a technocratic but a political exercise. In general terms, this appears to us to be the direction in which a radical political criminology should go. However, there are a number of serious problems with left realisms as it has been elaborated in Britain.

'Crime' as a unifier

The most fundamental problem in the realist theory, programme and methodology lies in the diminution of concern with the concept of 'crime' itself. This is not a theoretical luxury, but a strategic relaxation with important political effects. It is also closely related to the 'paramount' significance given to victim surveys (Young, 1986: 28).

Some sense of the importance attached to victim surveys by the new realists can be obtained from the following comments in the introduction to the (first) *Islington Crime Survey*:

> The question is how to develop policies which help protect women, ethnic minorities and the working class – those who suffer most from the impact of crime – who are the *natural constituents* of Labour, whilst refusing to accept the draconian policing policies and penal practice of the Tories. That is, how to develop policies which protect and give succour to the victims of crime, who are all the more affected because of their vulnerable position in the social structure, whilst controlling the urban offender who is himself often a product of the same oppressive circumstances. To do this demands humane policies which accurately reflect people's needs, which are guided by facts and which can be monitored effectively. All of this is provided by the local crime survey. (Jones et al., 1986: 6, emphasis added)

A closer examination of the realist surveys indicate that they have not been used to the extent they could to explore the range of possible meanings and articulations of the crime problem in local settings, but rather to prove a series of general propositions about crime and policing. As Gilroy and Sim argue as part of a more general left critique of realism '. . . public concern about crime must be understood as the outcome of a political process. This necessitates breaking down the abstract, general category "crime" into particular experiences, images and fear which correspond to city life' (1985: 46).

Such criticism does not carry the implication that public fears about crime are simply irrational, or that they are products of media sensationalism, or even that they are in any way necessarily exaggerated. The experiences of, fears and concerns about, crime are real enough. The crucial issue is what they signify, and how they are to be connected to other domains of experience and to alternative social practices and policies.

The available public discourses on crime elide a potential range of meanings and possible responses. There are few more loaded, persuasive and propagandistic terms than those, such as 'violence', 'vandalism', etc, which dominate the lexicon of crime. Eliciting popular opinion using such conceptual tools uncritically risks, at best, simply producing results that may be valid though trivial, or, at worst, concealing from view the most important strata of meaning. It has been the systematic and persistent way in which the available popular and official discourses of crime have, for example, failed to accommodate a recognition of the domestic nature of most violence that continues to foster the relative trivialization of this issue alongside violence involving strangers.

To take a specific example from the realist surveys themselves. The *Islington Crime Survey* found a very high level of agreement that sexual assaults on women should be, along with certain other crimes, given priority in terms of police time and resources (Jones et al., 1986: 106–10). This prioritization of crimes was consistent across all major social divisions, including class, gender, race, age, etc. However, does this really reflect a high level of consensus about the meanings of sexual assault? Is it consistent with what we know about patterns of sexual assault from other sources? – the traditional treatment of sexual assault victims at the hands of the criminal process, including juries; the degree to which legal recognition of victimization has depended, not on the actions of the alleged offender, but on the behaviour, demeanour, dress, reputation, etc, of the woman in question (Wilson, 1983: 67–72) and the ways in which sexual harassment and violence against women is rationalized by its perpetrators and by agencies of control.

The uncritical use of such general categories expunges the differences and divergences in meaning, intent and actual behaviour that arise as soon as we descend from the abstract to the context of situated and concrete judgements. A naive use of the survey method conceals the complexity of these problems behind a facade of consensus. And as Gilroy and Sim also point out: 'The easy resort to crime as an abstraction increases rather than diminishes the distance which the left has to travel if it is to articulate a credible politics of everyday life. Local factors are central to the pattern of fear about crime. This is always discontinuous, fluid and specific' (1985: 46).

The uncritical use of the concept 'crime' suggests that other purposes may underlie the realist project, or at least that it does not escape the effects of a certain essentialism – an essentialism that utilizes crime as an ideological unifier: a mode for expressing the 'real' and common interests of working-class people, '...the natural constituents of Labour...', as the earlier quote put it. The consensus of liberal criminology has been rediscovered, but with the added advantage that it is on the whole a progressive one. Thus, popular demands for policing, for interests in, and aspirations for, the democratic socialist solutions through which such demands will be realized (Taylor, 1981: 101–5). Policies, such as the democratization of policing, are thus articulated as the essential expression of a progressive consensus rather than in terms of the conditions required for their successful implementation (including political support) and their likely social effects, for example with regard to levels of crime (Hindess, 1983: 107–8). In short, the political problems of implementing progressive law and order policies are, to a considerable extent, defined out of existence (cf. Brown, 1987, 1988a).

The critique from the left

There have been a number of attacks launched against left realism by other left critics, which also emphasize that the label 'crime' conceals a diverse range of social phenomena, that the vast majority of criminalizable events are not in fact actually criminalized but are resolved in local and informal ways (Hulsman, 1986). Some have even argued for the abandonment of the concept altogether in favour of the more neutral language of 'troubles', 'conflicts', etc: 'It makes all the difference to frame the problems that are to be managed independently of criminal law and thus exclusionary terms and implications' (Steinert, 1985: 329).

A more concerted critique of left realism has emerged in Britain which rejects left realism in similar terms (Scraton, 1987). Gilroy and Sim (quoted above) point to '... the existence of normative conceptions of crime and wrongdoing which compete for popular allegiance with those which originate in police practice'. They argue that it '... is important to apply this insight and identify where such norms connect with a capacity for self-policing' (1985: 50).

These critiques imply that there is something approaching a total disconnection between formal discourses on crime and localized concerns and responses; or that to the extent that any articulation exists, it is the effect of the external imposition of legal and state control on community problems. The presumed 'real' interests of the community lie in eschewing state involvement as this necessarily embodies antithetical interests, those of capital, the ruling class, etc, and entails an extension of social control. The corollary of this is that strategies to deal with crime should be elaborated wholly autonomously of the state. This assumes that some authenticity resides in the immediate, often conflicting, definitions and perceptions of local parties to a conflict that is absent from legal categories and that the former never incorporate elements of the latter.

For many left critics of realism, crime is simply an expression of the divisions wrought by capitalism which will disappear within forms of community self-management directed at displacing capitalist social relations. However, the use of labels which express the anti-statism of their users merely represents an inversion of legal ideology. It comes no closer to describing the specific terms of the relationship between working-class communities and agencies of state, between legal and social definitions of crime or between informal and formal measures of control.

Gilroy and Sim, for example, ignore the apparent overlap between some rank and file police attitudes and some white male attitudes to certain forms of racial and sexual violence, which themselves operate as a source of demands on the state to provide genuine forms of protection *within* communities, to women and racial and sexual minorities in particular. The links between masculinity and violence, for example, about which the law and agencies of state are often ambivalent (Allen, 1988b), cannot be dismissed as somehow an inauthentic expression of class consciousness wrought by the divisive effects of capitalism (O'Donnell and Craney, 1982). It is a vain expectation that women and other groups would abandon struggles and demands on these fronts in favour of the sole, vague and dubious promise of forms of community self-policing in circumstances where it is precisely such traditional informal modes of control and policing (by men over women) that are at issue (Girdler, 1982: 146). Again, this essentialism simply defines away major political problems and differences, by positing as necessarily and objectively given some shared interests of communities *against* the state, although such interests and commonality often do not appear to be recognized by the groups in question.

Popular demands for policing are real, they give the lie to crudely instrumentalist conceptions of the state and they make it difficult to attribute progressive status to specific practices on the basis of an abstract dichotomy between state and civil society. The label 'crime' does express real relationships which have no essentialist foundations in capitalist social relations. To eschew it is simply evasion of disagreeable political terrain. To accept and analyse its various uses does not necessarily imply that they are not entangled in other social relationships, nor that they are immutable and unchanging.

The following sections will sketch out a brief history of post-war Australian criminology, the emergence of a radical or critical stream following British and American developments in the mid-1970s, and offer an assessment of the prospects of an explicitly left realist criminology in Australia. While necessarily truncated, such an overview may be of interest particularly to non-Australian readers interested in an account of developments 'down under'. The discussion will be conducted against the backdrop of the more general argument above, concerning the effects of essentialism in Marxism, radical criminology, left realist criminology and its left critiques.

A brief history of post-war Australian criminology

It is necessary first to identify a number of limitations affecting our ability to provide an adequate overview. Foremost among these perhaps is the absence of a reflexive tradition. Evaluations of the directions, character and contribution of Australian criminological research are rare and there are as yet no substantial criminological histories either in general or of particular areas, such as those provided in Britain by Taylor et al. (1973), Garland (1985), and Rock (1988). Even the 'footprints in the sand' exercise in assessment and classification provided by Cohen (1981) is largely absent. Of the few explicitly reflexive contributions, the most significant is that by Carson and O'Malley (1989) (but see also Wilson, 1973; Brown, 1978; Wilson and Braithwaite, 1978; Hiller and O'Malley, 1978; Prisoners' Action Group, 1979–80; O'Connor, 1980; Zdenkowski and Brown, 1982; Boehringer et al., 1983; Chappell, 1983; O'Malley, 1983, 1984, 1988; Chappell and Wilson, 1986; Wilson and Dalton, 1987; Howe, 1987; Hogg, 1988a).

Further, such evaluations as exist are restricted to post-war developments. Although lineages of crime-related themes can be found in the (mostly critical) social historical literature on transportation and convictism (McQueen, 1968; Hirst, 1983; Hughes, 1988), bush-ranging (McQuilton, 1979; O'Malley, 1979, 1980), aboriginal resistance, criminalization and welfare (Rowley, 1970; Reynolds, 1981, 1987), public order crime (Grabosky, 1977; Sturma, 1983), the state and social order (Sydney Labour History Group, 1982), imprisonment (Garton, 1988a), prison architecture (Kerr, 1988), crime trends (Mukherjee, 1980), prostitution (Daniels, 1984; Golder and Allen, 1979–80), drugs (McCoy, 1980), policing (Finnane, 1987; Allen, 1988b; Goodall, 1990), the rise of psychology, psychiatry and eugenics (Garton, 1988b) and crimes involving women (Allen, 1990), much of this work is largely outside officially constituted criminology. Indeed as we shall argue shortly, this is one of the sources of its considerable strength. But it seems likely that there is also a more explicitly 'criminological' history in Australia which awaits survey and reclamation (see for example *The ABC of Criminology*, by Anita Muhl, published in 1941 for the Australian Council for Educational Research by Melbourne University Press which invokes explicit notions of 'the Science of Criminology', although characteristically the author was an American Visiting Lecturer in Psychiatry at the University of Melbourne and the book is largely devoid of any reference to Australian conditions or literature).

Another feature often not appreciated outside Australia is the lack of contact and exchange between the small number of Australian criminologists working in different states, an indication of the very material effects of federalism, the distances and expense of travel, the predominantly state-based responsibility for criminal law, and the pertinence and diversity of local traditions and developments. As a result much criminological work is heavily weighted towards local state knowledges and events, as indeed this treatment is to NSW.

It should also be noted that to focus only on official, academic or professional criminology, neglects what Carson and O'Malley call 'perhaps the most influential exercises in criminological work... carried out... by the vast array of Royal Commissions, Boards of Inquiry, Law Reform Commissions and the like which produce a constant stream of interpretive analysis of crime' (1989: 352), to say nothing of a range of other popular cultural (for example a rich prison literature of biography, diary, plays and poetry) fictional, psychological and other discourses which contribute to the constitution of the object 'crime'. Journalistic accounts of 'organized crime', for example, in conjunction with and drawing on various Commissions of Inquiry, have been extremely influential in constituting a popular conception of 'crime as personal immorality' as well as strongly promoting expanded policing, criminal justice and penal 'solutions' (Bottom, 1979, 1984; Whitton, 1986; cf. Brown, 1984; Bersten, 1990).

Finally, to postulate a clear cut division between mainstream, official or administrative Australian criminology on the one hand and radical or critical criminology on the other arguably underplays both the continuities *between* Australian mainstream and radical criminologies and the discontinuities *within* radical criminologies. A change of editorship in 1980 in the *ANZ Journal* has led to a more open approach to contributions and the appearance of a minority stream of more radical and theoretically weighted articles. Indeed whether Australian criminology will develop the sort of 'convergence' between administrative and radical criminology detected in the British context by Rock (1988: 197) remains to be seen.

Mainstream criminology

Carson and O'Malley locate the foundations of post-war Australian criminology in the 1950s in the establishment of criminology departments within faculties of law at both Melbourne (1951) and Sydney (1959) Universities. They argue that these origins were characterized by a conservative social milieu in which the infant discipline was watched over by academic lawyers and state criminal justice and correctional officials. Criminology courses were heavily correctionalist in orientation and seen as an offshoot of criminal law. The institutional foundations of criminology in Australia remained 'miniscule' in the late 1960s (1989: 339) as evidenced by the need for two leading members of the Sydney Institute of Criminology to write an editorial in the *Australian Law Journal* entitled 'The need for criminology in Australia'. The editorial by Hawkins and Chappell (1967) argued for an 'applied' criminology 'aligned... with the pragmatic approach of Radzinowicz and the Cambridge school'. The two major justifications for criminology offered were the need for uniform crime statistics and for 'treatment research'. Carson and O'Malley see this pitch as part of a 'professionalising offensive' (1989: 340) aimed at lawyers and judges. By characterizing criminology as a service discipline to law, prestige and legitimacy was enhanced and autonomy from direct state control maximized. Further 'the strong alliance with the legal profession had been fostered inter alia in order to downplay, and even nullify, the associations of the discipline with the more disreputable social sciences' (1989: 341).

In 1967 the Australian and New Zealand Society of Criminology was established, followed a year later by the *Australian and New Zealand Journal of Criminology*. A content survey of the first decade of the *ANZ Journal* (O'Connor, 1980) found that most articles were 'either descriptive or research papers', predominantly within 'medical model, psychological or learning theory/socialisation' frameworks. O'Connor compared the range of topics and types of articles broadly with those then found in the *British Journal of Criminology* and *Federal Probation*. Theoretical articles were largely absent. O'Connor noted that 'particular American and British developments, e.g. labelling, conflict theory and radical deviancy theory, which occurred prior to and during the decade of publication were ignored' (1980: 16; see also White, 1975: 47).

In 1971 the Criminology Research Council (CRC) and the Australian Institute of Criminology (AIC) were established. Carson and O'Malley characterize the background to their emergence as an 'atheoretical, practical and policy oriented concern, not even the faintest whisper of the mounting northern hemisphere sociological debates about crime and criminology breaking through the dense ether of pragmatic zeal' (1989: 350). They argue that with one or two notable exceptions the work of the AIC 'throughout the early 1970s and early 1980s fell into the mold of conventional positivist criminology' (1989: 351); (for a different assessment see Chappell and Wilson 1986; and cf. O'Malley, 1984: 96–7). They place particular stress on the conservative political context in post-war Australia, the weakness and relatively late emergence of sociology as a discipline, and particular disciplinary policing operations for the 'protracted hegemony of relatively conventional and conservative criminology in Australia' (1989: 348) which they argue continued until the end of the 1970s. Carson and O'Malley argue that despite these constraints 'Australian criminology has begun to generate a genuinely critical discourse during the 1980s' (1989: 333).

Elements in the emergence of radical criminology

A number of forces led in the 1970s to cracks in mainstream correctionalist criminology in Australia. The broader political and cultural context was that of an upsurge of opposition to Australian involvement in the Vietnam war, particularly on the campuses; the establishment of the Aboriginal tent Embassy in Canberra which served as a focus for new-found Aboriginal militancy; the radical environmentalism of the NSW Builders' Labourers' Federation in the form of the 'green ban' policy through which builders' labourers and local residents' groups prevented the despoliation of historical and residential areas for commercial development; second wave feminism; the influence of anti-psychiatry and other anti-institutional movements which bolstered struggles by groups such as prisoners, psychiatric patients, and students; experimentation with recreational drugs, and the unfolding of a variety of lifestyle movements. This social ferment in the aftermath of the cultural stagnation of the long post-war economic boom was reflected in the election of the Whitlam national ALP government after 23 years of federal conservative Liberal/County Party rule (from 1949 to 1972). With the final abandonment of the 'white Australia' policy and the recognition of China, Australia emerged on to the international stage and into the international economy, revealing in the process the structural weaknesses of an economy previously sheltered from international competition by high levels of protection. While the social democratization programme of the Whitlam government gave expression to many reformist elements, it was brought to an economic halt by the withdrawal of capital reinvestment and the decline of the manufacturing sector and to an abrupt political halt by its dismissal by the Governor General in the 'constitutional coup' of November 1975.

In the criminological sphere a strong current of the 'crimes of the powerful' genre, informed by the post-1968 ferment in the new left and drawing on British and North American deviancy theory, interactionist, conflict and Marxist criminology emerged. In terms of the teaching of criminology younger academics, influenced by various of these developments, gained teaching positions and influence in a number of universities teaching criminology courses, predominantly in law faculties rather than sociology. While this legal location is seen as a weakness by Carson and O'Malley it arguably gave an interventionist impetus to the emerging radical criminology, aligning it to concrete criminal justice struggles and in particular prison movement and community legal centre organizations (Basten et al., 1982; Sallmann and Willis, 1984; Zdenkowski et al., 1987; Hogan et al., 1988). Wilson and Braithwaite's collection (1978) reflected the growing influence of interactionist (see also Edwards and Wilson, 1975) conflict and neo-Marxist perspectives. Throughout the 1980s a critical examination of white-collar crime, and the regulation of business and pollution by Hopkins, Braithwaite, Fisse and Grabosky in particular, has continued the crimes of the powerful focus but with a more empirically informed eye (Hopkins, 1978; Braithwaite, 1984; Grabosky and Braithwaite, 1986; Braithwaite and Fisse, 1988; Grabosky, 1989). A more explicitly radical, neo-Marxist current has kept the criminological focus firmly on the activities of agencies of the state, especially the police. The emphasis has been on the specific policing practices in relation to particular groups (Brown et al., 1984): Aborigines (Cunneen and Robb, 1987; Cunneen, 1990), bikies (Cunneen et al., 1989) and youth (White, 1989, 1990; Presdee, 1989).

While there is a danger of constructing a forced coherence and unity to the emergence of radical criminologies in Australia in the 1970s, it may be useful to identify very briefly some of the components shaping the emergence of radical criminology. One of these has been a strong abolitionist current forged out of an alliance between radical criminologists and prisoners' movement organizations. Another more general feature has been a range of attacks on the definition of criminology, an issue of continuing relevance in terms of our previous discussion of the essentializing effects of 'crime as a unifier' in left realist approaches. More recently, the influence of a strong radical tradition of social history, dealing with 'criminological' topics such as policing, prostitution, imprisonment, social order, but without explicitly invoking 'criminology', has been inflected by the political rather than academic, theoretical or criminological concerns of second wave feminism. The following discussion provides a brief guide to these developments as a prelude to a consideration of the prospects of an antipodean left realism in contemporary Australian criminology.

Abolitionism
One of the components shaping Australian radical criminology in the 1970s and 1980s was abolitionism. The *Alternative Criminology Journal* (ACJ) was established in 1975 under the auspices of the NSW Prisoners' Action Group (Boehringer, 1975) initially combining a Marxist/abolitionist politics with detailed and specific championing of prisoners' struggles, especially in NSW. Radical criminologists also contributed to social movements organizing around advocacy in the mental health area, community legal centres, Aboriginal criminal justice and land rights struggles and occupational health and safety issues. The ACJ published the NSW Prisoners' Action Group's (1979–1980) submission to the Nagle Royal Commission into Prisons (1978). The submission, drafted mainly by radical criminologists working in the group, mounted a strong attack on the correctionalist

and positivist nature of criminology, the repressive and counter-productive nature of the prison and the class or 'dual' society which spawned both. Thomas Mathiesen's *The Politics of Abolition* (1974) was taken up strongly by the PAG, particularly the concept of positive and negative reforms. 'Aggregate social harm' was suggested as a mechanism for reorienting the definition of the crime away from the activities of the marginalized and on to the harmful activities of the powerful. The later account of the NSW prison movement, *The Prison Struggle* (Zdenkowski and Brown, 1982), provides a detailed treatment of the previous decade of prison politics and offers a more theoretical introductory overview of radical and Marxist criminology. Other critical treatments of penal politics by academics (Findlay, 1982; Tomasic and Dobinson, 1979), prisoners (Anderson, 1989) and prison administrators (Vinson, 1982) added to both the interventionist character of radical criminology and the particular focus on the prison (for extended review articles of the four NSW prison books published in 1982 see Phillipps, 1983; Hogg, 1983b; Tomlins, 1985).

More recent work on penality has marked a shift away from abolitionism (Brown and Hogg, 1985; Brown, 1987; Hogg, 1988c) and exhibited a preparedness to examine statistical evidence in relation to an evaluation of decarceration (Chan and Zdenkowski, 1986) and current penal politics (Brown, 1989, 1990). It has included work on prison internal disciplinary practices (Brown, 1986) the jurisprudence of sanctions (Freiberg, 1986) 'models' of criminal justice (Hogg, 1983a) police accountability (Phillipps, 1982) and a critique of Cohen's (1979) 'dispersal of social control' thesis (Hogg, 1988d). This shift has come less from an explicitly left realist trajectory, which has until very recently been weak in the area of penality (cf. Garland, 1985; Ryan and Ward, 1986; but see Matthews, 1987, 1989a, 1989b), and more from the influence of Foucaultian perspectives (Wickham, 1987). This reassessment of abolitionism has been conducted at both an academic criminological and activist level through a critique of Mathiesen's (1974) very influential analysis. Three related problems in Mathiesen's analysis were apparent, leading to a questioning of the efficacy of the strategy of abolition itself (see especially Brown and Hogg, 1985). The first is the privilege that is accorded production relations as the determining principle in relation to the prison – thus the unproductive status of prisoners takes on a major significance in relation to the possibilities and nature of penal political struggle. Secondly, this economic criterion is the basis for asserting the essential unity, if not yet realized, of the struggle of workers and prisoners against the general capitalist system which oppresses them in different ways, in prison, in work, in the state, etc. Thirdly, the focus on production entails the putting to one side the question of power itself – it merely comes into existence to serve production by coercing, concealing and negating that which would threaten it.

Regarding the first of these problems in Mathiesen's analysis, the privileging of production inherent in the emphasis on prisoners' 'unproductive' status, it is significant that abolitionist appropriations of Foucault tended to concentrate on the (functionalist) role of the prison in the production of delinquency. But in *Discipline and Punish* (1977) the prison is not judged to have a determinate role which can be established by reference to its functions within the social relations of capitalism. Rather, the prison is merely the starting point for doing another history, or series of histories, dealing with the practices and techniques of regulating bodies which surface in the modern organization of imprisonment and in a diverse range of other locations. It is to the elaboration and extension throughout the social body of a whole range of disciplinary technologies and a micro-politics of the body dating from the eighteenth century onward that Foucault addresses himself. He demonstrates how disciplinary programmes and strategies aimed at the optimization of the forces, capabilities and movements of the body and the constitution of a 'docile and useful' subject penetrated a range of institutions including schools, factories, workhouses, monasteries, military barracks, etc, as well as the prison. The prison is not therefore understood as possessing some fixed and specific function determined elsewhere in the requirements of production. Thus the 'unproductive' status of prisoners is not in itself of overriding significance if we cease to define their struggle in terms of the requirements of capitalist production and thus as derivative and subordinate to some larger struggle.

Secondly, there is a tendency in Mathiesen's account with its emphasis on the 'unproductive' role of prisoners and the strategy of alliances with the 'radical part of the working class' to specify an underlying relation of unity which is merely to be realized. This raises a set of problems with the category of the unified subject, including a failure to acknowledge the importance of the discursive position within which every subject position is constituted (Laclau and Mouffe, 1985: 166–7), and the effects of internal segmentation and differentiation, in relation to both prisoners and 'the radical part of the working class', quite apart from the question of the principles and interests around which alliances are to be constructed. One of the sources of difficulty here is that abolitionist accounts have tended to underestimate the forms of power which have actually served to divide and differentiate populations. Those powers which classify, assign and normalize on the basis of sexual differentiation or grids of normality, age, health, etc, are real in their effects. In this respect the success of the prison, and other agencies such as the police, at constituting an 'alien and dangerous' criminal class is real and cannot be reversed by a simple assertion of common class interests. It is always a question of *constructing* alliances, often in very specific, localized and short-term ways. There is no necessary underlying unity merely waiting to be realized.

Finally, there is a tendency in abolitionist accounts to treat power as a negative, coercive and instrumental phenomenon. As soon as we begin to conceive of the body as a field of power relations it becomes difficult to confine our conception of power to that of negation. Apart from a recognition that power operates in positive terms and not merely as a denial of an essentialist subjectivity given in nature there must be a shift away from a notion of power as located in specific institutions as a property to be possessed and wielded, and thus in the final liberating instance destroyed. If the power operating through the prison is not to be regarded simply as repressive but as entangled in a whole network of power relations directed at the discipline and normalization of subjects; and if furthermore it is accepted that the disciplines take their place as one among a number of forms of the exercise of power in modern societies which together are co-extensive with society itself it is no longer helpful to talk of abolition in any simple terms. The prison can no longer simply be counterposed to some sphere of freedom and voluntariness outside the effects of power and it cannot be assumed that the sphere can be expanded as the state is gradually broken down. The operations of power cannot be suspended, and a vacuum created for the creation of 'genuine' alternatives, since we are always and already as political and social subjects products of power and constituted upon a field of power relations (for a critique of this position see Boehringer, 1987). At a more concrete level in NSW penal politics this has been reflected in the problems that have arisen in relation to Mathiesen's positive/negative reforms distinction and the inadequacy of the principle of 'voluntariness' as a guide to what is a genuine alternative as against that which merely reproduces or augments the prison system.

There is a convergence at points between this sort of Foucaultian-influenced critique of abolitionism which has been formulated in the Australian context by radical criminologists within prison movements who were previously exponents of abolitionism and some of the British left realist critiques of abolitionism (Matthews, 1987, 1989a, 1989b), although the latter were arguably initially less influenced by Foucault, less grounded in concrete penal movements, and less concerned with penality, the prison and sentencing policy. The object of left realist wrath has been an abolitionism with a wider meaning more akin to the 'left idealist' tag. Where there has been the strongest convergence has been in the critique of Cohen's (1979, 1985) influential extension and dispersal of social control and net-widening theories (Matthews, 1987;

Hogg, 1988d). Matthew's critique of the 'globalism, empiricism and impossibilism' (1987: 356) of the decarceration and social control literature
includes a warning of the dangers of 'reducing decarceration process to
an epiphenomenon' (p. 357), together with a plea for specificity and an
appreciation of the differential impact of policies on different populations. Matthews goes even further in *Informal Justice?* (1989a) reworking earlier more dismissive left realist approaches to Foucault's
power analysis in the direction of 'governmentality', 'the social' and of
'complexity and variation', including a critique of the dichotomous
oppositions of 'formal/informal; conservative/liberating; legalization/
delegalization' (1989a: 16). We would mischievously add left realism/
left idealism to his list. In short we would suggest that left realism itself
is far from unified in its various manifestations and that this new-found
opposition to 'exclusive oppositions' and to 'framing arguments in all-
or-nothing terms' and the new-found openness to complexity and
'post-modern conceptions of law' (1989a: 16) might usefully be applied
to other areas of left realist work, policing in particular.

Definitional questions
One element of the emerging radical challenge in Australian criminology in the early 1970s was a variety of calls for 'abolishing the
academic discipline of criminology' or at least that 'the politics and
priorities of research in criminology must be changed quite drastically'
(Wilson, 1973: 111, 113). Such attacks on definitions of crime and
criminology found their way into established mainstream collections.
Brown (1977: 489) followed the Schwendingers' (1975) call for a
redefinition of the criminal law based on the notion of 'historically
determined human rights' in arguing for a criminology which was
'more interested in studying for example the high mortality rate among
Aboriginal children than in studying Aboriginal "crimes". Criminology courses were taught focusing on unemployment, racism, sexism
and imperialism, rather than the usual working-class crime and criminological theory subject matter of traditional criminology courses.
Subsequent calls for a 'cognitive remapping' (Cohen, 1985: 1) of
criminology have included Harding's exhortation on becoming director of the Australian Institute of Criminology that 'there is no time
left for mini-criminology. Australian criminologists have an ability to
set an agenda for the 80s, one whose principal item is to save mankind
from extinction and to preserve the frame of life' (1983: 90), and
Howe's less apocalyptic suggestion to 'get out of criminology and to
reconceptualise the whole terrain as a sociology of law, crime and
criminalisation' (1987: 108). Hogg has argued that one of the formative
features of Australian criminology has been its 'refusal to define
criminology ... which in turn produced its extremely fluid and eclectic

nature', providing 'tremendous potential for the colonisation of areas of research and analysis (not to mention resources)' (1988a: xi).

The tendency in some of the 1970s radical criminology to insist on the methodological priority of definitional questions, requiring an analysis of the state, and the consequent political attempt constantly to re-orient both popular and professional criminological debates away from questions of the prevention and control of traditionally defined crime, are open in retrospect to the 'idealist' characterization, however unilluminating such labels may prove. For those criminologists engaged at a popular level in contributing to and intervening in media and political debates it ultimately became untenable, at least in its rather ritualist invocation, as the broader ideological and cultural conditions which had tended to overpoliticize traditionally defined crime by fusing it with expressions of political protest and dissent, recreational drug taking and lifestyle diversity, fractured. Ironically the conservative tendency to criminalize political opposition and conflate a range of departures from narrow conceptions of norms of appropriate behaviour and style provided one of the conditions for the maintenance of a militant refusal to acknowledge the harmful effects and intra-class nature of much officially defined crime. Nevertheless, though it remained possible at the level of academic and theoretical criminology to refuse to acknowledge the status of the category crime within Marxist theory (O'Malley, 1988), such positions became increasingly difficult to maintain at a popular level without appearing to be merely evasions. Arguably such difficulties are even more apparent in the context of the political dominance of the Australian Labor Party at both state and federal level in the 1980s, an argument which runs counter to the tendency to portray British left realism purely as a political response to Thatcherism.

The dangers of subordinating definitional questions lie in the ease with which the position being staked out can be assimilated to the pragmatic concerns of mainstream administrative criminology. There is a powerful common sense which brackets out any recognition of crime as an ideological artefact of the legal definitions of the state, the criminal law and its knowledge-producing processes. This common sense is sustained rather than challenged by the pragmatism of mainstream Australian criminology which has largely avoided any rigorous theoretical engagement with the object crime. Not only has this entailed considerable flexibility in the colonization of newly emerging areas of research and analysis as noted above, but also promoted the treatment of crime as a discrete phenomenon, a separate sphere of social practice organized around some internal unity, which establishes the basis of the discipline criminology. This danger, particularly the elision with popular commonsense notions of crime as a largely unproblematic concept, is a very real one for left realism and is potentially exacerbated by the methodological limitations of and heavy reliance on the crime victim survey.

In our view this assimilation can be avoided by rejecting the conception of a discrete and unitary notion of crime, whether its derivation be in the concern of mainstream criminology to 'bring science to bear' on its (pre-given) object or that of left realism to press crime into service in the interests of a class politics and a socialist programme. The implication of a rejection of a unity, however specified, is that it is no longer possible to sustain any general claims about criminology at all. Rather than 'crime in general', what confronts us is a heterogeneous range of conducts embedded in diverse sites of social practice which are most usefully examined by tracing the legal and ideological mechanisms through which particular events, conducts and individuals are constructed as targets of social intervention and objects of knowledge, and the terms in which this is carried out.

Feminism
An example of a recent sustained political and theoretical challenge to the traditional generic claims, concerns and theories of criminology is that of feminism. A growing stream of feminist-influenced work has been motivated not by a concern to advance the field of criminology in general but to raise issues of violence against women and its political, economic, ideological and conceptual conditions of both past non-recognition and contemporary 'discovery'. The work has focused on homicide (Wallace, 1985) domestic violence, sexual assault and child sexual assault (Scutt, 1980, 1983; Hatty, 1986), women in prison (NSW Task Force, 1985; Brown et al., 1988; Fitzroy Legal Service, 1988; Howe, 1989), crimes involving women (Mukherjee and Scutt, 1981; Allen, 1990) and the masculinity of criminology (Allen, 1988a). In a literature review Naffine (1986: 130–1) characterized the contribution of Australian criminology to the study of women and crime as 'weak', in contrast to the 'sophisticated' contributions of social historians. Arguably feminist concerns have impacted more strongly in the political and policy campaigning work around domestic violence, child abuse and sexual assault carried out by a wide range of rape crisis centres, women's refuges, community legal centres, victim support organizations, task forces, governmental special units and agencies, than in academic or theoretical criminology (but see Allen, 1988b, 1990; Howe, 1987; Naffine, 1987). One effect of this upsurge has been to pinpoint substantial disagreements with, and inadequacies in, the civil libertarianism dominant in Australian left liberal legal circles, and the former abolitionism of academic radical criminology and prison movement organizations.

More than this assessment, however, what much feminist research and analysis has demonstrated is that an adequate understanding and response to violence against women is not to be found in the exposure of one more 'crime problem' and the connection between work in this area and the study of crime in general or the traditional methods of criminology, but in locating it in an analysis of the family and gender relations. The following passage from Allen (1990: 254) makes the point well:

> The history of the crimes examined defy any attempt to construct a general theory of crime or policing. Instead, illegal practices are best analysed in relation to other historically available options for solving the same problems or securing the same experience. Prostitution is best analysed in relation to other work and support options for women and in relation to other sexual options for men. Spousal violence is situated in relation to divorce, desertion and other terminations of domestic relationships. Late nineteenth-century infanticide and abortion are considered in relation to 'natural' and 'artificial' contraception and demographic influences on patterns of reproduction. By the late twentieth century, infanticide is situated among mainstream discourses about crimes against children and within psychiatric categories and treatment, while abortion may be best reconsidered at least to a significant degree in relation to patterns in young women's sexual position and negotiations. Sexual offences involving girls under the age of consent have become evidence of poor socialization, parental neglect, justifying child welfare classification and surveillance. Rape, once related to male sexuality, is being fixed to the general options of violence in modern urban societies.

Allen goes on to argue that 'It is the investigation of these illegal practices in a social history framework that discloses their connections often with legal practices in the same domain. Alternatively, their investigation as part of the administrative category of "crime" obscures such social history connections. "Crime" history has been incapable of scrutinizing the use of laws, in theory and in practice, to regulate men's and women's options and experiences' (1990: 254). One of the political advantages of such a position is that it feeds into public campaigns around domestic violence, sexual assault and harassment not only a recognition that violence against women and children is a much more integral part of social relations in Australian society as against their popular portrayal as individual occurrences, but also challenges the popular notion of the victim as helpless, in that the emphasis on the differential capacity to positively influence, recon-struct or escape from violent relationships focuses attention on the availability and accessibility of a whole range of social, economic, political and material forms of support. In short it draws attention to the connections between victimization and a vast range of practical conditions which may inhibit or exacerbate it. This has the additional and beneficial effect of simultaneously challenging the traditional pathological portrayal of criminal offenders and of emphasizing the complex and relational nature of crime.

The prospects for left realism in Australian criminology

As mentioned earlier, little if any Australian radical criminology has been carried out explicitly under a left realist banner. Much of the Australian radical criminology emerging since the 1970s is susceptible to the same criticism of forms of essentialism made earlier of radical British criminology. It would be possible retrospectively to allocate particular work to a left idealist category (see especially Boehringer, 1977; Critique of Law, 1978; Brown, 1977, 1978; PAG, 1979–80), but there seems little point in such an exercise. Indeed certain of the aspects of the British left realist debate although not entirely absent in Australia (but confined largely to exchanges between mainstream and radical criminologists, Brown, 1978): tendencies to invective and caricature (Ryan and Ward, 1986), the substantial failure to acknowledge shifts as in part self-criticism, the unfair counter-charges of racism, hardly seem worth emulating in the Australian context, and indeed are hopefully being overcome in recent British developments (Matthews, 1989a, 1989b; Rock, 1988: 197).

In the light of the commonplace observation that left realism in Britain emerged as a specific response to law and order debates in the context of Thatcherism, it is interesting that realist resonances have emerged most strongly in NSW in the more popular interventions of the Campaign for Criminal Justice Group (CCJ *Bulletin*, 1988; Hogg, 1988a, 1988b). For it is in NSW that a state Liberal/National Party government of the right has most consciously attempted to implement free market deregulatory policies and sought to increase penalties, expand the law and order budget and intensify penal discipline (Brown, 1988b).

The CCJ Group, comprising mainly left lawyers, academics, youth workers and criminal justice system workers, have argued for a 'new direction for law and order'. Their first *Bulletin* provided a detailed outline and evaluation of the law and order policies of the two major political parties in NSW. Breaking from the dominant civil libertarian tendency in Australian left legal circles there is a clear and initial acknowledgement that crime is a serious problem and a recognition that, problems with the interpretation of criminal statistics notwithstanding, there has been a significant increase in the incidence of burglary, car theft, and robbery in NSW and that certain forms of violence, in particular those directed at women and children, are a pervasive and largely hidden problem. It is pointed out that crime and particularly violence disproportionately affects the poor, the elderly, Aborigines, women and children, not simply because these groups often suffer the highest rates of victimization, but because they are the most vulnerable in a whole range of other respects. Without specifically invoking left realism, this up-front recognition of the damaging effects of traditionally defined crime is a clear break with both the civil libertarianism which tries to play down the extent or significance of increasing crime rates and the leftist tradition which immediately points elsewhere to other sources of social harm sponsored by the state or by the powerful.

The CCJ Group goes on to argue that the almost exclusive focus on changing the criminal justice system is generally going to have little effect in terms of crime prevention and public safety, that limited gains can be expected from generalized demands of a qualitative nature – for more police, more powers, heavier sentences. The USA, and Britain under Thatcher are pointed to as an indication of the failure of an over-reliance on the criminal justice system and punitive, deterrent-based policies. Nevertheless particular areas are singled out where the performance of the criminal justice system could have clear crime reduction effects. One is the policing of domestic violence where sensitive police intervention in relation to identifiably violent relationships and situations could prevent serious crimes, including murder, from occurring. A second is in relation to the supervision and support of offenders on conditional liberty, such as parole and probation. On crime prevention the group argues that the locks and bars approach, promoted through neighbourhood watch schemes, is not a satisfactory one, representing an acceptance of, and a retreat from, an increasingly impoverished public life. Rather crime prevention needs to be linked to other policy areas such as employment and local industry policy, the environment and urban planning and the defence and enhancement of public goods and services such as public transport, public housing, child care and family and youth support schemes, as well as the development of specific crime prevention policies and measures.

Among the particular policies promoted by the CCJ Group are: a requirement that all new government policy be accompanied by crime impact statements; crime-related social impact to become a factor built into the urban planning process, so that the likely effects of new commercial and residential developments, roads, freeways, etc, be assessed as part of the public environmental impact process; the development of local safety strategies in areas with high-crime rates, aimed at integrating the provision of policing and other criminal justice services with other measures for crime prevention; that such strategies be based on the collection of local information through victim surveys (covering matters such as the patterns of victimization, expectations as regards policing, identification of trouble spots, existing informal crime control measures and resources); that the development and management of the strategies be built around the principle of community participation and involvement utilizing local organizations such as resident action groups, tenants' groups, refuges, etc; that such strategies be integrated with the assessment and provision of other community needs such as child care centres, home help, local youth employment schemes; the coordination of such a policy by a new central authority with the role of identifying and initiating local strategies and providing necessary levels of expertise and support in cooperation with local steering committees; the implementation of a whole range of specific measures such as the provision of low-cost security hardware and insurance to welfare recipients and low income earners, community arts policies directed at encouraging murals and other forms of art on railway stations, public housing estates and parks, enhancing and maintaining the physical and social environment of public areas, maintaining staffing levels on public transport, and so on.

The CCJ Group has attempted to inject these perspectives and policies into public debate. The NSW Labor Party opposition is currently formulating a crime prevention policy which takes up some of these issues and in particular provides for the setting-up of an administrative and political structure for crime prevention initiatives. Two Sydney local councils have embarked on crime prevention programmes initiated by CCJ members. A CCJ team including the authors is conducting a local crime victim survey in inner-suburban Sydney. So that although none of these initiatives has been sponsored under a left realist banner it can be seen that in its programmatic and policy aspects there are close affinities with British left realism and the Middlesex school. On the local political stage the point of departure is less with left idealism than with civil libertarianism, although the recognition that we cannot seriously fight crime with revolutionary demands or policies which dramatically inflate public expenditure (Hogg, 1988b: 18) invites repudiation by those who adhere to a variety of 'revolutionary' teleologies. Apart from anything else we would argue that governments and political movements of whatever persuasion cannot exercise full control of political and reform agendas and the conditions for realizing them, and that therefore the terrain of social change always tends to be more complex, contradictory and open than can be gleaned through the lens of any political ideology. The particular strength and hold of civil libertarianism can be seen in one of the few explicit and sympathetic invocations of left realism in the Australian context which in the course of an argument that the

Conservative and Labor Parties' policies on law and order in Victoria have converged, acknowledges only that 'the social perception that crime really is a serious problem had become widespread and entrenched' and states that 'clearly a victim ideology aligns with conservative law and order policies' (Corns, 1989: 12–13).

In considering the prospects for left realism in Australian criminology it is important to note major differences in national contexts. Apart from significant differences in the structure of the Australian state, federalism being foremost among them (an important issue given that the responsibility for policing and criminal justice rests predominantly with the states), the Australia of the 1980s has seen the unprecedented electoral hegemony of the Australian Labor Party at both federal and state levels. The centrepiece of the programme of the federal Labor government has been the Accord with the peak council of Trade Unions (ACTU) organized around orderly wage adjustments, price control, enhancement of the social wage, and an active investment and industry policy. While there have been many criticisms from the left of the failure of the ACTU to enhance the position of marginalized groups outside the workforce there has been a shift from a defensive, economistic posture on the part of both the ACTU and the federal Labor government to the adoption of a social leadership role within Australian society, although it could hardly be said that this has led to a recognition that violence and criminal victimization in Australian society are bound up with the conditions of economic, social and political marginality of certain groups in the society, especially female, child and Aboriginal dependency (Hogg and Brown, 1990).

These major differences in context lead us to argue that the specific problems and tasks facing Australian criminology are not necessarily advanced by the promotion of a left realist/left idealist dichotomy or an explicitly left realist 'paradigm' or current. Indeed, given the traditionally derivative status of Australian criminology, its predominantly liberal, reformist and administrative character and trajectory, the tendency to replicate British and American debates and fashions in both liberal and radical Australian criminology is an indication of the continuance of a colonialism of the intellect, what used to be called the 'cultural cringe'. This is not to assert a crude cultural nationalism nor to adopt an isolationist stance in relation to significant international developments (Taylor, 1990) and comparative research (Braithwaite, 1979; Pratt, 1988), but rather to suggest reflexively that the obligation felt by radical Australian criminologists to authorize their work by reference to key conceptual frameworks lifted from other national contexts constitutes an impediment to the development of a more specific, nuanced and autonomous Australian criminology. A key example of this tendency has been the increasingly widespread adoption of Stuart Hall and colleagues' analysis of crime debates as an ideological component of a Thatcherite 'authoritarian populism'. The authoritarian populism thesis has come under increasingly convincing challenge in Britain (Hirst, 1989) and in any event cannot just be imported for instant application in different national and state contexts without the risk of constituting an evasion of the more difficult task of a specific analysis of local conditions and politics.

There are dangers, in our view, of claims (common to various streams of radical criminology) to be establishing 'new paradigms' or signifying 'paradigm shifts'. Such claims are often underpinned by techniques of 'critique' (Hirst and Jones, 1987; Rose, 1987) and forms of dialectical or dichotomous thinking rendered increasingly problematic both in the light of developments in social theory (the challenge of postmodernism) and in the current redrawing of the political landscape taking place in the aftermath of 40 years of international cold war politics. The collapse of statist authoritarian socialism in Eastern Europe provides a context for a revitalization of arguments for a radical political pluralism in a mixed economy and a recognition of some of the considerable benefits of a genuine social democracy, notions previously treated with derision by western Marxists. But these developments also provide a context for the rise of religious and ethnic fundamentalism and national chauvinism, left and right.

This is not to deny the positive features of the left realist response: the move back into empirical research, often eschewed in the attack on positivism and empiricism, and the concern for purity evident in some (particularly Marxist, cf. interactionist) radical criminology of recent decades; the move away from a predominantly oppositional and in some instances abstentionist politics overplaying the dangers of 'incorporation', 'strengthening the state', 'extending social control' or mistaking a 'positive' for a 'negative' reform; the recognition in the alliance with local left-wing councils of the need to develop forms of relationship and sponsorship with popular institutions and forms of political organization other than minority left sects.

It seems likely that there will be an increase in Australian local crime victim surveys resulting in part from an interest in the left realist 'second generation' (Crawford et al., 1990: 4) surveys, in part from increasing frustration with the monotonously opportunist manipulation of crime statistics by all Australian political parties. Most of these victim surveys will be carried out by mainstream criminologists or by statistics bureaux for governments or government departments such as the police. Radical criminology has not acquired the 'powerful patrons' (Rock, 1988: 196) of its British counterparts. In particular the prospects of alliances with and funding by local government, itself far less influential or radical, are limited. (For discussions of existing Australian crime victim surveys see: ABS, 1979, 1984; Wilson and Brown, 1973; Congalton and Najman, 1974; Minnery and Veal, 1981; Minnery, 1986, 1988; Grabosky, 1982; Braithwaite et al., 1982; Braithwaite and Biles, 1980a, 1980b, 1980c; 1986; Hogg, 1988a; Grabosky, 1989; van Dijk et al., 1990). Some, including a small sample, victim crime survey in inner-suburban Sydney currently being conducted by a research team including the authors, will be more explicitly concerned to connect fear of crime to the local social and economic organization of particular communities and the quality of the local environment, as well as attempting to re-orient the growing debate over the needs of victims of crime away from individual responses and towards the social structural aspects of victimization.

The conduct of such surveys, while providing a better knowledge basis from which to intervene in local crime prevention and political debates, nevertheless throws up a number of problematic aspects of left realist claims to a new and distinctive paradigm. First, as Mugford and O'Malley (1990) in a critique of left realist heroin policy arguments point out, the epistemological claims to be privileged to divine 'the real' and to 'be faithful to the phenomenon' (Young, 1987: 337) are arguably no more convincing than knowledge claims of previous radical criminologists. What might at first appear as simple empiricism – 'the most fundamental tenet of a realist criminology is to be faithful to the phenomenon' (Young, 1987: 337) – is rescued by the acknowledgement that the task is not to accept the views of inner-city crime victims at face value but to recognize 'a rational core to public concerns and images.... Realist criminology involves an act of deconstruction', taking 'the phenomenon of crime apart, breaking it down to its component pieces and sequences' before placing 'these fragments of the shape of crime in their social context over time'. The criteria for reassembly or 'recontextualisation' of the 'fragments' which are recycled from the last chapter of *The New Criminology* (Taylor et al., 1973) are marked by the claim of totality, in contrast to the 'partiality' of previous criminologies. Though clearly useful, the various criteria and methodological prescriptions are themselves open to a range of interpretations and arguably the emphasis on capturing a totality paves the way for forms of essentialism which the process of 'deconstruction' might otherwise appear to be mitigating. That the left critics of British left realism have chosen not to contest its epistemological claims may indicate an agreement with the realist philosophy of science (Bhaskar, 1978, 1989) invoked at points by the left realists. If so, it illustrates another convergence between the warring parties, namely the concern to defend and recuperate Marxism.

Secondly, the realist crime victim surveys privilege the experience of inner-city residents (or more accurately the inner-city working class) over suburban residents. Thirdly, despite the useful advances in methodology and interpretation of victimization achieved in the second generation surveys, especially the differential character of victimization and the effect of risk, vulnerability, the compounding effects of crime, and the location of victimization within particular patterns of social relationships (Young, 1988; Phipps, 1986), there are still many methodological difficulties involved in the conduct and interpretation of the surveys. In this respect the openness and detail of the discussion of these difficulties in earlier surveys (Sparks et al., 1977; Sparks, 1981; Genn, 1988) is exemplary. However sophisticated the development of victim surveys and however important the new knowledge base they may provide, they are clearly skewed to certain forms of personal victimization as against crimes whose effects are so dispersed that no clear-cut individual victim is produced. Forms of corporate fraud, price fixing, loan sharking, asset stripping, tax avoidance, false advertising, medifraud, the manufacture and sale of dangerous products, corruption in obtaining development approval, industrial pollution and negligence, etc, in short the crimes of the powerful, tend to be excluded from crime victim survey results. Their costs are borne disproportionately by the same social groups most victimized by burglary, assault, robbery and the more traditional (individual) forms of crime. The risk here is of reproducing the power/knowledge relations inscribed within existing criminal justice practices which in both policing and knowledge-producing aspects tend to yield up the poorest and most powerless offenders to public view and penal control, while those occupying more privileged positions largely elude scrutiny and control.

Conclusion

This chapter has been directed at a critical review of the debates around left realist criminology in Britain and has offered a brief assessment of the prospects for left realism in Australia, against the backdrop of an overview of Australian post-war criminology and the emergence of a radical or critical criminology following on from British and American developments. Though we support the general realist position and programme we have been critical of what we take to be the inadequate break with past critical positions within radical criminology. The effect of this has been to oversimplify the political tasks that the realist project poses. Taking crime seriously from a left perspective is seen to be primarily a matter of formulating policies and strategies which express the true interests of the working class and other groups in socialist solutions to crime problems. These solutions are focused on democratization of criminal justice, especially policing. Thus it is argued that democratic accountability of police forces through locally elected police committees will increase the efficiency of local policing because 'a force trusted by the local community will be one to which the community will be prepared to yield a high flow of information concerning crime ... A democratically accountable police force would have a higher clear up rate' (Lea and Young, 1984: 260).

Such arguments exaggerate the extent to which the flow of general information to the police can be significantly influenced one way or another by such democratic arrangements. For detection is not so much influenced by the general flow of information as by particular forms of information, usually that which is available from the scene of an offence by victims or witnesses or that which is provided (or allegedly provided) by those involved in crime themselves. Greater democratic accountability over the pervasive and institutionalized practice of police verballing, for example, could well lead to *decreased* clear-up rates. Police/informant relationships, to give another example, consist of a series of exchanges, which may be read as either corruption or effective policing, depending on prevailing political and ideological circumstances (Hogg, 1987). Our point is not to oppose the left realist's emphasis on increasing the local democratic account-ability of the police but to warn of overstating its capacity to influence policing decisions, the majority of which will not be subject to demo-cratic mechanisms and, moreover, take place in low visibility settings (Hindess, 1983: ch. 2). For one of the key dimensions of policing rather neglected in left realist approaches – but which is apparent from many of the interactionist accounts – is the effective power that resides in the lower ranks of the police. Far from policing being a transparent mechanism for the implementation of ruling-class strategies, or being susceptible to the mandate of a democratically elected executive or authority, the critical task that has always confronted police adminis-trators themselves is how to control effectively the conduct of the police on the ground. Democratic control, whatever the particular form(s) it might take, cannot of itself adequately deal with the policy questions posed by policing. As Reiner points out 'The task of reform is neither just laying down the law, nor achieving majority control. It is knowing what policy changes could achieve their desired objectives, bearing in mind the refracting effects of the rank and file subculture' (1985: 176).

This is not meant to indicate that greater democratic control over policing is undesirable or irrelevant, but it is important, as Hindess (1983) argues of democratic strategies generally, to assess their likely effects in terms of the specific conditions under which they operate. It is necessary to formulate specific regulatory proposals in relation to specific objectives and sites of policing. Different policing contexts and practices present different opportunities for internal supervision and systems of review, record keeping, etc, and hence also different opportunities for connecting these with external measures of scrutiny and accountability. In the Australian context the potential for demo-cratic reforms (especially at a local level) in relation to policing is limited, by comparison with Britain.

Finally, it is important to emphasize that effective crime control depends as much on the reconstruction of social policy as it does on criminal justice policy. The concentration on policing in left realist criminology contrasts with the lack of attention devoted to the operation of other criminal justice institutions such as the courts and penal agencies, informal mechanisms of control, and non-criminal justice responses to crime (although this is being remedied in relation to penality: Matthews, 1989a, 1989b). In relation to the last of these, Hogg has previously suggested that it is time many of the dimensions of public safety were explicitly located within debates over the size and content of the social wage (Hogg, 1988a: 46). This should take place at many sites including greater attention to the crime-related impact of private residential, commercial and other planning developments, landlord and tenant laws, youth employment programmes, insurance policy, liquor licensing, public transport, the provision of child care and recreational facilities and so on.

A reconstruction of social policy in the Australian context would necessarily entail a confrontation with the legacy of residualism in public welfare provision, founded on the particular history and traditions of Australian labourism and industrial arbitration which emphasized the 'family wage', the benefits of which would flow indirectly to those outside the labour market. A gender and racially based division of labour institutionalized a residual conception of social policy which has contributed to the patterns of dependency and economic, social and political marginality of certain social groups in Australian society, in particular single mothers, children and Aborigines.

Important dimensions of public policy and the political culture have contributed to the widespread evasion of the fact that most violence occurs in private, despite the popular focus on street crime and violence, reproducing the invisibility of many of the victims most affected by patterns of violence. The conditions which cast certain categories into positions of extreme economic and social marginality in Australian society also expose them to increased risks of victim-ization–criminalization. Victims are frequently stigmatized as much as offenders by the intervention of the criminal law. Where family relationships are concerned, the economic consequences of criminalization are likely to be visited as heavily on the family as the individual offender. Thus, the impact of criminalization, most baldly apparent in Aboriginal communities, is often to reproduce and exacerbate conditions of poverty, dispossession, and violence. Addressing the problems of crime and violence necessitates addressing the conditions of marginality of its most frequent and vulnerable victims. The relation between economic and social marginality and victimization is also mediated by a wide range of more specific factors, such as the availability of firearms and patterns of alcohol use. Popular ideologies of crime often serve to disconnect patterns of violence from these cultural and situational factors and associated public policies as much as they do from wider social and economic policy debates.

In arguing the limitations of, and tendencies to essentialism in, general theories of state, policing and crime, the implication of this chapter is that the left must concern itself with specific, realizable policies for effective crime prevention and control and the conditions for their implementation by reform governments and other organizations and movements here and now. One of these conditions is the fracturing of unitary notions of both crime and law and order. Left realist criminology provides some of the means towards such a fracturing but then, in its concern to utilize crime as a vehicle or unifier for expressing the common interests of the working class in a democratic socialist programme and future, tends to belie its promise.

References

Allen, J. (1988a) 'Policing since 1880: some questions of sex', in M. Finnane (ed.), *Policing in Australia: Historical Perspectives*. Sydney: University of NSW Press.

Allen, J. (1988b) 'The "masculinity" of criminality and criminology: interrogating some impasses', in M. Findlay and R. Hogg (eds), *Understanding Crime and Criminal Justice*. Sydney: Law Book Co.

Allen, J. (1990) *Sex and Secrets: Crimes Involving Australian Women since 1880*. Melbourne: Oxford University Press.

Anderson, T. (1989) *Inside Outlaws: A Prison Diary*. Sydney: Pluto Australia.

Australian Bureau of Statistics (1979) *1975 General Social Survey: Crime Victims*. Canberra: ABS.

Australian Bureau of Statistics (1984) *Crime Victims Survey, Australia 1983*. Canberra: ABS.

Bankowski, Z., Mungham, G. and Young, P. (1977) 'Radical criminology or radical criminologist?', *Contemporary Crises*, 1(1).

Basten, J., Richardson, M., Ronalds, C. and Zdenkowski, G. (eds) (1982) *The Criminal Injustice System*. Sydney: Australian Legal Workers Group/Legal Service Bulletin.

Bersten, M. (1990) 'Defining organised crime in Australia and the USA', *ANZ Journal of Criminology*, 23: 39.

Bhaskar, R. (1978) *A Realist Theory of Science*. Brighton: Harvester.

Bhaskar, R. (1989) *Reclaiming Reality*. London: Verso.

Boehringer, G. (1975) 'Alternative criminology and prisoners' movements: partnership or rip-off', *Alternative Criminology Journal*, 1(1): 24–45.

Boehringer, G. (1977) 'The law and class struggle: a critique of Andrew Frazer', *Arena*, 46: 90–97.

Boehringer, K. (1987) 'Radical criminology and media regulation', in G. Zdenkowski, C. Reynolds and M. Richardson (eds), *The Criminal Injustice System* Vol 2. Sydney: Pluto Press.

Boehringer, G., Brown, D., Edgeworth, B., Hogg, R. and Ramsey, I. (1983) 'Law and order for progressives? An Australian response', *Crime and Social Justice*, 9: 2–12.

Bottom, B. (1979) *The Godfather in Australia*. Sydney: A.H. and A.W. Reed.

Bottom, B. (1984) *Without Fear or Favour*. Melbourne: Sun Books.

Braithwaite, J. (1979) *Inequality, Crime and Public Policy*. London: Routledge.

Braithwaite, J. (1984) *Corporate Crime in the Pharmaceutical Industry*. London: Routledge.

Braithwaite, J. and Biles, D. (1980a) 'Overview of findings from the first *Australian National Crime Victims Survey*', *ANZ Journal of Criminology*, 13(1): 41–51.

Braithwaite, J. and Biles, D. (1980b) 'Crime victimisation rates in Australian cities', *ANZ Journal of Sociology*, 16(2): 79–85.

Braithwaite, J. and Biles, D. (1980c) 'Women as victims of crime: some findings from the first *Australian National Crime Victims Survey*', *The Australian Quarterly*, 52: 329–39.

Braithwaite, J. and Biles, D. (1986) 'Victims and offenders: the Australian experience', in R. Block (ed.), *Victimization and Fear of Crime: World Perspectives*. Washington: Department of Justice.

Braithwaite, J. and Fisse, B. (1988) 'Accountability and the control of corporate crime', in M. Findlay and R. Hogg (eds), *Understanding Crime and Criminal Justice*. Sydney: Law Book Co.

Braithwaite, J., Biles, D. and Whitrod, R. (1982) 'Fear of crime in Australia', in H. Schneider (ed.), *The Victim in International Perspective*. Münster: Walter de Gruyter.

Brown, D. (1977) 'Criminal justice reform: a critique', in D. Chappell and P. Wilson (eds), *The Australian Criminal Justice System*. Sydney: Butterworth.

Brown, D. (1978) 'Some notes on the state of play in criminology', *Alternative Criminology Journal*, 2(3): 81–100.

Brown, D. (1984) 'Organised crime: changing practices, markets and relations', *Australian Left Review*, 90.

Brown, D. (1986) 'Prison Discipline, Legal Representation and the NSW V.J. Courts', in R. Tomasic and R. Lucas (eds) *Power, Regulation and Resistance*. Canberra: Canberra College of Advanced Education.

Brown, D. (1987) 'Some preconditions for sentencing and penal reform', in G. Wickham (ed.), *Social Theory and Legal Politics*. Sydney: Local Consumption.

Brown, D. (1988a) 'The politics of reform', in G. Zdenkowski, C. Ronalds and M. Richardson (eds), *The Criminal Injustice System* Vol 2. Sydney: Pluto Press Australia.

Brown, D. (1988b) 'Post election blues: law and order in NSW Inc', *Legal Service Bulletin*, 13: 99.

Brown, D. (1989) 'Returning to sight: contemporary Australian penality', in P. O'Malley and P. Beilharz (eds), *The Politics of Empowerment in Australia. Social Justice*, 16(3): 141–57.

Brown, D. (1990) 'Are we sending too many people to gaol?', in A. Gollan (ed.), *Questions for the Nineties*. Sydney: Left Book Club Co-op.

Brown, D. and Hogg, R. (1985) 'Abolition reconsidered: issues and problems', *Australian Journal of Law and Society*, 2(2): 56.

Brown, D., Hogg, R., Phillipps, R., Boehringer, G. and Zdenkowski, G. (eds) (1984) *Policing: Practices, Strategies and Accountability*. Sydney: ACJ.

Brown, D., Kramer, H. and Quinn, M. (1988) 'Women in prison: task force reform', in M. Findlay and R. Hogg (eds), *Understanding Crime and Criminal Justice*. Sydney: Law Book Company.

Campaign for Criminal Justice (1988) *Bulletin*. Nos. 1 and 2, Sydney: CCJ.

Carson, K. and O'Malley (1989) 'The institutional foundations of contemporary Australian criminology', *ANZ Journal of Sociology*, 25(3): 333–55.

Chambliss, W. (1976) 'The state and criminal law', in W. Chambliss and M. Mankoff (eds), *Whose Law, What Order?* New York: John Wiley.

Chan, J. and Zdenkowski, G. (1986) 'Just alternatives: trends and issues in the de-institutionalization of punishment', *ANZ Journal of Criminology*, 19: 67–90, 131–54.

Chappell, D. (1983) 'Australia', in E.H. Johnson (ed.), *International Handbook of Contemporary Developments in Criminology, Europe, Africa, The Middle East and Asia*. Westport: Greenwood Press.

Chappell, D. and Wilson, P. (1986) 'Introduction: Australian crime and criminal justice at a time of national alarm', in D. Chappell and P. Wilson (eds), *The Australian Criminal Justice System: The Mid 1980s* (3rd edn). Sydney: Butterworth.

Cohen, S. (1979) 'The punitive city: notes on the dispersal of social control', *Contemporary Crises*, 3: 339–63.

Cohen, S. (1981) 'Footprints in the sand', in M. Fitzgerald, G. McLennan and J. Pawson (eds), *Crime and Society*. London: Routledge.

Cohen, S. (1985) *Visions of Social Control*. Oxford: Polity Press.

Conglaton, A. and Najman, J. (1974) *Unreported Crime*. Sydney: NSW Bureau of Crime Statistics.

Corns, C. (1989) 'Claiming the victim territory: the politics of law and order'. Paper presented at the Australian Law and Society Conference, La Trobe University, Melbourne.

Crawford, A., Jones, T., Woodhouse, T. and Young, J. (1990) *Second Islington Crime Survey*. Middlesex Polytechnic: Centre for Criminology.

Critique of Law Editorial Collective (1978) *Critique of Law: A Marxist Analysis*. Sydney: Red Pen Press.

Cunneen, C. (1990) 'Aborigines and law and order regimes', *Journal for Social Justice Studies*, 3: 37–50.

Cunneen, C. and Robb, T. (1987) *Criminal Justice in North-west NSW*. Sydney: Bureau of Crime Statistics and Research.

Cunneen, C., Findlay, M., Lynch, R. and Tupper, V. (1989) *The Dynamics of Collective Conflict*. Sydney: Law Book Company.

Currie, E. (1985) *Confronting Crime*. New York: Pantheon.

Cutler, A., Hindess, B., Hirst, P. and Hussain, A. (1977) *Marx's Capital and Capitalism Today* Vol. 1. London: Routledge.

Cutler, A., Hindess, B., Hirst, P. and Hussain, A. (1978) *Marx's Capital and Capitalism Today* Vol. 2. London: Routledge.

Daniels, K. (ed.) (1984) *So Much Hard Work: Women and Prostitution in Australian History*. Sydney: Fontana.

Edwards, A. and Wilson, P. (1975) *Social Deviance in Australia*. Melbourne: Cheshire.

Findlay, M. (1982) *The State of the Prison*. Bathurst: Mitchellsearch.

Finnane, M. (ed.) (1987) *Policing in Australia: Historical Perspectives*. Sydney: University of NSW Press.

Fitzroy Legal Service (1988) *Women and Imprisonment in Victoria: A Report*. Melbourne: FLS.

Foucault, M. (1977) *Discipline and Punish*. London: Allen Lane.

Freiberg, A. (1986) 'Reward, law, power: towards a jurisprudence of the carrot', *ANZ Journal of Criminology*, 19.

Garland, D. (1985) *Punishment and Welfare: A History of Penal Strategies*. London: Heinemann.

Garton, S. (1988b) *Medicine and Madness: A Social History of Insanity in NSW*. Sydney: University of NSW Press.

Garton, S. (1988a) 'The state, labour markets and incarceration', in M Findlay and R. Hogg (eds), *Understanding Crime and Criminal Justice*. Sydney: Law Book Co.

Genn, H. (1988) 'Multiple victimisation', in M. Maguire and J. Pointing (eds), *Victims of Crime: A New Deal*. Milton Keynes: Open University Press.

Gilroy, P. and Sim, J. (1985) 'Law and order and the state of the left', *Capital and Class*, 25: 15–51.

Girdler, M. (1982) 'Domestic violence: social solutions', in C. O'Donnell and J. Craney (eds), *Family Violence in Australia*. Melbourne: Longman Cheshire.

Golder, H. and Allen, J. (1979–80) 'Prostitution in NSW, 1870–1932', *Refractory Girl*, 18/19.

Goodall, H. (1990) 'Policing in whose interest: local government, the TRG and Aborigines in Brewarrina, 1987–88', *Journal of Social Justice Studies*, 3: 19–36.

Grabosky, P. (1977) *Sydney in Ferment. Crime, Dissent and Official Reaction, 1788–1973*. Canberra: Australian National University Press.

Grabosky, P. (ed) (1982) *National Symposium on Victimology: Proceedings*. Canberra: Australian Institute of Criminology.

Grabosky, P. (1989) *Wayward Governance: Illegality and its Control in the Public Sector*. Canberra: Australian Institute of Criminology.

Grabosky, P. and Braithwaite, J. (1986) *Of Manners Gentle: Enforcement Strategies of Australian Business Regulatory Agencies*. Melbourne: Oxford University Press.

Gross, B. (1982) 'Some anti-crime strategies for progressives', *Crime and Social Justice*, 17: 51–4.

Hall, S., Critcher, C., Jefferson, T., Clarke, J. and Roberts, B. (1978) *Policing the Crisis*. London: Macmillan.

Harding, R. (1983) 'Nuclear energy and the destiny of mankind – some criminological perspectives', *ANZ Journal of Criminology*, 16: 90–91.

Hatty, S. (ed.) (1986) *National Conference on Domestic Violence, Seminar Proceedings*. Canberra: Australian Institute of Criminology.

Hawkins, G. and Chappell, D. (1967) 'The need for criminology in Australia', *The Australian Law Journal*, 40: 307–14.

Hiller, A.E. and O'Malley, P. (1978) 'Symposium on deviance, crime and legal process', *ANZ Journal of Sociology*, 14(1): 20–24.

Hindess, B. (1977) 'The concept of class in Marxist theory and Marxist politics', in Communist University of London (eds), *Class Hegemony and Party*. London: Laurence and Wishart.

Hindess, B. (1983) *Parliamentary Democracy and Socialist Politics*. London: Routledge.

Hindess, B. (1987) *Politics and Class Analysis*. Oxford: Blackwell.

Hirst, J.B. (1983) *Convict Society and its Enemies: A History of Early NSW*. Sydney: Allen and Unwin.

Hirst, P. (1975) 'Marx and Engels on law, crime and morality', in I. Taylor, P. Walton and J. Young (eds), *Critical Criminology*. London: Routledge.

Hirst, P. (1989) *After Thatcher*. London: Collins.

Hirst, P. and Jones, P. (1987) 'The critical resources of established jurisprudence', *Journal of Law and Society*, 14(1): 21–32.

Hogan, M., Brown, D. and Hogg, R. (1988) *Death in the Hands of the State*. Sydney: Redfern Legal Centre Publishing.

Hogg, R. (1983a) 'Perspectives on the criminal justice system', in M. Findlay, S. Egger and J. Sutton (eds), *Issues in Criminal Justice Administration*. Sydney: Allen and Unwin.

Hogg, R. (1983b) 'Review article', *Australian Journal of Law and Society*, 1(2): 122–33.

Hogg, R. (1987) 'The politics of criminal investigation' in G. Wickham (ed.), *Social Theory and Legal Politics*. Sydney: Local Consumption.

Hogg, R. (1988a) 'Taking crime seriously: left realism and Australian criminology', in M. Findlay and R. Hogg (eds), *Understanding Crime and Criminal Justice*. Sydney: Law Book.

Hogg, R. (1988b) 'Law and order policy: a new direction', *Current Affairs Bulletin*, October.

Hogg, R. (1988c) 'Sentencing and penal politics: current developments in NSW', in *Proceedings of the Institute of Criminology, No. 78: Sentencing*, Sydney University Law School.

Hogg, R. (1988d) 'Criminal justice and social control: contemporary developments in Australia', *Journal of Studies in Justice*, 2(1): 89–122.

Hogg, R. and Brown, D. (1990) 'Violence, public policy and politics in Australia', in I. Taylor (ed.), *The Social Effects of Free Market Policies*. London: Harvester Wheatsheaf.

Hopkins, A. (1978) *Crime, Law and Business*. Canberra: Australian Institute of Criminology.

Howe, A. (1987) 'Toward critical criminology – and beyond', *Law in Context*, 5: 97–111.

Howe, A. (1989) 'Sentencing women to prison in Victoria: a political and research agenda. Paper delivered at the Law and Society Conference, La Trobe University, Melbourne.

Hughes, R. (1988) *The Fatal Shore*. London: Pan Books.

Hulsman, L. (1986) 'Critical criminology and the concept of crime', *Contemporary Crises*, 10: 63–80.

Jones, T., MacLean, B. and Young, J. (1986) *The Islington Crime Survey*. Aldershot: Gower.

Jones, T., Lea, J. and Young, J. (1987) *Saving the City: The First Report of the Broadwater Crime Survey*. London: Middlesex Polytechnic, Centre for Criminology.

Kerr, J.S. (1988) *Out of Sight, Out of Mind: Australia's Places of Confinement, 1788–1988*. Sydney: S.H. Ervin Gallery.

Kinsey, R. (1985) *The Merseyside Crime Survey*. Liverpool: Merseyside County Council.

Kinsey, R., Lea, J. and Young, J. (1986) *Losing the Fight against Crime*. Oxford: Blackwell.

Laclau, E. and Mouffe, C. (1985) *Hegemony and Socialist Strategy*. London: Verso.

Lea, J. and Young, J. (1984) *What is to be Done about Law and Order?* Harmondsworth: Penguin.

Lea, J. and Young, J. (eds) (1986) *Confronting Crime*. London: Sage.

Lea, J. (1987) 'In defence of realism', *Contemporary Crises*, II: 357–70.

Lea, J., Matthews, R. and Young, J. (1987) *Law and Order: Five Years on*. London: Middlesex Polytechnic, Centre for Criminology.

McCoy, A. (1980) *Drug Traffic: Narcotics and Organised Crime in Australia*. Sydney: Harper and Row.

McQueen, H. (1968) 'Convicts and rebels', *Labour History*, 15: 3–31.

McQuilton, J. (1979) *The Kelly Outbreak, the Geographical Dimensions of Social Banditry*. Carlton: Melbourne University Press.

Maguire, M. and Pointing, J. (1988) *Victims of Crime: A New Deal*. Milton Keynes: Open University Press.

Mathiesen, T. (1974) *The Politics of Abolition*. Oslo: Martin Robertson.

Matthews, R. (1987) 'Decarceration and social control: fantasies and realities', in J. Lowman, R.J. Menzies and T.S. Palys (eds), *Transcarceration: Essays in the Sociology of Social Control*. Aldershot: Gower.

Matthews, R. (1989a) *Informal Justice?* London: Sage.

Matthews, R. (1989b) *Privatising Criminal Justice*. London: Sage.

Minnery, J.R. (1986) *Crime Perception and Victimisation of Inner City Residents*. Brisbane: Queensland Institute of Technology.

Minnery, J.R. (1988) *Crime Perception, Victimisation and Reporting in Inner Brisbane*. Brisbane: Queensland Institute of Technology.

Minnery, J.R. and Veal, G. (1981) *Crime Perception and Residential Mobility in an Inner City Suburb*. Brisbane: Queensland Institute of Technology.

Mugford, S. and O'Malley, P. (1990) 'Heroin policy and deficit models. The limits of left realism'. Unpublished paper.

Mukherjee, S.K. (1980) *Crime Trends in Twentieth Century Australia*. Sydney: Allen and Unwin.

Mukherjee, S.K. and Scutt, J. (eds) (1981) *Women and Crime*. Sydney: AIC and Allen and Unwin.

Mungham, G. (1984) 'Review of *What is to be Done about Law and Order?*', *Journal of Law and Society*, 11(3).

Naffine, N. (1986) 'Women and crime', in D. Chappell and P. Wilson (eds), *The Australian Criminal Justice System: The Mid 1980s*. Sydney: Butterworth.

Naffine, N. (1987) *Female Crime*. Sydney: Allen and Unwin.

New South Wales Women in Prison Task Force (1985) *Report of the NSW Women in Prison Task Force*. Sydney, NSWGPS.

O'Connor, M. (1980) 'A decade of the *Australian and New Zealand Journal of Criminology*, 1968-1977', *ANZ Journal of Criminology*, 13: 11-21.

O'Donnell, C. and Craney, J. (1982) *Family Violence in Australia*. Melbourne: Longman Cheshire.

O'Malley, P. (1979) 'Class conflict, land and social banditry: bushranging in nineteenth century Australia', *Social Problems*, 26: 271-83.

O'Malley, P. (1980) 'The class production of crime, banditry and class strategies in England and Australia', in S. Spitzer (ed.), *Research in Law and Sociology* Vol. 3. New York: JAI Press.

O'Malley, P. (1983) *Law, Capitalism and Democracy. A Sociology of the Australian Legal Order*. Melbourne: Allen and Unwin.

O'Malley, P. (1984) 'Trends in the sociology of Australian legal order', *British Journal of the Sociology of Law*, 11: 91-103.

O'Malley, P. (1988) 'The purpose of knowledge: pragmatism and the praxis of Marxist criminology', *Contemporary Crises*, 12: 65-79.

Painter, K. (1988) *Lighting and Crime: The Edmonton Project*. Middlesex Polytechnic: Centre for Criminology.

Painter, K., Lea, J. and Young, J. (1988) *The West Kensington Estate Survey*. Middlesex Polytechnic: Centre for Criminology.

Painter, K., Lea, J., Woodhouse, T. and Young, J. (1989) *The Hammersmith Crime Survey*. Middlesex Polytechnic: Centre for Criminology.

Phillipps, R. (1982) 'Law rules OK?', in P. Botsman (ed.), *Theoretical Strategies*. Sydney:

Local Consumption.

Phillips, R. (1983) 'Prison politics', in J. Allen and P. Patton (eds), *Beyond Marxism? Interventions after Marx*. Sydney: Local Consumption. pp. 184–93.

Phipps, A. (1986) 'Radical criminology and criminal victimisation: proposals for the development of theory and intervention', in R. Matthews and J. Young (eds), *Confronting Crime*. London: Sage.

Platt, T. and Takagi, P. (1981) 'Law and order in the 1980s', *Crime and Social Justice*, 15: 1–7.

Pratt, J. (1988) 'Law and order politics in New Zealand 1986: a comparison with the United Kingdom 1974–79', *International Journal of the Sociology of Law*, 16: 103–26.

Presdee, M. (1989) 'Made in Australia: youth policies and the creation of crime', in D. Edgar, D. Keane and P. McDonald (eds), *Child Poverty*. Australian Institute of Family Studies: Allen and Unwin.

Prisoners' Action Group, (1979–80) 'Submission to the Royal Commission into NSW Prisons', 3(2): 1–74; 3(3): 1–67; 3(4): 1–74.

Quinney, R. (1974) *Critique of Legal Order*. Boston: Little Brown and Co.

Reiner, R. (1985) *The Politics of the Police*. Brighton: Wheatsheaf.

Reynolds, H. (1981) *The Other Side of the Frontier. An Interpretation of the Aboriginal Response to the White Settlement of Australia*. Townsville: James Cook University.

Reynolds, H. (1987) *Frontier: Aborigines, Settlers and Land*. Sydney: Allen and Unwin.

Rock, P. (1988) 'The present state of criminology in Britain', in P. Rock (ed.), *A History of British Criminology*. Oxford: Clarendon Press.

Rose, N. (1987) 'Beyond the public/private division: law, power and the family', *Journal of Law and Society*, 14(1): 61.

Rowley, C.D. (1970) *The Destruction of Aboriginal Society*. Canberra: Australian National University.

Ryan, M. and Ward, T. (1986) 'Law and order: left realism against the rest', *The Abolitionist*, 22: 29–33.

Sallmann, P. and Willis, J. (1984) *Criminal Justice in Australia*. Melbourne: Oxford University Press.

Schwendinger, H. and Schwendinger, J. (1976) 'Defenders of order or guardians of human rights?' in I. Taylor, P. Walton and J. Young (eds) *Critical Criminology*. London: Routledge.

Scraton, P. (1987) *Law, Order and the Authoritarian State*. Milton Keynes: Open University Press.

Scutt, J. (ed.) (1980) *Rape Law Reform*. Canberra: AIC.

Scutt, J. (1983) *Even in the Best of Homes*. Ringwood, Victoria: Penguin.

Sparks, R. (1981) 'Surveys of victimisation', in M. Tonry and N. Morris (eds), *Crime and Justice Review* Vol 3. Chicago: University Press. pp. 1–58.

Sparks, R., Genn, H. and Dodd, D. (1977) *Surveying Victims*. Chichester: Wiley.

Steinert, H. (1985) 'The amazing new left law and order campaign', *Contemporary Crises*, 9: 327–33.

Sturma, M. (1983) *Vice in a Vicious Society: Convicts in Mid-nineteenth Century New South Wales*. St. Lucia: Queensland University Press.

Sumner, C. (1976) 'Marxism and deviancy theory', in P. Wiles (ed.), *The Sociology of Crime and Delinquency in Britain* Vol 2. *The New Criminologies*. London: Martin Robertson.

Sydney Labour History Group (eds) (1982) *What Rough Beast? The State and Social Order in Australian History*. Sydney: Allen and Unwin.

Taylor, I., Walton, P. and Young, J. (1973) *The New Criminology*. London: Routledge.

Taylor, I. (1981) *Law and Order: Arguments for Socialism*. London: Macmillan.

Taylor, I. (1990) *The Social Effects of Free Market Policies*. London: Harvester Wheatsheaf.

Tomasic, R. and Dobinson, I. (1979) *The Failure of Imprisonment*. Sydney: Allen and Unwin.

Tomlins, C. (1985) 'Whose law? What order? Historicist interventions in the "war against crime" ', *Law in Context*, 3: 130–47.

van Dijk, J., Mayhew, P. and Killias, M. (1990) *Experiences of Crime across the World: – Key Findings from the 1989 International Crime Survey*. Deventer, Netherlands: Kluwer.

Vinson, A. (1982) *Wilful Obstruction*. Sydney: Methuen.

Wallace, A. (1985) *Homicide: The Social Reality*. Sydney: NSW Bureau of Crime Statistics and Research.

White, S. (1975) 'Criminological theory: a review article', *ANZ Journal of Criminology*, 8: 47–56.

White, R. (1989) 'Making ends meet: young people and the criminal economy', *ANZ Journal of Criminology*, 22(3): 136.

White, R. (1990) *No Space of their Own: Young People and Social Control in Australia*. Melbourne: Cambridge University Press.

Whitton, E. (1986) *Can of Worms*. Sydney: Fairfax Library.

Wickham, G. (ed.) (1987) *Social Theory and Legal Politics*. Sydney: Local Consumption.

Wilson, E. (1983) *What is to be Done about Violence against Women?* Harmondsworth: Penguin.

Wilson, P. (1973) 'The politics of research and reform in criminology', *ANZ Journal of Criminology*, 6: 107–13.

Wilson, P. and Brown, J. (1973) *Crime and the Community*. St Lucia: Queensland University Press.

Wilson, P. and Braithwaite, J. (1978) *Two Faces of Deviance*. St Lucia: Queensland University Press.

Wilson, P. and Dalton, V. (eds) (1987) *Review of Australian Criminological Research*. Canberra: AIC.

Young, J. (1975) 'Working class criminology', in Taylor, I., Walton, P. and Young, J. (eds), *Critical Criminology*. London: Routledge.

Young, J. (1986) 'The failure of criminology: the need for a radical realism', in R. Matthews and J. Young (eds), *Confronting Crime*. London: Sage.

Young, J. (1987) 'The tasks of a realist criminology', *Contemporary Crises*, 11: 337–56.

Young, J. (1988) 'Risk of crime and fear of crime: a realist critique of survey-based assumptions', in M. Maguire and J. Pointing (eds), *Victims of Crime: A New Deal?* Milton Keynes: Open University Press.

Zdenkowski, G. and Brown, D. (1982) *The Prison Struggle*. Melbourne: Penguin.

Zdenkowski, G., Ronalds, C. and Richardson, M. (1987) *The Criminal Injustice System* Vol 2. Sydney: Pluto Press Australia.

Index